Dialogue and Decolonization

Also Available from Bloomsbury

A Practical Guide to World Philosophies,
by Monika Kirloskar-Steinbach and Leah Kalmanson
Interpreting Chinese Philosophy, by Jana S. Rošker
Interrelatedness in Chinese Religious Traditions, by Diana Arghirescu
Toward a New Image of Paramārtha, by Ching Keng

Dialogue and Decolonization

*Historical, Philosophical, and
Political Perspectives*

Garrick Cooper, Sudipta Kaviraj, Charles W. Mills,
Sor-hoon Tan, and James Tully

Edited by Monika Kirloskar-Steinbach

BLOOMSBURY ACADEMIC
LONDON • NEW YORK • OXFORD • NEW DELHI • SYDNEY

BLOOMSBURY ACADEMIC
Bloomsbury Publishing Plc, 50 Bedford Square, London, WC1B 3DP, UK
Bloomsbury Publishing Inc, 1385 Broadway, New York, NY 10018, USA
Bloomsbury Publishing Ireland, 29 Earlsfort Terrace, Dublin 2, D02 AY28, Ireland

BLOOMSBURY, BLOOMSBURY ACADEMIC and the Diana logo
are trademarks of Bloomsbury Publishing Plc

First published in Great Britain 2023
Paperback edition published 2025

Copyright © Monika Kirloskar-Steinbach and Contributors, 2024

Monika Kirloskar-Steinbach has asserted her right under the Copyright, Designs
and Patents Act, 1988, to be identified as Editor of this work.

For legal purposes the Acknowledgments on p. vi constitute
an extension of this copyright page.

Cover image: Oxygen/Getty Images

All rights reserved. No part of this publication may be: i) reproduced or transmitted
in any form, electronic or mechanical, including photocopying, recording or by
means of any information storage or retrieval system without prior permission in
writing from the publishers; or ii) used or reproduced in any way for the training,
development or operation of artificial intelligence (AI) technologies, including
generative AI technologies. The rights holders expressly reserve this publication
from the text and data mining exception as per Article 4(3) of the
Digital Single Market Directive (EU) 2019/790.

Bloomsbury Publishing Inc does not have any control over, or responsibility for,
any third-party websites referred to or in this book. All internet addresses given
in this book were correct at the time of going to press. The author and publisher
regret any inconvenience caused if addresses have changed or sites have
ceased to exist, but can accept no responsibility for any such changes.

A catalogue record for this book is available from the British Library.

A catalog record for this book is available from the Library of Congress.

ISBN: HB: 978-1-3503-6081-5
PB: 978-1-3503-6085-3
ePDF: 978-1-3503-6082-2
eBook: 978-1-3503-6083-9

Typeset by Integra Software Services Pvt. Ltd.

For product safety related questions contact productsafety@bloomsbury.com.

To find out more about our authors and books visit www.bloomsbury.com
and sign up for our newsletters.

Contents

Acknowledgments   vi

1   Deparochializing Political Theory and Beyond: A Dialogue Approach to Comparative Political Thought   *James Tully*   1
2   A Conversation with James Tully's "Deparochializing Political Theory and Beyond"   *Garrick Cooper*   41
3   Whose Tradition? Which Practices?   *Sor-hoon Tan*   47
4   Historicizing Political Theory   *Sudipta Kaviraj*   53
5   Dialogues in Black and White   *Charles W. Mills*   81
6   Continuing the Dialogue   *James Tully*   101

Afterword: Concluding Reflections   *Monika Kirloskar-Steinbach*   183

Notes on Contributors   200
Index   202

Acknowledgments

This volume continues a conversation on intellectual decolonization that began in the pages of the *Journal of World Philosophies*. It includes James Tully's article "Deparochializing Political Theory," that was published in 2016 in the journal's inaugural issue, and Garrick Cooper's and Sor-hoon Tan's responses that were published in 2017 in the journal's second volume. These essays are complemented by Sudipta Kaviraj's and Charles W. Mills' hitherto unpublished, revised, interventions to Tully's article as well as Tully's response to the whole debate. The latter has been especially composed for this volume. I am grateful to all the authors for working with me to materialize this collection.

I would like to warmly thank James Tully for agreeing to initiate a conversation on deparochializing theory in the pages of the *Journal of World Philosophies*. I would also like to acknowledge the contribution of the journal's former co-editor James Maffie in implementing the debate in the journal's pages. I am grateful to Judy Dunlop for copyediting the collection. My thanks to Bloomsbury's editor Colleen Coalter for guiding us through the publication process. Finally, many thanks to Charles W. Mills' estate manager, Chike Jeffers, for kindly granting permission to include Mills' essay in the volume.

Charles W. Mills was very keen that an extended version of the journal debate be published in book form. Due to his untimely passing in 2021, he will, unfortunately, not be able to see the final version of the debate in print. I do hope though that he would have considered the volume as furthering his thought-provoking and boundary-pushing work, work that consistently underscored why it is worthwhile to resist the standard narrative that sustains the dominance of the European and Euro-American philosophical tradition.

Monika Kirloskar-Steinbach
Amsterdam, September 2022

1

Deparochializing Political Theory and Beyond: A Dialogue Approach to Comparative Political Thought

James Tully

Introduction: Clarification

The objective of this article is to deepen our understanding of transformative engagement in comparative and critical dialogues of comparative or transnational political thought. The objective is *not* to develop a "globalized discourse about moral standards for judging politics."[1] The first five sections discuss the challenges of dialogical comparative political thought. The following three sections discuss how a dialogue approach responds to these challenges and generates comparative and critical mutual understanding and mutual judgment. This objective is well expressed by Michel Foucault[2]:

> [W]hat is philosophy today—philosophical activity I mean—if it is not the critical work that thought brings to bear on itself? In what does it consist, if not in the endeavor to know how and to what extent it might be possible to think differently, instead of legitimating what is already known? .... [I]t is entitled to explore what might be changed, in its own thought, *through the practice of a knowledge that is foreign to it*. The "essay"—which should be understood as the assay or test by which, in the game of truth, one undergoes changes, and not as the simplistic appropriation of others for the purpose of communication—is the living substance of philosophy, at least if we assume that philosophy is still what it was in times past, i.e., an "ascesis," *askesis*, an exercise on oneself in the activity of thought.

In addressing this objective, I will also say something about another aim: what are the best methods for decentering western traditions? If we introduce our students to a global conversation or dialogue that is focused on the moral bases of political relationships, then we may inadvertently fail to decenter western traditions. A focus on moral principles that are said to provide the foundations of political relationships, like the earlier response to globalization of focusing on moral standards of political judgment, are both constitutive and orienting features of dominant western theories. If we prescribe that the response to globalization has to be a conversation focused on these questions of moral principles, then we may well continue the dominance of this western orientation to politics, rather than decenter it, and constrain students and participants from other traditions to formulate their engagement in these terms. It would then not be a genuine dialogue among traditions, but an assimilative monologue masquerading as a global dialogue. Much of the so-called cosmopolitan dialogue on globalization is monological in precisely this sense, as we all know.

Therefore, the first step in decentering western political traditions is to set aside the prescriptive search for moral standards of judgement or moral principles of political association as the telos of global dialogue. I am not against moral standards coming up in dialogues, and participants from some traditions proposing that they be the focus of the dialogue.[3] I am just warning against it being prescribed as the focus.

On Understanding Engagement in Genuine Dialogues Among Traditions

If we wish to deepen our understanding of engagement in meaningful or genuine dialogue among and across different traditions of political thought then we should enquire into the conditions of meaningful or "genuine" dialogue.[4] These conditions include the ethical practices of openness and receptivity to the otherness of others that enable participants to understand one another in their own traditions (mutual understanding) and to appreciate the concerns of one another regarding globalization and the injustices and suffering it causes (mutual concern). The participants may discuss moral standards of judgment and moral bases of political relationship at times in the dialogue, but these are meaningless unless and until through deep listening each comes to understand and appreciate the concerns of others as they experience and articulate them in the terms of their own traditions without inclusion, assimilation, or subordination.

The problem of the "meaninglessness" of abstracted moral principles is even worse than this. Abstract moral principles can literally mean anything the user wishes them to mean unless they are grounded and articulated in relation to the experiential self-understanding of those to whom they are applied. Take these dominant moral standards as examples: treat each other as free and equal; as ends in themselves, never only as means; and the difference principle of organizing politics to the benefit of the least well-off. These moral principles have been and continue to be used to justify the greatest inequalities in human history; modern wars of intervention, conquest, subjugation, and modernization; environmental destruction and climate change. They also have been and continue to be used to criticize these injustices of globalization by equally elaborate and well-defended critiques of the dominant justificatory theories.

This is one of the contemporary problems to which the turn to the understanding of the grounded ethical practices of engagement in multi-tradition dialogue is the response. If we can explicate the conditions of genuine dialogues then the participants themselves will work out their understanding of and responses to globalization themselves. That is, a genuine dialogue is not prescriptive: the participants co-articulate their own scripts democratically.

Six Obstacles to Deparochialization and Genuine Dialogue[5]

I propose that the project of deparochializing political theory can be seen as the work of creating genuine dialogues among and across traditions of political thought and practice. Engagement in genuine dialogues can accomplish much more than deparochializing political theory, as we will see, but it must achieve this first if the other benefits of genuine dialogue are to be achieved.

Deparochializing conversations are exceptionally difficult to engage in yet exceptionally rewarding if we do so.[6] The conditions of a genuine conversation or dialogue are difficult to explicate because it is so easy to finesse the demands of such a dialogue: that is, to appear to engage in them while all the time remaining within one's own tradition (as much of the global dialogue literature does today). Engagement in what we can call non-genuine or "false" dialogues is as common as rain and it conceals the demanding conditions of genuine dialogue from view. Like Gadamer, I distinguish genuine dialogue (mutual or reciprocal understanding) from two main types of false dialogue that fail to live up to the demands of genuine dialogue: strategic-instrumental (strategic) and deliberative-imperative (legislative). Also like him, I discuss both face-to-face dialogues and dialogues between interpreter and the texts of other traditions of political thought, although I place more emphasis on the first.[7] Allow me to mention six ways in which genuine dialogue is suppressed by false dialogue.

First, it is often simply a matter of a person or a dominant tradition being aware that they are pretending to engage in a genuine dialogue with people from other traditions, but continue to do so to get the upper hand (strategic dialogues). However, the problem of false dialogue is much deeper than this.

Second, in other cases, the individual or collective agents who engage in a false dialogue deceives themselves into believing that they are engaged in a genuine dialogue, so there is the psychological problem of self-deception to overcome. This problem is common in many of the participatory dialogues employed in the World Bank and IMF policies of democratization and transitional justice, and, indeed, it is seen by many as a deeply embedded feature of western traditions of dialogue with non-westerners, brought to awareness only in times of crises, such as after World War, Decolonization, 9/11 and the war on Iraq, and then quickly forgotten. Yet, the difficulty of false dialogue is more fundamental.

Third, the fundamental reason we get off on the wrong foot is that the very condition of being in a meaningful world with others in any tradition is that humans always and pre-emptively project over, interpret, and try to understand the other in the terms and ways of their own tradition. This is an ontological condition of sense-making. Our living traditions disclose the world to us as an actually and potentially meaningful world. Unless there is some awareness that the horizon of understanding of one's own tradition, which discloses the other and their way of life as meaningful in its terms, has to be called into question in the course of dialogue with others, who, as a matter of course, enter dialogue under the horizon of their tradition, then the dialogue, by definition, will remain a false dialogue in which each misunderstands the other and responds to this misunderstanding by reimposing—often unconsciously—their traditional understanding over others. Unless there is a critical practice within a tradition or within the course of the dialogue that brings this problem to self-awareness and addresses it by bringing aspects of one's background horizon of disclosure into the space of questions at the center of the dialogue, genuine dialogue cannot begin.[8]

In addition, this disclosure and projection of our form of pre-understanding over the world (and interpreting and acting under its sway) is not only true with respect to human beings but also over all living beings including the earth itself. We must somehow learn to listen to and understand the norms of self-organization of all forms of life and of the animate earth as a whole if we are not to destroy it by disclosing and acting on them under our traditions that disclose them as externalities or resources for the use and abuse of one species.[9]

Fourth, even when tradition-critical practices are present in traditions or dialogues among them, there is a multiplicity of factors that override or undermine them: psychological, military, economic, religious, rationalistic, political, face-saving, and so on. Fifth, these weighty factors are in turn legitimated by a multiplicity of "secondary explanations" that, as Franz Boas argued, every tradition gives to itself; such as the grand theories of civilization, modernization, and globalization generated by the west over the last half millennium of global expansion.[10] These are called "secondary" explanations because they often redescribe and conceal what is really going on in false dialogues and the escalating struggles that result from them in the terms of acceptability and approval of that tradition; terms such as progress, modernization, liberty, necessary means to world peace and justice, and so on. For example, Rousseau pointed out that "slavery" and "subordination" are often redescribed as "liberty."[11] These secondary explanations give us a false picture of our histories of interactions with other traditions.

The demand that global dialogues follow certain allegedly universal rules and be oriented to allegedly universal ends is often said to be a kind of textbook example of this failure to see what one's traditional form of representation conceals from view and of the failure to call the form of representation into the space of questions, even though it has a critical dimension within it. The reason this occurs is that the juridical language of representation of the tradition presents itself as meta-traditional from the outset, conceptually and historically, giving rise to "legislative" rather than genuine dialogues.[12]

As a result of these five factors (and a sixth below), a natural disposition to see the world in the terms of one's own tradition in the first instance is continually finessed, rather than faced and addressed, at each stage of interaction, as false dialogues escalate to the submission of one participant to another, or to conflict. These escalating misunderstandings and conflicts in turn are then legitimated by the secondary explanations of modern politics: namely, that peace cannot be brought about by peaceful means and democracy cannot be brought about democratic means: both require violence and authoritarian rule to bring less-advanced others to see the superiority or universality of the particular form of peace and democracy on offer.

These secondary explanations and their effects in practice lend credence to a global norm of modern politics: in time of peace prepare for war. Once this becomes the norm, even those traditions that are disposed to peaceful means of dispute resolution through genuine dialogue see that it is strategically rational to prepare for war in response to the others who have already done so. This security dilemma at the center of modern politics discredits genuine dialogue and undercuts the mutual trust on which it depends because it becomes rational to enter into dialogue in a distrustful way: that is, pretending to engage in genuine dialogue, in hopes it might work out, yet openly preparing for conflict if it does not. The dialogical effect of the open hand on the other—the nonviolent power of genuine dialogue—is undermined by the hidden fist in the background, affecting others to do the same in response. As Nietzsche argued in "The Means to Real Peace," and generations of IR scholars and game theorists ever since, this logic leads to the security dilemma and ever-escalating arms races, world without end.[13]

Accordingly, it is not difficult to see that if the logic of finessing genuine dialogue by means of the secondary explanations that comprise the language of development and globalization is not confronted, it will lead to the destruction of billions of *Homo sapiens* and other forms of life on earth, as Hannah Arendt forewarned in the 1960s and many others have since substantiated.[14]

Thus, in conclusion to this section, if this analysis is even partially accurate, there is no way to address the multiple crises of globalization that does not pass through engagement in genuine dialogues among and across the traditions of political thought present on this small planet.[15] Moreover, as these five obstacles show, engagement in deparochializing dialogues is not a simple task that we can do in a year or two. Many have failed, not only for the five reasons given above, but also for the sixth reason. The long, slow, intergenerational crafts of teaching, acquiring, and exercising the ethical practices of engagement in genuine, deparochializing dialogues have been ignored, and fast-time teaching, dialogues, negotiations, bargaining, and pre-scripted, transitional processes have proliferated.[16]

Given these six obstacles, the cultivation of genuine conversations and dialogues is one of the most important yet difficult tasks in the world. It requires learning and acquiring the ethical practices of genuine dialogue despite our human, all-too-human, dispositions to overlook the requisite critical work on our self-understandings and the self-understandings of others, and on all the factors piled up to dispose us to finesse these ethical practices of mutual understanding and concern. But, if genuine dialogue were to succeed in some future generation of people educated and proficient in the requisite ethical practices of engagement (the students of our students' students perhaps), then, in virtue of their sustained engagement in these dialogical relationships, they just might be able to bring into being another world of possible ways of living together peacefully and democratically that we can scarcely even imagine today. We can scarcely imagine these possibilities because our imaginations are constrained by the traditions and false dialogues we inhabit and the factors that hold them in place. Nevertheless, we can begin to explore some of the first steps of engagement, and teaching engagement in genuine dialogues of deparochializing, mutual understanding and concern, and critical comparison.[17]

Recognizing the Parochiality of Political Theory

To begin these steps, I will clarify how I am using the term "deparochialize." The sense I wish to explicate consists of steps that bring us to recognize the parochial character of modern political theory. Deparochializing shares many similarities with projects to "decolonize," "provincialize," and "de-imperialize" political theory.[18]

First, most political theories are written in ways that hide the spatial-temporal parochial contexts in which they are written and the locations of authors within them. This so-called "transitive" or even "transcendental" feature of political theory is a direct result of the grammar of the written phonetic language in which it is written. That is, a theory is standardly presented in general or universal terms and concepts that are presumed to apply across the range of parochial cases or instances to which the general concepts of the theory refer. The grammar generalizes local problems, arrangements, groupings, forms of speech, genres of reasoning, and senses of terms such as justice, freedom, citizen, oppression, and so on. The contextual or parochial conditions of possibility of the theory are concealed by the transitive character of most written languages.

The abstraction and reification of written meaning (called "literal" meaning) from the enveloping lifeworld of oral language usage and its meaning-in-use (practical meaning) began with the development of written alphabetical language in the west.[19] The Platonic dialogues are written during the first generation of users of Greek as a written language. The prior generation of oral language users and many of Socrates' interlocutors, especially Meletus in the *Apology*, connect the explication of terms like justice and courage to specific instances, places, and stories when and where they are spoken by concrete individuals: that is, to events in specific circumstances. Meletus explains that (participatory) democracy consists in dialogues with fellow citizens over the differing senses of political concepts in differing circumstance, judging, agreeing, and disagreeing in particular cases, while acting together.[20] In contrast, Socrates asserts that, if they are to know what these terms mean they have go beyond giving examples and find a definition that transcends all its instances and contains within itself a set of criteria common to all uses. Once the few possess this general knowledge over, rather than within, the field of politics, Socrates immediately concludes, it legitimates the use of power-over the many, rather that participatory democratic power-with, like any other craft.[21] With these two moves to knowledge-over and power-over, the dominant tradition of western political theory (and practice) is founded and participatory knowledge-with and power-with eclipsed.[22]

Accordingly, the first step in deparochializing political theories is to "reparochialize" them: to recontextualize their presumptively general or universal terms back into the parochial contexts in which they make sense. This is a step common to decolonization and provincialization as well. Moreover, it is also an insight of the tradition of philosophy of language initiated by Wittgenstein: sense-making is contextual. Here, the aim is to bring us to see that the great political theories that presume to be general or universal rest on quite specific and limited senses of the terms in question; senses that in turn make sense given the circumstances in which they are normally used.[23]

Second, some local theories are internally related to global power: that is, they are employed to describe, justify, legitimate, or operate systems of power that modernize or globalize the world (politically, legally, militarily, economically, subjectively, etc.). In this sense, the generalization of parochial institutions in these theories of modernization is made general *de facto* by the spread of these institutions and practices of western imperialism. At the same time, other traditions of political thought are changed by their interaction with the spread of this knowledge/power/subjectification ensemble: rendered marginal, lower, particular, primitive, exotic, assimilated, and subordinated, etc., by processes of modernization. Accordingly, the second step in deparochializing political theories is the hard work of studying the complex relationships between political theories and forms of power.[24]

These two steps show the sense in which political theories are parochial. What I mean by deparochializing is coming to realize that political theories, which are always presented in the language of abstraction and generalization (of not being parochial), are parochial: that is, partial and limited in their sense and reference. Once "we" who take these steps become aware of the limited and partial scope of any political theory, we have deparochialized our understanding of it. We are now not so parochial as to presume our local theories are general or universal in either sense or reference. This difficult form of self-awareness is the first condition of opening oneself to genuine non-imperial dialogues among different traditions.[25]

As a result of this parochial feature of modern political theory and our awareness of it, genuine dialogue among traditions of political thought becomes all the more important. Humans literally need dialogue with other limited traditions of political thought to see their own limitations and to see beyond them by means of the perspectives of others. Hence, it is dialogue itself that deparochializes, as I will argue below.

The third step is to realize that the genre of political theory in the west is only one species of the larger family of forms of political "thought." Political theory, as theory, is a quite peculiar way of reflecting on the world of politics. As Aristotle responded to Plato, the study of politics, which I will call political thought, cannot be theoretical in the sense Plato gave to it: that is, of universal validity. Political thought, in contrast, is practical, not theoretical, and it holds only for a limited number of cases and contexts. It holds "for the most part," as Aristotle put it, not for all time and place. If students of political theory are not to be parochial in the negative sense, then we need to study many other types of political reflection, not only the highly specialized and abstract academic genre called political theory. So, we should replace "political theory" with the phrase "political thought," as the more general category, in which political theory is one species. If we fail to do this, then we are going to continue the dominance of one genre of political thought by only accepting types of political thought in other traditions that approximate the parochial features of western political theory.

The central distinction between political theory and political thought more generally is that political theory presupposes that its central terms are rigid designators; concepts that have necessary and sufficient conditions for their application in every case. If this were not the reigning presumption, then theorists would not build general theories in the sense that this term has come to have in the west over the last half millennium: that is, the theory sets out the necessary and sufficient conditions for the application of political concepts in every case.

Political thought makes no such presumption. It is based on the presumption that political vocabulary is composed of terms that have an indeterminate number of criteria of application, and thus of uses (sense, reference, and evaluative force) and these are fought over and altered in the course of political struggles. They are modifiable "family resemblance" terms, as Wittgenstein puts it, or, in the fields of rhetoric and discourse analysis, metaphors, and cluster concepts. They have a range of senses and references and complex relationships among them, but no invariable set of properties in every instance. Accordingly, political judgment—the employment of these terms in actual cases—is akin to aesthetic judgement, not to the determinate judgment of theoretical reason that employs concepts with necessary and sufficient conditions for their application.[26]

Political thought in this broad sense emerges everywhere and anywhere that people converse on the ways they govern and are governed in all their activities. It is not restricted to a type of theory or a particular place of composition, such as within the institutions of higher education, or to reflection on a canonical set of institutions. Political thought develops in countless conversations and contexts. A mantra of the World Social Forum captures this crucial point of genuine global dialogue: "there is no global justice without epistemic justice."[27] That is, wherever there are people involved in practices of governance of oneself and others—and this is in every form of society, small or large—there is political thought in and about those practices of governance. They are co-extensive. Communities are epistemic communities with distinctive forms of knowing. These take many forms: all forms of written reflection, oral traditions, music, art, theater, direct action and inaction, private scripts, and so on can all be forms of political thought in this broad and "global" sense, both historically and in the contemporary period.[28]

It follows that the range of "texts" that should be included in the study of transnational political thought must be much broader than the narrow range of texts that conform to the canons of western political theory.[29] This is not only to decenter western political theory or any other form of official political theory in any other civilization. It is also to democratize local/global genuine dialogues among traditions of political thought by not privileging one authoritative type. And, it follows from this conclusion, that the form of genuine dialogue cannot be prescribed beforehand, because, to be true to these considerations of global justice, is to develop genuine dialogues from the ground up: from the dialogue-genres of the world's communities of political thought.

Political Thought *Takes Place* in Traditions

The next feature is that comparative political thought should always place political texts in their background traditions in order to make sense of them. A genuine dialogue is a dialogue across and among the world's traditions in which particular instances and genres of political thought have their homes. To ignore this and cherry-pick interesting ideas out of other peoples' traditions is to commit an epistemic and social injustice.

Oral and written traditions, in my opinion, are the background "modes of disclosure" of the world in which political thought emerges and takes place.[30] There is a multiplicity of political thought within any tradition, given the indeterminacy of the vocabulary, the standpoints of individual political thinkers, the problems of the times, and so on. Traditions are ongoing dialogues among their members, who accept, question, negotiate, and modify the aspects of their traditions as they carry them on. Thus, what functions as a "background" shared intersubjective presupposition and what functions as a "foreground" subject of discussion can vary over time. Members of traditions also engage, directly or indirectly, in dialogues with members of other traditions, exchange ideas, and use them in novel ways. Traditions are rarely or ever completely closed by a frontier. This "diffusion thesis" of the co-evolution of human traditions was advanced in nineteenth-century Berlin and substantiated by anthropologists in the twentieth.[31]

Political theorizing and political thinking more generally thus take place seamlessly within broader traditions in this sense and are meaningful in virtue of so being. This is why transnational comparative political theory and thought has to be dialogues among and across traditions if it is to avoid false dialogues of pre-judging and interpreting the political thought of other traditions within the background of one's own.[32]

For a comparative dialogue across traditions to be genuine the participants have to be able to call into the space of questions of the dialogue (to foreground) constitutive background features of the traditions involved in the course of the dialogue.[33] This is a condition of mutual understanding. These features are constitutive features of political thinking which members of traditions normally take for granted. Given the fact that traditions change, interact, and learn from each other, we know that this practice of foregrounding and mutual understanding is not only possible but actual.[34] However, we also know it is exceptionally difficult. As both Gadamer and Bohm underscore, calling into question a deep-seated prejudgment of one's traditional horizon of understanding goes against that person in a demanding sense. It brings an aspect of her or his identity and tradition (their "world" in Arendt's sense) into question and opens it to testing for what it both reveals and conceals. Initial reactions are often defensiveness, resentment, aggressive response, or finesse.[35] It requires the virtue of the courage of truthfulness for the participants to open themselves to each other in this self-critical and often self-transformative experience.[36]

Moreover, traditions of political thought, and members within them, are radically differently situated in relation to each other under the long and complex historical processes of globalization.[37] These massive inequalities along many axes would seem to make genuine dialogue across traditions impossible. However, the resiliency of traditions and the practices in which they are lived enables humans to continue to inhabit the processes of globalization differently.[38] It is not the case that globalization constructs the identities of individuals and groups all the way down, as early post-structuralism presumed. Rather, the relations between processes of globalization and their hegemonic forms of political thinking and the diverse traditions in which people live are immensely complex and irreducible to simple generalizations, as contextual studies of communities of non-assimilation show. Global inequalities and injustices make genuine dialogue and the exercise of the virtue of courage reciprocally across traditions exceptionally difficult, and the pretense of inclusion and dialogue is often simply the assimilating and subordinating ruse of the hegemonic partner.[39] Nevertheless, these conditions do not render genuine dialogue impossible or fruitless. As I will argue in the following sections, as difficult as it is, it is the only way that global injustices can be brought to light from the perspectives of the lived experience of the people who suffer them, and, reciprocally, call into question the deeply entrenched constitutive features of the hegemonic traditions and their secondary explanations that legitimate these injustices.[40]

Traditions Are Grounded in Practices and Places

One of the reasons traditions are resilient and billions of people are able to live diversely in the contemporary world, despite all the grand theories of convergence, is that traditions are grounded in practices. These practices include the following: first, everyday practices of the embodied, sensuous, emotional, reasonable, and unreasonable human beings in dialogical relationships to themselves, each other, the living earth, and the spiritual realm (practices of the self); and, second, the larger practices or forms of organization, interaction, and conflict resolution in which these self-practices are exercised. Furthermore, practices are grounded in places: in the ecosystems in which humans live. Thus, political theory makes sense in light of the conventions of political thought in which it is grounded, political thought in light of the traditions in which it is spoken and written, traditions in light of the practices in which they are embedded, and practices in the places in which they "take place."

It is not that these "circumstances" or "contexts," or some subset of them, determine political thought causally. Phenomenologically, the lived experience and lived meaning of political thought makes sense in light of embodied human interaction with tradition, practice, and place: the "lifeworld." On this view, humans are always already in a "perceptual dialogue" with the living earth that surrounds them by means of all their senses. "This perceptual reciprocity between our sensing bodies and the animate, expressive landscape both engenders and supports our more conscious, linguistic reciprocity with others."[41] If, in contrast, persons take the meaning of political thought to be a function of an autonomous system of signs, it can mean anything or nothing. They then give an abstracted spoken or written text of political thought meaning by placing and interpreting it in their background traditions, practices, and places without noticing they do so.

The striking consequence of this phenomenological view of meaning for genuine dialogue is the following. Not only do participants in a genuine dialogue have to enter into the dialogue with this practice-based and place-based view of the scope of the meaning of their own and others' political thought. The dialogue itself also should take place, as much as is humanly possible, where the interlocutors' utterances have their meaning in this worldly sense: that is, in each other's traditions, practices, and places if they are to achieve mutual understanding. If they meet only at conferences, public spheres, the United Nations, universities, or on Skype, their dialogues will be abstract, manipulative, and false. Thus "back to the rough ground" of meaning-in-use in traditions, practices, and places if we wish to understand one another.[42]

Despite the growing evidence for this view of meaning-in-use, the vast majority of global dialogue literature continues to take the model of an abstract, official public sphere as the appropriate site for global dialogues. In the exchange of disembodied speech-acts over presumptively tradition-transcendent norms in these empty spaces, each pre-interprets others in the terms of their background, and, while they appear to agree or disagree earnestly, simply agree or disagree with the proposed norm as they understand it within their tradition. They thus bypass the mutual understanding of the very differences the dialogue is supposed to clarify and reconcile. If there is apparent agreement, the underlying differences reappear when the norm is applied differently in practice, and then each accuses the other of not following the norm as they agreed in the exchange.[43]

Locating dialogues of comparative political thought in the places where they are practiced, especially for the less-powerful, is not only an issue of epistemic justice. It also gives oppressed minorities confidence and courage to speak truthfully to the powerful in their own languages and ways. This enactment in turn is empowering for younger members of the community who witness it. Taking the class out of the classroom, community-based and land-based course-work and workshop dialogues, study abroad and exchange programs are examples of meeting this condition.[44]

When such dialogue options are unavailable, it is the role of scholars of comparative political thought to simulate them, as much as possible, in their scholarship and teaching. This is done by situating texts in their contexts (traditions, practices, and places) in edited editions and in lectures. Publications, lectures, assignments, and class presentations are often in dialogical form among texts from different traditions in order to deparochialize western political theory and initiate cross-tradition understanding. Scholars of comparative political thought are either from the traditions they study and teach or spend years engaged in dialogues with members of the traditions and dialogues with the texts of the traditions (in Gadamer's sense). Comparative political thought draws on dialogue methods in contextual history of political thought, anthropology, comparative philosophy, linguistics, hermeneutics, postcolonial studies, gender studies, Indigenous studies, and community-based research, as well as developing new methods.[45]

Therefore, in these ways and others, the research and teaching of comparative political thought is dialogical all the way down in order to meet the challenges surveyed in the first five sections and generate meaningful knowledge. The following sections discuss ways that participation in genuine dialogues brings about comparative political knowledge.

Deep Listening and Non-Attachment

How does participation in genuine multi-tradition dialogues of comparative political thought overcome the six obstacles to deparochialization, bring to awareness the parochiality of political thought, take into account the four contexts of sense-making (secondary explanations and global power relations, broader language of political thought, political traditions, practices, and places), enable practices of openness and courage of truthfulness, bring about mutual understanding and mutual concern, and enable comparative and critical political judgments? This is the work of the next three sections. If participation is successful, it lays the intersubjective groundwork not only for thinking together across traditions but also for living together and conciliating disputes together nonviolently.[46]

To bring out the *way* that participation in these genuine dialogues bring about the transformative self-understanding of the participants I prefer the phrase dialogues of "reciprocal elucidation." It brings into focus the central feature of interdependency. The participants co-depend upon the reciprocal speech acts of listening and responding with each other to free themselves from their habitual mode of disclosure, to move around and see the field of the political from other limited disclosures, and thus to see the limits of their own in comparison and contrast. The intersubjective relationships of listening and responding in turn are gift-gratitude-reciprocity relationships, and, when successful, virtuous cycles of reciprocal elucidation and enlightenment that the participants bring into being and co-sustain by the ways they exchange speech acts of various kinds.[47]

A preparatory exercise is to become aware of and reflect on the problems with western political theory and the difficulties they create for understanding other traditions canvassed in the previous sections. The first participatory step is to practice the art of "deep listening" to the political thought of other traditions.[48] This involves cultivating an ethos of openness and receptivity to others.[49] One of the best ways of doing this is to disclose the dialogue, not initially as a comparative or critical question and answer game, but as an exchange of storytelling and narratives in which the participants say or perform where they are coming from and why they are here so they come to know each other, the ways they are comfortable talking to each other, the languages they prefer to use, and so on.[50] Deep listening also attends to the embodied and place-based dimensions of dialogue: being response to where the dialogue takes place, the setting, and the linguistic and non-linguistic interactions that make the participants feel comfortable with each other.[51] For example, when Indigenous people meet with other tribes or with settler governments in North America, practices of reciprocal deep listening and storytelling often lay the groundwork of relationships of peace and friendship before the contentious dialogue begins.[52]

All the genres of speech-acts in genuine dialogues of reciprocal elucidation share one feature with exchanging stories. They are nonviolent forms of conversation. They are "invitations" or "proposals" to the listeners to consider the issue at hand this way rather than that, and request their thoughtful response; trying again in another way if listeners do not understand, and so on. Imperatives (commands), strategic manipulation, and coercive threats have no place in genuine dialogue because they are modes of false dialogue (legislative and strategic). These relationships treat dialogue partners as means, rather than as reciprocally respect worthy ethical beings, and they lead to victory, defeat, or compromise, not to mutual understanding.[53]

Ethical practices of deep listening, of openness and receptivity, are partly but not fully cultivated through participation in dialogue. They also require preliminary practices of the self that prepare the participants for engagement. These are meditative practices on the importance of the dialogue for oneself and others, how its success depends on how one attends to what others say or do, controls one's emotions, and conducts oneself. The initial rounds of getting to know one another eases novitiates into the exercise of these dispositions because challenging questions are not raised.[54]

Finally, the practice of deep listening cultivates one of the most important dispositions of dialogue: non-attachment. As we have seen, humans are deeply attached to their background view of the world and the assumptions that compose it. It appears not as *a* view but *the* comprehensive view. It is attached not just to ways of thinking, but also to feelings, emotions, and the body.[55] When it is challenged, the immediate impulse or charge is anger and defensiveness or aggressiveness, and the depth of attachment can be seen in body language. This is "attachment." Pema Chodron explains its importance[56]:

> [*Shenpa*], the Tibetan word for "attachment" points to a familiar experience that is at the root of all conflict, cruelty, oppression, and greed. I think of *shenpa* as "getting hooked." Another definition is [...] the "charge"—the charge behind our thoughts and words and actions, the charge behind "like and don't like" [For example:] Someone criticizes you [...] or says a harsh word and immediately you feel a shift. There's a tightening that rapidly spirals into mentally blaming this person, or wanting revenge, or blaming yourself. Then you speak and act. The charge behind the tightening, behind the urge, behind the story line or action is *shenpa*.

Attachment forecloses genuine dialogue. The antidote is to cultivate the counter-disposition of non-attachment or "suspension" by means of ethical practices of meditation, patience, and deep listening. This is not to abandon one's own views or embrace relativism. It is simply to suspend one's attachment to them so one can listen deeply to others and enter into dialogue with them without prejudging what they say. Meditation, deep listening, and initial storytelling cultivate and strengthen non-attachment for the agonistic dialogue to come.

Empathy and Interdependency

Non-attachment, deep listening, openness, and receptivity create the pre-conditions for empathy; the intersubjective ground of comparative dialogues of genuine mutual understanding. Empathy is generated and sustained by participation in dialogues of reciprocal elucidation, but, there usually has to be beforehand a certain awareness of the need for empathy and a willingness to take the risks and exercise the courage it involves. If not, attachment and its vicious cycles of defensive-aggressive and counter defensive-aggressive misunderstanding and distrust hold sway. No one has given a better explanation of the need for empathy to open oneself to the difficult transformative experience of genuine dialogue than Franz Boas, the founder of dialogical anthropology in Germany, Canada, and the United States[57]:

> [T]he activities of the human mind exhibit an infinite variety of form among the peoples of the world. In order to understand these clearly, the student must endeavor to divest himself entirely of opinions and emotions based upon the peculiar social environment into which he is born. He must adapt his own mind, so far as feasible, to that of the people whom he is studying. The more successful he is in freeing himself from the bias based on the group of ideas that constitute the civilization in which he lives, the more successful he will be in interpreting the beliefs and actions of man. He must follow lines of thought that are new to him. He must participate in new emotions, and understand how, under unwonted conditions, both lead to action.

There are four more or less sequentially learned modes of empathy in dialogical interactions: (1) the coupling or pairing of one's living body with others' living body in perception and interaction in the course of dialogue (affective and sensorimotor coupling); (2) the imaginary movement of transposition of oneself into the places of other partners in dialogue (imaginary transposition); (3) the perspectival understanding of dialogue partners as others to oneself, and of oneself as another to them (mutual self- and other-understanding); (4) the ethical realization of the partners as ethical beings, similar in this regard to oneself (ethical awareness).[58]

The reciprocal logic of deep listening and responding moves the partners through these steps of imaginary transposition. They come to imagine and understand the experiences of each other to a considerable extent so that each participates in a new, intersubjective viewpoint that deparochializes their own first-person singular experience and places it in the field with others (modes 2 and 3). The fourth mode is the ethical perception of the other as a living being who deserves reciprocal concern and respect (manifested in deep listening). This concern is not abstract and general but an embodied and emplaced capacity of concern in response to the understanding of the lived experience (of modes 2 and 3). Mutual understanding and concern come together (in 3 and 4).

There are two distinct ways in which the movement of imaginary transposition, of putting oneself in the shoes of another, is understood.[59] In the first, "false" empathy, a person imagines herself or himself in the shoes of another, but does not change their self-understanding. This move displaces the other and discloses the other's situation through their own, transposed, parochial worldview, masquerading as universal, thereby bypassing deparochialization. In the second, genuine, Boasian empathy, through participation in genuine dialogue, partners are mutually drawn out, and draw themselves out, of their prejudgments, and drawn, and draws themselves, imaginatively into the lived experiences and lifeworlds of each other, as much as is humanly possible. This empathetic experience is imaginary transposition into another mode of being in the world with others. It is a "limit experience" in the double sense of neither complete departure from the limits of one's own lifeworld nor complete assimilation into the lifeworld of other partners, but a kind of intermediacy: being-with (*Mitsein*).[60]

The first point of empathetic imaginary transposition for comparative political thought is that it is not possible to know (or even to imagine) how to treat another concrete human being as an ethical human being unless we come to understand their suffering and well-being as they experience and articulate them in their traditional ways—in comparison with others. The ethical norms of "treating each other as ends rather than means" or "do unto others as you would have them do unto you" either hang in the air as vague, universal pronouncements or they are operationalized by linking them to the background prejudgments of the theorist, policy specialist, or activist.[61] Non-attachment and empathy deparochialize this imperious disposition and enable the mutual understanding that is the basis of appropriate ethical and political action.

It may seem that empathy is necessary in practical dialogues but inappropriate for dialogues with theoretical texts and traditions of political thought. I demur. Quentin Skinner and Sheldon Wolin have shown in different ways that political theories are written by living authors deeply engaged in responding to problems of injustice (suffering) and justice (well-being) of their times. Understanding texts in the ways that they were understood at the time, or in different contexts, requires explicating the problems and their contexts and enabling readers to imaginatively transpose themselves imaginatively into them. This differs in degree but not in kind from real-time dialogues.[62]

Empathetic imaginary transposition is not only the basis of reciprocal understanding. Meditation on the experience in dialogue of the lived experience of other ways of being begins to bring to awareness the interconnectedness and interdependency of all the participants and, by extension, all human beings. This is the infinite variety of forms of being human Boas mentions above. Ways of life of humans are seen perspectively, as one moves around; neither as independent, all the same, nor antagonistic; but, rather, interconnected and interdependent by infinitely complex webs of similarities and dissimilarities expressed in the languages of the world. This is the participatory experience of diversity awareness, of the lifeworld as a multiverse rather than universe, and of being-human *as* both being-there (*Dasein*) and being-with (*Mitsein*). This experience is expressed in different ways in many traditions.⁶³ For example, Thích Nhất Hạnh refers to this experience as "interbeing," his translation of *Tiep Hien*. He too argues that it comes to awareness through meditation, deep listening, empathy, and mutual understanding.⁶⁴

As ecologists and political ecologists argue, imaginary transposition can be extended through dialogues with non-human lifeforms: animals, plants, ecosystems, and the living earth as a whole (Gaia). These are participatory dialogues within and with the places in which political thought, traditions, and practices take place and on which they depend for their well-being. With deep listening, we too can imaginatively "think like a mountain," as Aldo Leopold argued we must do to save the planet, as Indigenous peoples have been doing for over thousands of years, and as teachers and students are learning to do today.⁶⁵

This experience of interconnectedness and interdependency calls into the space of questions the presupposition of much of modern western political thought that human beings are basically independent and antagonistic. From the empathetic dialogue perspective, this presupposition appears to be the manifestation of an underlying attachment (*shenpa*) to the modern western worldview as a whole; an aggressive refusal of non-attachment, openness, empathetic dialogue, and so of deparochialization.⁶⁶

It is important not to conflate empathy and compassion. Empathy enables mutual understanding and awareness of interdependency through dialogue. However, it does not provide motivation for acting together in response to the sufferings and injustices that empathetic dialogue discloses: that is, for ethical and political action. This requires the further step of compassion. Compassion is cognitive, sensible, and emotional repertoire of dispositional capacities that moves human from mutual understanding of concrete situations of suffering to appropriate forms of mutual action in response.⁶⁷ "Com-passion" (*Mitleiden*) means sharing the passions of suffering and well-being (*Mitfreude*) with others, not only imaginatively, as with empathy, but actually, in modes of acting ethically and politically together. It comes into praxis through empathy and dialogues of reciprocal elucidation.⁶⁸

In summary, deep listening and empathetic dialogue bring forth the dawning awareness of an ethical attitude or orientation among participants of being members in a world of human diversity and biodiversity. In contrast, as we have seen, the dominant tradition of modern moral and political theory from Socrates to Habermas, in contrast, discloses the world from a basically legislative stance over the moral and political world and nature. As a result, dialogue takes place within this juridical orientation, universalization, obligation and coercion displace empathetic dialogue, reciprocal elucidation and compassion. Both Peter Kropotkin and Albert Schweitzer argued that the modern ethical orientation of being-in-the-world-with diverse others developed in response to the parochialism and resulting injustices of the legislative orientation, and many have followed in their footsteps.[69]

This ethical orientation to comparative political thought is a manifestation of an ethical maxim common to many ethical and spiritual traditions: "do unto others as you would have them do unto you." As we have seen, there are two ways to interpret this norm. The first is the false—imperial colonizing or parochial—way of transposing yourself and your traditional worldview into the shoes of the other and thus arguing that others and their institutions should be made over in the image of yours, for this is what you would want. This is the standard modernist moral justification of both imperial globalization and violent resistances to it.[70] The second is the genuine way deep listening and empathetic dialogue. It assumes that what human beings would want to have done to them is for others not to impose their ways on them, but, rather to listen carefully to their own understanding of the situation they inhabit, in their own ways and traditions, until they imaginatively understand it as much as is humanly possible, then, in reciprocity, enter into a dialogue of comparison and contrast with other similar and dissimilar situations to work up good responses. In addition to enacting this famous maxim, the ethical orientation lays the indispensable groundwork for one of the oldest political norms in the western tradition, "what touches all must be agreed to by all," as well as for the newest, "all affected by any exercise of power should have a say (and often a hand) in the exercise of power."[71] As Schweitzer argued, it brings into being a basic "reverence for all forms of life."[72]

Reciprocal Elucidation and Transformation

The previous sections survey the complex conditions or stage-setting of the central activity of dialogical comparative political thought: translation.

Translation brings with it an additional set of conditions that need to be borne in mind by participants along with the previous ones. Translators today are situated in the dense relationships of translation constituted by the last five hundred years of translation across traditions among translators from hegemonic societies and the counter-translations of translators from subalternized societies ("writing-back"). That is, relationships of translation and counter-translation are located within the larger global "contrapuntal ensemble," as Edward Said called it, surveyed in Sections 2 and 3.[73]

These are not simple self/other relationships of translation. Translators are situated within an ensemble of different ways of using the language of political thought in their own societies along intersectional lines of inequality and difference: class, gender, ethnicity, race, region, language, sexual orientation, settler-indigeneity, and, as the same time, they are translating spoken and written texts from similarly complex societies.[74] These inequalities and differences are now so great that there is often little communication or understanding across them. The interweaving of political thought and traditions is yet more complex, due to the vast increase in "diffusion" since Boas and brought about by immigration from former colonies to metropole societies under postcolonial conditions, and *vice versa*, and the deeper penetration of settler-colonial societies, such as Canada and the United States, into the still colonized Indigenous Fourth World. Furthermore, the networkization of global communication; the global spread of capitalist modes of production, commodification, strategic-instrumental forms of thought, subjectivity and dialogue; the rise of institutions of global governance; the spread of international law and its presumptively universal language of commerce, human rights, and the good life; and the militarization of conflict and conflict resolution all bring with them complex relationships of communication.[75]

The great dangers in this situation are not only incomprehension and misunderstanding due to inequality and difference. They also include the ever-present danger of the reign of a global network Esperanto that brings about, at best, a fast-time listening and superficial communication, but not understanding. Interlocutors often use the same words, and so presume they understand each other, but, as we have seen, they understand the words differently because they interpret them in light of their own background form, or forms, of life. Or, they can barely cling to a meaningful form of life, as in the massive cases of impoverishment, forced migration, war refugees, climate refugees, and genocide.[76] In addition to the proliferation of strategic-instrumental and legislative dialogues, another danger is what might be called the dialogue of hegemonic ventriloquism in which the more powerful partners consult with and listen to the less-powerful others and then translate what they hear into the presumptively universal or higher language of their hegemonic discourses.[77] Yet another danger is the influence neo-liberal universities that promote many of these trends have on academic research.[78]

Bearing all these conditions and dangers of translation in mind, what are the distinctive features of translation dialogues of transformative reciprocal elucidation?

First, participation in translation dialogues of reciprocal elucidation "elucidates" or clarifies texts being translated in light of their contexts. In so doing, participants "enlighten" or bring enlightenment to each other.[79] This is a transformative experience consisting of the following six steps. Through dialogue they: (1) free each other partially from deep attachment to their worldviews; (2) move each other around to see the phenomenon (text) in question from each other's perspectives as much as humanly possible; (3) from these other perspectives each sees their own and others' perspectives as limited perspectives (mutual deparochialization); (4) through further dialogue they come to see similarities or commonalities, as well as dissimilarities, in the different ways they disclose the phenomenon from different perspectives; (5) they then go on to exchange critical and comparative judgments, and to see if these too share commonalities through negotiation or deliberation; and (6) thus, participation in this dialogical work of translation transforms and transposes the participants into its nonviolent, conciliatory mode of being-in-the-world-with-others and, *eo ipso*, into the pluriverse that participation both brings to light and teaches them how to be its enlightened citizens. This is the dialogical deparochialization of, and alternative to, the monological tradition of enlightenment and cosmopolitanism.[80]

The most important set of capabilities that participants acquire through participation—in addition to deep listening, empathy and, eventually, compassion—is called the intersubjective virtue of the courage of truthfulness: *parrhesia* and *satyagraha*.[81] The first and best known feature is the disciplined capacity to speak as truthfully as possible to others in the dialogue. This is not to speak "the truth," as it is commonly translated, for the obvious reason that participation in dialogue teaches the partners that no one person or tradition knows the whole truth, but only a limited perspective on it. Each participant *needs* the participation of all others, also speaking truthfully, to get as close to the truth as is humanly possible by sharing perspectives. They are interdependent in this radical sense. The second, less-known yet equally crucial, reciprocal feature is the courage to listen truthfully to what the others are saying no matter how difficult this is: that is, deeply and openly by means of non-attachment. When speakers and listeners exercise these reciprocal kinds of courage of truthfulness in taking turns, a third feature comes into being: a "parrhesiastic pact."[82] This is just the term for a genuine dialogical relationship among them. Being reciprocally truthful binds the parrhesiastic partners together in the search for truth. Each dialogue with others who see the situation differently is an "experiment in truth" in Gandhi's famous phrase.[83]

Next, how do truth-seeking participants proceed to bring about mutual understanding? The translating participants elucidate the phenomena (texts) in question (Q) by drawing analogies and dis-analogies to other phenomena with which the listeners are already familiar (F). They suggest, for example, that Q is similar to F in their tradition in the following aspects, yet dissimilar in other aspects. The two phenomena Q and F share what Wittgenstein calls one or more "family resemblances," just as members of families share different characteristics, but none is common to all members. A similarity is a criterion, or set of criteria, for identifying Q and F among the whole cluster of contestable criteria used to identify Q and F.

The dialogue continues with other analogies and dis-analogies, similarities and dissimilarities, with different phenomena of comparison and contrast, until a whole web of crisscrossing and overlapping similarities and dissimilarities between Q and series of Fs comes to light. Each similarity and dissimilarity forms an "intermediate step" that enables listeners and questioners to begin to get a sense of the meaning of Q in its traditional contexts relative to their own. These intermediate steps enable these partners to "see connections" between the phenomenon in question and the phenomena invoked in comparison and contrast. That is, they begin to see how Q is used in various contexts and shades of meaning, and so begin to acquire the ability to use the concept themselves: that is, to understand it in its context. These are steps one and two in reciprocal elucidation.

The reason why participants are able to acquire this kind of participatory ability and mutual understanding of other texts and traditions of political thought is that, *mutatis mutandis*, this is how humans acquire the ability to use and understand language in general. According to this view, humans acquire these abilities through examples and practice, not through the acquisition of a rule stating the necessary and sufficient criteria for the application of the concept in every case, because there is no such essential set of criteria. Wittgenstein illustrates this thesis by taking his readers through various examples of games, showing that there is no one criterion common to all of them, but similar and dissimilar criteria are invoked in different instances of games. He concludes the following: "we see a complicated network of similarities overlapping and crisscrossing: sometimes overall similarities, sometimes similarities of detail." He then goes on to show how participants learn meaning-in-use through examples and practice. They not only learn how concepts are used in different contexts by invoking crisscrossing and overlapping criteria. They also go on to learn how to give contextual reasons to contest habitual uses and to present novel uses. The dialogical work of translation is the extension of this ability to learn meaning-in-use by means of examples and practice in different traditions of political thought and to present translations of them that bring understanding to others. Wittgenstein calls such a translation a "surveyable representation (*uebersichtliche Darstellung*) that brings understanding in the sense of 'diversity-awareness' or 'seeing-as.'"[84]

As we have seen, interpretation and translation of particular "texts" has to include interpretation and translation of the contexts in which they make sense. This is especially important in comparative political thought. Political contests over the practices of politics are always also over the languages of political thought that are used to describe, evaluate, defend, and contest these practices. Although the contests of political theories appear more abstract, they are responses to them, and contributions that enter into the history of the languages of political thought. This ongoing contestedness of political concepts explains why Nietzsche says they have histories, not definitions.[85] Translation dialogues of reciprocal elucidation are no exception. They too are in these relations of contestation, of agreement and disagreement, of understanding and misunderstanding, of the languages of politics.[86] They bring to this field a distinctive nonviolent *way* of contestation.

The acquisition of the abilities of mutual judgment is much the same as mutual understanding. Practitioners of languages of political thought are always already involved in judgments because political concepts are never purely descriptive. They are terms that describe and evaluate at the same time: they "characterize" the phenomena. Think of "democracy," "freedom," "oppression," and so on. In addition, in learning how to use a concept in various contexts, they learn judgments of correct and incorrect uses, and how to give reasons to contest, criticize, and legitimate dominate uses, as well as to extend the use of concepts in new ways and give reasons *pro* and *contra*.

Moreover, in dialogues of reciprocal elucidation, standards and ways of judging are placed in the intersubjective space of translation and compared and contrasted, as in mutual understanding. Standards and ways of judgment are judged and counter-judged, critiqued and counter-critiqued, from various perspectives, within this being second-order.[87] Comparative insights and limits and strengths and weaknesses of various types are brought to light from various perspectives and the family resemblances and dissimilarities among them explored. When people learn a language or tradition of political thought they learn how to make judgments and counter-judgments, critique and counter-critique within a background structure of prejudgments that constitutes a worldview or form of representation.[88] As participants move through the six steps of translation dialogues of reciprocal elucidation they free each other from their background prejudgments to varying degrees and draw them into the foreground of comparison and critique.

The revolutionary feature of mutual understanding and mutual judgment is that they are not oriented to transcending the multiplicity of traditions and languages of political thought in order to understand and judge them from a universal viewpoint. They aim to deparochialize and de-transcendentalize this imperious disposition and place it in the field where it belongs, with other limited viewpoints. They orient the participants to learn how to understand and judge multi-perspectively from within the lifeworld of living theories, traditions, practices, and places of comparative political thought by learning their way around within them, and with each other. It is the practice of a worldly, *immanent* critique.

The practice of translation dialogues of reciprocal elucidation can be illustrated by three examples. Boaventura de Sousa Santos sees the "work of translation" as the disclosure of the political world as a pluriverse capable of being disclosed from multiple modes of disclosure in comparison with each other. He uses the example of the work of translating concerns over human dignity in terms of the western concept of human rights, the Islamic concept of *umma*, and the Hindu concept of *dharma*.[89]

In this case, the work of translation will reveal the reciprocal shortcomings or weaknesses of each one of these conceptions of human dignity once viewed from the perspective of any other conception. Thereby, a space is open in the contact zone for dialogue, mutual understanding and for identification, over and above conceptual and terminological differences, of commonalities from which practical combinations for action can emerge.

The lifelong work of Dennis Dalton in translating Gandhi's political thought is an exemplar of the reciprocal elucidation approach. He carefully situates Gandhi's political thought and practice in the historical context of Indian traditions and shows what is traditional and novel. He then compares and contrasts these translations and interpretations of Gandhi's thought and practice with equally careful, contextual interpretations of similar and dissimilar political thought and practice in the west. Readers are thus able to come to understand such complex concepts and practices as *swaraj* and *swadeshi* by way of their similarities and dissimilarities with freedom and economic self-reliance in western traditions, and thus go on to make comparative judgments themselves.[90] Last but not least, the most famous example of a decolonizing dialogue of reciprocal elucidation of comparative political thought is Gandhi's *Hind Swaraj* of 1909.[91]

In summary, mutual understanding and judgment that can be achieved in dialogues of reciprocal elucidation is neither a comprehensive view nor a consensus. It consists in bringing to light background forms and ways of thought and being from various traditions and becoming able to view and discuss them comparatively from different limited perspectives. They become meaningful for the participants. This is what Gadamer calls the "fusion of horizons" and Bohm describes as exposing and sharing of tacit meanings in common in dialogue.[92] The diverse forms and ways of thought and being are no longer isolated and foreign. They are *meaningful* precisely because the participants have elucidated the webs of similarities and dissimilarities (family resemblances) that connect them in their diversity.

To borrow a metaphor from Wittgenstein, the languages of comparative political thought compose a "labyrinth of paths. You approach from *one* side and know your way about; you approach the same place from another side and no longer know your way about."[93] The participants in a dialogue of reciprocal elucidation learn their way around the places and connecting paths and the labyrinth becomes full of meaning to them. Thus, a "genuine dialogue" of reciprocal elucidation is meaningful in this sense.[94] The "dia" in "dialogue" does not mean "two." It means to partake in and of *logos* (meaning) with others.[95]

Dialogues of reciprocal enlightenment exist in many cultures and they too exhibit webs of family resemblances and dissimilarities.[96] For example, in many Indigenous North American traditions, there are somewhat similar practices of dialogue that bring about similar transformative meaningfulness among participants. This is often called "being of one mind." To begin, they usually give thanks in reciprocity to Mother Earth for all the interdependent ecological relationships of gift-reciprocity (symbiosis) that sustain life.[97] Then, they listen carefully and quietly to each other's stories of where they come from and how they see from their different perspectives the situation that has brought them together. They understand these dialogue relationships as gift-reciprocity relationships, derived from dialogues with the living earth. The Nootka word for participation in such dialogues on the Northwest coast is "*Pa-chitle*" (tr. Potlatch), the verb "to give."[98] Moreover, within stories, there is usually a character, such as Raven on the Northwest Coast, who has the ability to transform him or herself in the ways of thought and being of other living beings, human, and more-than-human. The gift exchange of stories and mask dances transform the listeners into the ways of life narrated in the stories. Through engagement in these dialogues they become able to understand and share all the different meanings of their situation in common. This is to be of one mind. It lays the groundwork for negotiating and acting together in response to the situation they share.[99]

Finally, dialogues of reciprocal elucidation have a telos beyond mutual understanding and mutual judgment. First, the intersubjective world of shared meanings brings to light ways of thinking, judging, deliberating, and acting together in response to the situation they share that were *unimaginable and unthinkable* prior to the dialogue. This is often the practical reason for the dialogue. According to Aeschylus and Protagoras, the democratic system of justice in Athens was founded on this insight.[100] Even more importantly, the complex repertoire of nonviolent, contestatory, and conciliatory ways of being-with-each-other that the participants acquire in dialogue prefigure and dispose the participants to relate to others in similar ways when they respond to suffering, disagreement, and conflict in the lifeworlds they inhabit. In taking this further, compassionate step, they become the change they experience in dialogue.[101] They extend nonviolent practices of deparochializing political thought into the world of nonviolent practices of deparochializing and transforming unjust political action.[102]

Notes

1 This article was originally presented at the conference on "De-Parochializing Political Theory: East Asian Perspectives on Politics; Advancing Research in Comparative Political Theory," University of Victoria, Victoria BC, Canada, August 2–4, 2012. The conference literature suggested the focus on "moral standards for judging politics" that I decline in the opening sentence. I would like to thank Melissa Williams, Project Leader, East Asian Perspectives on Politics, and the main organizer of the conference for inviting me to participate and for her comments on my presentation. I would also like to thank Akeel Bilgrami, Paul Bramadat, Nikolas Kompridis, Anthony Laden, Andrew March, Tobold Rollo, Gina Starblanket, Heidi Stark, Yasuo Tsuji, and Feng Xu for their comments. I am also grateful to Monika

Kirloskar-Steinbach and Jim Maffie for their editorial comments on the draft. I am deeply indebted to John Borrows, Aaron Mills, and Joshua Nichols for discussions on all aspects of the article since 2012 and especially the sections on Indigenous peoples and their traditions of political thought and practice.

2 Foucault, *Use of Pleasure*, 8–9 (my italics). For my interpretation of this aim, see Tully, "To Think and Act Differently."

3 See Section 8.

4 I borrow the term "genuine" dialogue from the conference agenda. I mean by this term the type of dialogue I describe in this article. The participants engage in genuinely trying to understand each other and their concerns. I take this to mean what most people mean by a "meaningful" dialogue. See Section 8 for this sense of "meaningful."

5 I discuss the points in this and the following section in more detail in Tully, *Public Philosophy*, in dialogue in Tully, *Global Citizenship* and in Nichols and Singh, *Freedom and Democracy*.

6 I sometimes use "conversation" and "dialogue" interchangeably to emphasize that these conversations occur in everyday interactions. However, "conversation" is the broader term, including everyday dialogues that include some but not all of the conditions of genuine dialogue, yet are the intersubjective ground of genuine dialogue. For this type of distinction, see Laden, *Reasoning*.

7 Gadamer, *Truth and Method*, especially 341–80. For interpretations of Gadamer close to my own, see Davey, *Unquiet Understanding* and Benson, *Improvisation of Musical Dialogue*.

8 This is the central insight of Martin Heidegger's early *Being and Time* and it became the starting point for Edmund Husserl, Maurice Merleau-Ponty and the field of phenomenology, as well as for Gadamer. Ludwig Wittgenstein states that it is the central problem he addresses in the *Philosophical Investigations*, 109–15. He uses the terms "picture" and "form of representation" for mode of disclosure.

9 Capra and Luisi, *Systems View of Life*; Esbjorn-Hargens and Zimmerman, *Integral Ecology*.

10 Boas, *Mind*. In this classic text and his methodological articles, he used the example of how the unjust treatment of Indigenous peoples of the Northwest coast of North America by Europeans was redescribed by them in ways that legitimated it to explain how secondary explanations function. See Tully, "Rediscovering the World of Franz Boas."

11 Rousseau, *Discourse*.

12 This is a central problem of the Kantian tradition. See Allen, *End of Progress*.

13 Nietzsche, "Means to Real Peace." in "Wanderer and His Shadow." remark 284, 380–1.

14 Arendt, *On Violence*. For a recent restatement, see Dilworth, *Too Smart for Our Own Good*.

15 The anthropologist Wade Davis estimates that there are roughly 7000 traditions around the world. See his *Wayfinders*.
16 See Bohm, *Dialogue* for this sixth, crucial feature, and Mountz et al., "For Slow Scholarship."
17 One of the best known examples of an attempt at dialogues across traditions as a worldwide educational project is the United Nation's *Alliance of Civilizations*. It was set up by Turkey and Spain after 9/11/2001 to replace the military clash of civilizations with a dialogue of civilizations through cross-civilization education in dialogue from an early age. I was involved in the early drafting and I draw on this experience. See *United Nations Report on the High-Level Group on The Alliance of Civilizations* (2006).
18 de Sousa Santos, *Epistemologies of the South*; Tlostanova and Mignolo, *Learning to Unlearn*; Allen, *End of Progress*; Chakrabarty, *Provincializing Europe* for provincialization; Tully, *Democracy and Civic Freedom*, 15–132, *Imperialism and Civic Freedom*, 125–222 for de-imperialization; and Nichols, *World of Freedom* for the problem of deparochialization of western philosophy through Heidegger and Foucault.
19 Abram, *Spell of the Sensuous*, 93–136.
20 Arendt, *Human Condition*, 175–206.
21 Plato, "Apology," 24b–25c.
22 Socrates embodies the courage of truthfulness and the dialogical way of practicing it. He (or Plato) does not recognize the perspectival character of all individual practical knowledge claims (including his) and thus the need for the dialogical (democratic) negotiation of them to reach a truth acceptable to all, whereas Meletus and Protagoras (and the rhetorical tradition) do realize this. Arendt, "Socrates," 5–40; and Skinner, *Reason and Rhetoric* on the rhetorical tradition that follows from Aristotle on practical knowledge (and Section 8).
23 Temelini's *Wittgenstein and the Study of Politics* presents a careful survey of this tradition. Wittgenstein cites Socrates for the craving for generality and disregard of particular cases in *The Blue and Brown Books*, 20, 26–7. The later *Philosophical Investigations* is a dialogue with interlocutors who enact this craving for generality in different contexts.
24 For an introduction to this scholarship, inspired by Edward Said and Michel Foucault among others, see Tully, *Imperialism and Civic Freedom*, and Nichols and Singh, *Freedom and Democracy*.
25 In the modern period, Johann Herder was among the first to articulate this critical step in his response to the imperialism of Immanuel Kant's political philosophy and European political theory more generally. See Barnard, *Herder on Nationality*. Kant's replies are in his *Political Writings*, 192–220.
26 See Temelini, *Wittgenstein and the Study of Politics*; Laden, *Reasoning*; and Section 8.

27 See de Sousa Santos, *Epistemologies of the South*.
28 Tully, "Global Multiplicity of Public Spheres," and Tully, *Democracy and Civic Freedom*, 291–316.
29 I will continue to use "text" for the broad range of phenomena that are interpreted, translated and discussed in dialogues; such as political thought, speech, enactments, practices and activities, problems, traditions and places below. This is for the sake of simplicity; not to privilege written texts.
30 For "modes of disclosure" see above at Section 2.
31 Boas, *Mind*, 155–91. The diffusion thesis is associated with Alexander von Humboldt (1769–1859) and Adolf Bastian (1826–1905). These features of traditions are discussed by Wittgenstein in *On Certainty*. See Tully, *Democracy and Civic Freedom*, 39–70.
32 See section 2 for this problem.
33 This is the third obstacle to genuine dialogue introduced briefly in Section 2.
34 For a detailed examination of the possibility of foregrounding and mutual understanding in early modern treaty dialogues between Indigenous people and European settlers in North America, see Asch, *Being Here to Stay*.
35 Gadamer, *Truth and Method*, 341–57; Bohm, *Dialogue*, 70–95. They both argue that this kind of critical reflection cannot be carried out on one's own, monologically, or in dialogues within a tradition. They also argue that it does not bring about definitive or universal knowledge but openness to the experience of unexpected experience (insight). For the importance of this for global mutual understanding see Section 8.
36 See Foucault, *Courage of Truth*, for the origins of this ethical virtue in the west. See Section 8.
37 See the second step in Section 3 for this feature.
38 Scott, "Traditions of Historical Others," See also Tully, *On Global Citizenship*, 33–84.
39 The liberal norm of inclusion and process of transitional justice often function in this way. See, for example, Rajagopal, *International Law from Below*; Emon, and Tully, "Editors' Introduction."
40 This is one meaning of the mantra "there is no global justice without epistemic justice."
41 See Abram, *Spell of the Sensuous*, 89–90. He traces the development of this embodied, dialogical view of meaning from Edmund Husserl through Maurice Merleau-Ponty to eco-phenomenology. Wittgenstein refers to these four dimensions of meaningful human thought and action "forms of life." For substantiation of this view of meaning from other disciplines, see Thompson, *Mind in Life* and Capra and Luisi, *The Systems View of Life*. Abram became aware of this view of meaning through his dialogues with Indigenous peoples in North America and Asia.

42 Wittgenstein, *Philosophical Investigations*, 107. I am indebted to Tobold Rollo for discussions of this issue.
43 For concrete examples of how this occurs in the European Union see Wiener, *Invisible Constitution of Politics*. She has gone on to develop a global research project on conditions of genuine dialogue. See Wiener, *Theory of Contestation*.
44 For example, this is at the heart of community-based research and teaching with Indigenous peoples throughout Canada. The Faculty of Law and the Indigenous Governance Graduate Program at the University of Victoria have a number of exemplary programs: www.uvic.ca/igov, www.uvic.ca/law/ILRC.
45 For example, the *Cambridge Texts in the History of Political Thought* series, under the editorship and methodology of Quentin Skinner, classifies the texts as "thought" not theory, includes marginal texts and contextual introductions, and is expanding beyond the western canon.
46 This has been the aim of most dialogue approaches to world understanding and peace, as, for example, in the UN *Alliance of Civilizations* in the 2000s (see note 17). See Melchin and Picard, *Transforming Conflict Through Insight*.
47 I borrowed the term "reciprocal elucidation" from Foucault, "Polemics, Politics and Problematizations" and developed it in Tully, *Strange Multiplicity*. See Tully, *Democracy and Civic Freedom*, 15–38.
48 I discuss the features of dialogue primarily, but not exclusively, with reference to embodied linguistic dialogues. I believe most of these features apply with modification to reading dialogues with texts from other traditions and discussing them through writing and conversing with others (See Section 8).
49 Kompridis, "Receptivity, Possibility, and Democratic Politics."
50 Listening to and telling stories and narratives often brings insight into the modes of disclosure and traditions of the participants more clearly and unguardedly than question and answer. More importantly, it enables each participant to bring forth the world of the dialogue in terms of their background understanding, and "own" the space of dialogue when they speak, rather than being forced to speak within a set of prescribed norms.
51 For an excellent survey of literature on these features of deep listening and her own examples, see Beausoleil, "Responsibility as Responsiveness."
52 See Lessard, Johnston, Webber, *Storied Communities*; Miller, "Gifts as Treaties"; Alfred, *Wasase*, 13–17. See further Section 8.
53 This is a fundamental feature of the analysis of conversational reasoning-together advanced by Laden, *Reasoning*. See also Bohm, *Dialogue*, 24–9.
54 For these practices of deep listening in the Engaged Buddhist tradition of conflict resolution and reconciliation, see Thích Nhất Hạnh, *Interbeing*.
55 See Section 2. Attachment and non-attachment are studied under the terms subjectification (interpolation) and de-subjectification in western social sciences.

56 Chodron, *Practicing Peace in Times of War*, 55–6. Compare Bohm, *Dialogue*, 27–9. Bohm's conception of non-attachment (proprioception) includes the ability to reflect on one's presuppositions and their roots. Since this complex ability requires comparative dialogue, I associate it with that later phase of dialogue (Section 8).

57 Boas, *Mind*, 98. See Tully, "Rediscovering the World of Franz Boas," and Wilner, "A Global Potlatch."

58 For the neuroscience, phenomenological and ethical research that substantiates this account of empathy, see Thompson, *Mind in Life*, 382–412, and Johnson, *Moral Imagination*. Obviously, the first step does not apply in the dialogue with written texts, but, as we have seen, these are often based on embodied dialogues in the field (Section 5).

59 For a recent survey of the vast contemporary literature on these two senses of empathy, and the popularity of the false sense, to which I am indebted, see Nelems, "What Is This Thing Called Empathy."

60 See further Section 8.

61 This is the main thesis of Johnson, *Moral Imagination*.

62 Skinner, *Visions of Politics*; Wolin, *Politics and Vision*.

63 See Temelini's *Wittgenstein and the Study of Politics* for a study of this experience in Wittgenstein.

64 Thích Nhất Hạnh, *Interbeing*. See also Nelems "What Is This Thing Called Empathy"; Thompson, *Mind in Life*, and Merleau-Ponty, *Phenomenology of Perception*, for similar views.

65 See also Leopold, *Sand County Almanac*, 137–41; Harding, *Animate Earth*, 35–62; Abram, *Spell of the Sensous*, 73–92.

66 Dialogues of reciprocal elucidation bring this deep attachment to light and subject it to critical scrutiny: See section 8.

67 See, for example, Dalai Lama's *Beyond Religion* for how compassion builds on empathy and goes beyond abstract justice to action. For the importance of compassion and the failure of legislative morality to understand it, see Schopenhauer, "On the Basis of Morals."

68 See Section 8.

69 Kropotkin, *Ethics*; Schweitzer, *Civilization and Ethics*. For more recent work, see references at notes 57–68, and for a comparative discussion, see Lambeck, Das, Fassin, Keane, *Four Lectures on Ethics*.

70 See, Tully, "Rethinking Human Rights and Enlightenment" and Tully, *Imperialism and Public Philosophy*, 127–65, and Sections 2–3.

71 The Latin is *Quod omnes tangit ab omnibus approbari debet*. Another touchstone that plays the same role of consulting "all those who are affected" is *audi alteram partem*, always listen to the other side.

72 Schweitzer, *Civilization and Ethics*, 240–60.

73 Said, *Culture and Imperialism*.
74 Dhamoon, *Identity/Difference Politics*; Tuck and Yang, "Decolonization Is Not a Metaphor."
75 Tully, "Communication and Imperialism."
76 See Section 3 for this problem.
77 This is perhaps the most common form of colonizing translation, which includes only to subordinate and assimilate, while allowing a patina of multicultural differences to be recognized and celebrated. See Tully, *Democracy and Civic Freedom*, 291–316. Media panels of talking heads after protests are classic examples of this danger.
78 Mountz et al., "For Slow Scholarship."
79 Enlightenment in French, *L'Éclaircissement*, has these two senses as well and Foucault probably had this in mind when he coined the phrase "reciprocal elucidation." See Foucault, *The Foucault Reader*.
80 See Tully, "Diverse Enlightenments." For an influential articulation of a dialogue view of enlightenment, see Buber, *I-Thou* and *Between Man and Man*.
81 *Parrhesia* is the Greek term for this virtue. See Foucault, *Fearless Speech*; Foucault, *Courage of Truth*; Hénaff, *Price of Truth*, 101–55. *Satyagraha* is the term Gandhi invented to characterize holding on to and being moved by (*graha*) truthfulness (*satya*) in everything one says and does. See Gandhi, *Satyagraha* and Dalton, *Mahatma Gandhi*, 12–30.
82 Foucault, *Fearless Speech*, 11–20.
83 Gandhi, *Experiments with Truth* and note 102.
84 Wittgenstein, *Philosophical Investigations*, 65–8, 122. This is Wittgenstein's knowing-with alternative to Socrates' knowing-over in Section 3. In *Wittgenstein and the Study of Politics*, Temelini explicates Wittgenstein's account and shows how Charles Taylor uses it to explain cross-cultural understanding and judgment and Quentin Skinner to contextualize the history of political thought.
85 This internal relationship between political theory and political practice is the basis of the contextual schools of political thought since Nietzsche.
86 See Owen, "Reasons and Practices of Reasoning."
87 Wittgenstein compares this to the way orthographers deal with the word "orthography among others, without being second-order" (Wittgenstein, *Philosophical Investigations*, 121).
88 Wittgenstein explores the learning and questioning of judgments in *On Certainty*, remarks 104–52. "We do not learn the practice of making empirical judgments by learning rules: we are taught *judgments* and their connexion with other judgments. A *totality* of judgments is made plausible to us" (*On Certainty*, 140).
89 de Sousa Santos, "The Future of the World Social Forum," 17. He suggests that this kind of translation dialogue takes place at the World Social Forum.

90 See McDermott, Gordon, Embree, Pritchett, and Dalton, *Sources of Indian Traditions*, 183–452; Dalton, *Mahatma Gandhi* and Dalton, "Gandhi's Significance at the Center of Indian Political Discourse."
91 Gandhi, *Hind Swaraj and Other Writings*.
92 Gadamer, *Truth and Method*, 306–7; Bohm, *Dialogue*, 29–31. For a careful analysis of this "limit experience" in the case of Foucault (and Max Weber), see Szakolczai, *Max Weber and Michel Foucault*.
93 Wittgenstein, *Philosophical Investigations*, 203.
94 This answers the question at note 4 above.
95 Bohm, *Dialogue*, 6–7.
96 As noted in Sections 6 and 7.
97 See, for example, the "Rotinoshonni Thanksgiving Address of the Haudenosaunee," in Alfred, *Wasase*, 13–17.
98 Clutesi, *Potlatch*, 9–10.
99 See Borrows, *Drawing out Law*; Kimmerer, *Braiding Sweetgrass*; Atleo, *Tsawalk*; Wilner, "A Global Potlatch"; Napoleon, *Ayook*; Wilson, *A Post-Delgamuukw Philosophical Feast*.
100 Athenians introduced the jury system when they realized that a single agent could not judge justly and devolved judgment to the *demos* in the form of juries. Aeschylus, "Eumenides," and see Manderson, "Athena's Way: The Oresteia and the Rule of Law" for this interpretation; Plato, *Protagoras*. This background makes sense of Meletus' disagreement with Socrates in the *Apology* (see Section 3).
101 For the role of compassion, see Section 7.
102 Gandhi's nonviolent mode of contesting and transforming violent oppressors, *Satyagraha*, for example, is interpreted in this way by Gandhi's good friend, Gregg, *Power of Nonviolence*. For an enlightening example of how to take dialogues of reciprocal elucidation into the world of cooperative responses to neo-liberal globalization, see Ouziel, *Vamos Lentos Porque Vamos Lejos*.

References

Abram, David. *The Spell of the Sensuous*. New York: Random House, 1996.
Aeschylus. "Eumenides." In *Oresteia*. Translated by Alan Sommerstein. 354–486. Cambridge MA: Harvard University Press, 2009.
Alfred, Taiaiake. *Wasase: Indigenous Pathways of Action and Freedom*. Peterborough: University of Toronto Press, 2005.
Allen, Amy. *The End of Progress: Decolonizing the Normative Foundations of Critical Theory*. New York: Columbia University Press, 2015.
Arendt, Hannah. *On Violence*. New York: Harcourt, 1970.

Arendt, Hannah. *The Human Condition*. Chicago: Chicago University Press, 1998.
Arendt, Hannah. "Socrates." In *The Promise of Politics*. Edited by Jerome Kohn. 5–39. New York: Schocken Books, 2005.
Asch, Michael. *On Being Here to Stay*. Toronto: University of Toronto Press, 2014.
Atleo Sr., Richard. (*Umeek*), *Tsawalk: A Nuu-chah-nulth Worldview*. Vancouver: UBC Press, 1996.
Barnard, Frederick M., ed. *Herder on Nationality, Humanity and History*. Montreal: MacGill Queen's University Press, 2003.
Beausoleil, Emily. "Responsibility as Responsiveness: Enacting a Dispositional Ethics of Encounter." *Political Theory*, 45, no. 3 (June 2017): 291–318.
Benson, Bruce. *The Improvisation of Musical Dialogue: A Phenomenology of Music*. Cambridge: Cambridge University Press, 2003.
Boas, Franz. *The Mind of Primitive Man*. New York: Macmillan, 1911.
Bohm, David. *On Dialogue*. London: Routledge, 2014.
Borrows, John (*Kegedonce*). *Drawing Out Law: A Spirit's Guide*. Toronto: University of Toronto Press, 2010.
Buber, Martin. *I-Thou*. Translated by Walter Kaufmann. New York: Simon & Shuster, 1970.
Buber, Martin. *Between Man and Man*. London: Routledge, 1993.
Capra, Fritjof and Pier L. Luisi. *The Systems View of Life*. Cambridge: Cambridge University Press, 2014.
Chakrabarty, Dipesh. *Provincializing Europe: Postcolonial Thought and Historical Difference*. Princeton: Princeton University Press, 2000.
Chodron, Pema. *Practicing Peace in Times of War*. Boston: Shambala, 2007.
Clutesi, George. *Potlatch*. Vancouver: Sidney, 1969.
Dalai Lama. *Beyond Religion: Ethics for the Whole World*. Toronto: McClelland & Stewart, 2012.
Dalton, Dennis. *Mahatma Gandhi: Nonviolent Power in Action*. New York: Columbia University Press, 2012.
Dalton, Dennis. "Gandhi's Significance at the Center of Indian Political Discourse." Lecture given at the Gandhi Workshop, Reed College, Portland Oregon, April 16, 2016.
Davey, Nicholas. *Unquiet Understanding: Gadamer's Philosophical Hermeneutics*. Albany: State University of New York Press, 2006.
Davis, Wade. *The Wayfinders: Why Ancient Wisdom Matters in the Modern World*. Toronto: House of Anansi Press, 2009.
de Sousa Santos, Boaventura. "The Future of the World Social Forum: The Work of Translation." *Development* 48, no. 2 (2005): 15–22.
de Sousa Santos, Boaventura. *Epistemologies of the South: Justice against Epistemicide*. London: Taylor and Francis, 2015.
Dhamoon, Rita. *Identity/Difference Politics: How Difference is Produced and Why It Matters*. Toronto: UBC Press, 2009.

Dilworth, Craig. *Too Smart for Our Own Good: The Ecological Predicament of Humankind*. Cambridge: Cambridge University Press, 2010.
Esbjorn-Hargens, Sean and Michael E. Zimmerman, eds. *Integral Ecology: Uniting Multiple Perspectives on the Natural World*. Boston: Integral Books, 2009.
Emon, Anver and James Tully, eds. "Editors' Introduction: Pluralism, Constitutionalism, and Governance." *Middle East Law and Governance* 4, nos. 2–3 (2012): 189–93.
Foucault, Michel. "Polemics, Politics and Problematizations." In *The Foucault Reader*. Edited by Paul Rabinow. 381–90. New York: Pantheon Books, 1984.
Foucault, Michel. *The Use of Pleasure*. Translated by Robert Hurley. New York: Pantheon Books, 1985.
Foucault, Michel. *Fearless Speech*. Los Angeles: Semiotext, 2001.
Foucault, Michel. *The Courage of Truth*. New York: Palgrave Macmillan, 2011.
Gadamer, Hans-Georg. *Truth and Method*. Translated by Joel Weinsheimer and Donald G. Marshall. New York: Continuum, 1999.
Gandhi, Mohandas K. *Satyagraha: Non-violent Resistance*. Boston: Shocken, 1961.
Gandhi, Mohandas K. *Hind Swaraj and Other Writings*. Edited by Anthony J. Parel. Cambridge: Cambridge University Press, 2009.
Gandhi, Mohandas K. *My Experiments with Truth*. London: Fitzhenry & Whiteside, 2011.
Gregg, Richard. *The Power of Nonviolence*. Edited by James Tully. Cambridge: Cambridge University Press, 2018.
Hạnh, Thích Nhất. *Interbeing: Fourteen Guidelines for Engaged Buddhism*. Berkeley: Parallax, 1993.
Harding, Stephan. *Animate Earth: Science, Intuition and Gaia*. Cambridge MA: Green Books, 2013.
Hénaff, Marcel. *The Price of Truth: Gift, Money, and Philosophy*. Translated by Jean-Louis Morhange. Stanford: Stanford University Press, 2010.
Johnson, Mark. *Moral Imagination: Implications of Cognitive Science for Ethics*. Chicago: Chicago University Press, 1996.
Kant, Immanuel. *Political Writings*. Edited by Hans S. Reiss. Cambridge: Cambridge University Press, 1991.
Kimmerer, Robin W. *Braiding Sweetgrass: Indigenous Wisdom, Scientific Knowledge, and the Teachings of Plants*. Minneapolis: Milkweed Editions, 2013.
Kompridis, Nicholas. "Receptivity, Possibility, and Democratic Politics." *Ethics and Global Politics* 4, no. 4 (2011): 255–72.
Kropotkin, Peter. *Ethics: Origin and Development*. London: George F. Harrap, 1924.
Laden, Anthony. *Reasoning: A Social Picture*. Oxford: Oxford University Press, 2012.
Lambeck, Michael, Veena Das, Didier Fassin, and Webb Keane. *Four Lectures on Ethics: Anthropological Perspectives*. Chicago: Hau Books, 2015.
Leopold, Aldo. *Sand County Almanac*. New York: Oxford University Press, 1966.
Lessard, Hester, Rebecca Johnston, and Jeremy Webber, eds. *Storied Communities: Narrative of Contact and Arrival in Constituting Political Community*. Vancouver: UBC Press, 2010.

Manderson, Desmond. "Athena's Way: The Jurisprudence of *Oresteia*." *Law, Culture and the Humanities* 15, no. 1 (2019): 253–76.
McDermott, Rachel F., Leonard A. Gordon, Ainslie T. Embree, Frances W. Pritchett, and Dennis Dalton. *Sources of Indian Traditions*. Volume 2, Third Edition. New York: Columbia University Press, 2013.
Melchin, Kenneth R. and Cheryl A. Picard. *Transforming Conflict Through Insight*. Toronto: Toronto University Press, 2008.
Merleau-Ponty, Maurice. The *Phenomenology of Perception*. Translated by Donald A. Landes. London: Routledge, 2012.
Miller, Cary. "Gifts as Treaties." *American Indian Quarterly* 26, no. 2 (Spring 2002): 221–46.
Mountz, Alison et al. "For Slow Scholarship: A Feminist Politics of Resistance Through Collective Action in the Neoliberal University." *ACME: An International E-Journal for Critical Geographies* 14, no. 4 (2015): 1235–59.
Napoleon, Valerie R. *Ayook: Gitksan Legal Order, Law and Legal Theory*. Ph.D. dissertation, Faculty of Law, University of Victoria, 2009.
Nelems, Rebeccah, J. "What Is This Thing Called Empathy?" In *Exploring Empathy: It Propagations, Perimeters, and Potentialities*. Edited by Rebeccah Nelems and Nic Theo. 17–38. London: Brill, 2017.
Nichols, Robert. *The World of Freedom: Heidegger, Foucault, and the Politics of Historical Ontology*. Stanford: Stanford University Press, 2014.
Nichols, Robert and Jakeet Singh, eds. *Freedom and Democracy in an Imperial Context: Dialogues with James Tully*. New York: Routledge, 2014.
Nietzsche, Friedrich. "The Means to Real Peace." in "The Wanderer and His Shadow." In *Human, All Too Human: A Book for Free Spirits*. Translated by R. J. Hollingdale. 380–1. Cambridge: Cambridge University Press, 1986.
Ouziel, Pablo. *Vamos Lentos Porque Vamos Lejos: Towards a Dialogical Understanding of Spain's 15M*. Ph.D. Dissertation, University of Victoria, Victoria BC, 2015.
Owen, David. "Reasons and Practices of Reasoning." *European Journal of Political Theory* 15 (2016): 172–88.
Plato. *Protagoras*. Edited by Gregory Vlastos. Indianapolis: Bobbs Merrill, 1956.
Plato. "The Apology." In *The Trial and Death of Socrates*. Translated by George M. A. Grube. 21–43. Indianapolis: Hackett, 1975.
Rajagopal, Balakrishnan. *International Law from Below: Development, Social Movements, and Third World Resistance*. Cambridge: Cambridge University Press, 2003.
Rousseau, Jean-Jacques. *Discourse on the Origin of Inequality*. Translated by Franklin Philip. Oxford: Oxford University Press, 1994.
Said, Edward. *Culture and Imperialism*. New York: Knopf, 1993.
Schopenhauer, Arthur. "On the Basis of Morals." In *Two Fundamental Problems of Ethics*. Translated by David E. Cartwright and Edward E. Erdmann. 210–75. Oxford: Oxford University Press, 2010.
Schweitzer, Albert. *Civilization and Ethics*. London: A & C Black, 1946.

Scott, David. "Traditions of Historical Others." *Symposia on Gender, Race and Philosophy* 8, no. 1 (Winter 2012): 1–8, http://mit.edu/sgrp.

Skinner, Quentin. *Reason and Rhetoric in the Philosophy of Hobbes*. Cambridge: Cambridge University Press, 1996.

Skinner, Quentin. *Visions of Politics: Volume I: Regarding Method*. Cambridge: Cambridge University Press, 2002.

Szakolczai, Arpad. *Max Weber and Michel Foucault: Parallel Life-Works*. London: Routledge, 1998.

Temelini, Michael. *Wittgenstein and the Study of Politics*. Toronto: University of Toronto Press, 2015.

Thompson, Evan. *Mind in Life: Biology, Phenomenology and the Sciences of Mind*. Cambridge MA: Belknap Press, 2007.

Tlostanova, Madina V. and Walter D. Mignolo. *Learning to Unlearn: Decolonial Reflections from Eurasia and the Americas*. Columbus: Ohio State University Press, 2012.

Tuck, Eve and K. Wyane Yang. "Decolonization Is Not a Metaphor." *Decolonization: Indigeneity, Education, Society*, http://decoloniziation.org/index.php/des/article/view/18630, August 12, 2020.

Tully, James. *Strange Multiplicity*. Cambridge: Cambridge University Press, 1995.

Tully, James. "Diverse Enlightenments." *Economy and Society* 32, no. 3 (2003): 485–505.

Tully, James. "To Think and Act Differently." In James Tully. *Democracy and Civic Freedom, Public Philosophy in a New Key*, Volume I, 71–132. Cambridge: Cambridge University Press, 2008.

Tully, James. *Imperialism and Civic Freedom, Public Philosophy in a New Key*, Volume II, Cambridge: Cambridge University Press, 2008.

Tully, James. "Rethinking Human Rights and Enlightenment." In *Self-Evident Truths? Human Rights and the Enlightenment*. Edited by Kate E. Tunstall. 3–35. London: Bloomsbury, 2012.

Tully, James. "On the Global Multiplicity of Public Spheres." In *Beyond Habermas: Democracy, Knowledge and the Public Sphere*. Edited by Christian J. Emden and David Midgley. 169–204. New York: Berghahn, 2013.

Tully, James. "Communication and Imperialism." In *Critical Digital Studies*. Edited by Arthur Kroker, and Marilouise Kroker. Second Edition, 257–82. Toronto: University of Toronto Press, 2013.

Tully, James. *On Global Citizenship: James Tully in Dialogue*. London: Bloomsbury, 2014.

Tully, James. "Rediscovering the World of Franz Boas: Anthropology, Equality/Diversity and World Peace." In *Indigenous Visions: Rediscovering the World of Franz Boas*. Edited by Ned Blackhawk and Isaiah Wilner. 111–46. New Haven: Yale University Press, 2016.

United Nations Report. "The Alliance of Civilizations." 2006. Accessed August 11, 2020. www.unaoc.org.

Wiener, Antje. *The Invisible Constitution of Politics: Contested Norms and International Encounters*. Cambridge: Cambridge University Press, 2008.
Wiener, Antje. *A Theory of Contestation*. Heidelberg: Springer, 2014.
Wilner, Isaiah. "A Global Potlatch: Identifying Indigenous Influence on Western Thought." *American Indian Culture and Research Journal* 37 (2013): 87–114.
Wilson, Vernon. *A Post-Delgamuukw Philosophical Feast: Feeding the Ancestral Desire for Peaceful Coexistence*. MA thesis, Trinity Western University, Langley BC, 2015.
Wittgenstein, Ludwig. *The Blue and Brown Books*. Oxford: Blackwell, 1972.
Wittgenstein, Ludwig. *On Certainty*. Edited by G. E. M. Anscombe and G. H. von Wright. Oxford: Blackwell, 1974.
Wittgenstein, Ludwig. *Philosophical Investigations*. Translated by G. E. M. Anscombe, P. M. S. Hacker and Joachim Schulte. Oxford: Wiley Blackwell, 2009.
Wolin, Sheldon. *Politics and Vision*. Princeton: Princeton University Press, 2004.

2

A Conversation with James Tully's "Deparochializing Political Theory and Beyond"

Garrick Cooper

In "Deparochializing Political Theory and Beyond," James Tully puts forward, what appears on the face of it, a humble request: to engage in a *genuine dialogue*. The request appears humble in the sense that it simply seems like a very human endeavor to communicate genuinely and to genuinely communicate. However, such a proposal becomes increasingly less humble and more elusive when resources and power are at stake, or in other words, when matters are political. Tully though temporarily suspends analyses of power to explore some of the psycho-cognitive challenges of achieving a *genuine dialogue* between and across political thought systems with the aim of generating "critical mutual understanding" (Tully 1). Further, he calls for *translations* of political thought that move beyond the linguistic to the phenomenological dimensions of dialogue. Notwithstanding some of the obstacles that he identifies in part two—in particular the discussion of "false" dialogues (Tully 3)—the premise then of his paper is that there is indeed a willingness and commitment to engage in a dialogue. To engage in a dialogue is to begin a relationship open to hitherto unexplored possibilities.

Is it possible though that Tully's *genuine dialogue* is a contradiction or paradox? The word *genuine* comes from the Latin word *genuinus*, meaning "native, natural, innate" which in turn comes from the root word *gignere* meaning "to beget."[1] To beget something signals that a set of forces and energy have been coalesced leading to the creation of something. "Natural" suggests that something would come into existence by itself, or free from an external or "unnatural" intervention. An unnatural intervention often means human intervention. Think here for example of an animal documentary where an animal might be injured, and rather than humans intervening, the prevailing logic is "to let nature take its course." A dialogue here though demands human intervention otherwise you would just be talking to yourself, even if other humans were present. Perhaps then, dialogues if they are to be truly genuine, or at least not unnatural, are premised upon a relationship with, and commitment to, the other? Here, we return to Tully. Dialogical relationships are his central theme. These are not merely cognitive or intellectual exercises or exchanges, but matters of the heart and the stomach.[2] Through dialogues we give a little of ourselves to the other while simultaneously opening our hearts to the other and relationships form. Complicating things further however is that the new relationship is often mediated through and by our existing sets of relationships. A re-examination of our existing relationships in the context of a burgeoning new relationship is called for.

Genuine dialogues, for Tully have liberatory potential for participants, and can "free each other partially from *deep attachments* to their worldviews" (Tully 22). To be free though is presented with the caveat "partially," and with the distinction between a "deep attachment" and being completely detached from those ideas. It is indeed difficult to imagine how one might completely detach from an idea once we have become conscious of that idea, let alone an idea that we have a significant investment politically. For Tully, attachments we have to ideas about the world can be both a barrier to and an enabler of understanding; in other words, they can serve both positive and negative functions. "Deep" attachments that convey a greater sense of certainty and completeness are more problematic for translations across political thought systems than simply "attachments," which conversely convey more tentativeness and incompleteness; in short, possibilities are kept alive.

Deep attachments have the effect of concealing something. To keep something concealed requires an effort, even if we are not always conscious of such efforts, nor of that which we conceal. Such an effort smacks of Sartrean bad faith.[3] Lewis R. Gordon states that "Bad faith is a lie to the self, one that involves an effort to hide from one's freedom."[4] The act of concealing something through deep attachments is bad faith because we are not willing to confront a reality over which we have no control over—the acceptance of which might require us to change. Deep attachments require less of a relationship with reality. Because they are hidden in our deepest recesses, they are not readily accessible or available for reality's scrutiny. It takes courage to face reality.

Tully turns to Foucault's discussion of the ancient Greek idea of *parrhesia* and Gandhi's concept of *satyagraha* which he describes as the "intersubjective virtue of the courage of truthfulness" (Tully 22) to explore a more open relationship with reality in building dialogical relationships with one another. His proposal is put forward against a backdrop of human relationships a completely different sort, which are established through and perpetuated by patriarchies, aristocracies, colonialism and imperialism, and normative gender social roles and labor divisions. Under the logic of these regimes, the "other" is always lacking—not completely human, not completely a man, just not complete. This logic was famously diagnosed by Frantz Fanon in *Black Skin, White Masks*. The colonized black man and woman are always striving to be recognized as completely human. To be completely human was to acquire white language, white culture, and a white lover or partner. Whilst clearly the colonizer-colonized relationship is oppressive for the colonized, Fanon shows that it was also problematic for the colonizer, for their inability to imagine a being outside of a relationship was also characterized by an inability to see the other as fully human.[5]

Tully has a completely different relationship in mind which is indeed a radical departure from the Manichean master-slave relationship just described. He describes a relationship that is based on interdependence, where "Each participant needs the participation of all others" (Tully 22). The starting point is that each other is already fully human, and as such both have the full range of human faculties; the ability to feel and experience emotions, to think deeply about the world in ways that are meaningful and efficacious. We have something to offer one another, as "parrhesiastic partners" in "truth-seeking" premised on an openness in how we engage with one another through listening, questioning, and speaking.

In Māori communities (indigenous people of New Zealand) we have a form of "truth-seeking" when negotiating where the body of a relative will be interred. When kin die outside of our tribal regions, we have a tradition of making a *tono tūpāpaku,* or a request for the deceased's remains, at the funeral so that they may be returned to their ancestral lands for burial. For Māori, death rites are seen as perhaps the most important of all. Over the last thirty years or so there have been a number of cases that have received significant national media attention in New Zealand; largely where the partner of the Māori deceased was a Pākehā (white person) and disputes arose over where the deceased would be finally laid to rest. Such cases are euphemistically referred to as "body-snatching," the implication being that bodies taken were done so without "permission." One recent case is still unresolved after nearly ten years.[6]

The term "body-snatching" though implies a particular type of intent; that is, the body was going to be taken whether or not the immediate family acquiesced to the request. It implies that a request was more a violent demand. This despite the fact that *tono* are made quite regularly within Māori communities without any public furor. The request is read as having only one of two possible answers: "yes, you may take the body" or "no, you can't." And just as likely, the intent of the request is read so that only an affirmative response to the request would be accepted. To be clear, there can be quite "rigorous" debates arising from a *tono*, and the debates can go on for a very long time, particularly if the deceased was prominent. The intent of the *tono* was not to have the body returned necessarily. Rather it was to find out where the rightful resting place for the body was. The request does presuppose a view about that rightful resting place but not that it was the only rightful place. Even very "rigorous" requests leave open possibilities, otherwise the request would be in bad-faith—by denying its premise—and also an example of a "false dialogue"; in which case the charade should be done away with and the body should just be "snatched." "Truth-seeking" here, which takes the form of speaking as faithfully possible about one's connections to the deceased, reciting genealogies, telling stories about the deceased and her or his deeds and wishes, but above all, looking for who would metaphorically *fight* for the body; the implication being that they would likely then look after the body once interred. The rightful resting place then was genuinely a negotiated outcome, and to be in good faith, all parties are required to make an earnest case while keeping open the possibility that their case might not be "successful." "Success" here though is measured by both parties being assured that the deceased's body will be cared for and looked after for in death. Further, by both parties engaging in making a strong case to look after the dead body, they were also both honoring the deceased. Bonds between kin and in-laws are often reaffirmed and strengthened by *tono tūpāpaku*.

Bonds and relationships, can indeed be forged, tested, and strengthened by the most rigorous of discussions. Dialogical relationships as set out by Tully with the purpose of "truth-seeking" have the potential to bring scrutiny to ideas that are located in our archaeological middens of thought. There may be treasures worthy of holding onto and there may just be the remnants of waste; yet all have the capacity to provide us with greater understanding of our thought systems and generate "critical mutual understanding." Tully's proposal should however come with a warning: genuine dialogues if they are to be truly transformative will require us to change, and change can be painful and traumatic, for some, more than others.

Notes

1. Barnhart, *Chambers Dictionary of Etymology*, 428.
2. In Māori (indigenous people of New Zealand) thought, the pit of the stomach is where emotions reside and are manifest.
3. See Chapter 2 of Sartre's *Being and Nothingness*, 47–70. Also see Gordon's *Bad Faith and Antiblack Racism*. In particular, in this paper I draw from Chapter 1 "A 'Determined' Attitude That Involves Lying to Ourselves," 8–9 and Chapter 4 "The Elusiveness of Transcendence and the Comfort of Facticity," 16–18.
4. Gordon, *Existentia Africana*, 75.
5. Gordon, *Fanon and the Crisis of the European Man*.
6. See Mika, "Body-Snatching," for a discussion on some recent cases and analysis of the New Zealand law dealing with the bodies of deceased.

References

Barnhart, Robert, ed. *Chambers Dictionary of Etymology*. Edinburgh: Chambers Harrap Publishers Ltd, 2008.

Fanon, Frantz. *Black Skin, White Masks*. New York: Grove Press Inc, 1967.

Gordon, Lewis R. *Bad Faith and Antiblack Racism*. New Jersey: Atlantic Press International, 1995.

Gordon, Lewis R. *Fanon and the Crisis of the European Man: An Essay on Philosophy and the Human Sciences*. New York: Routledge, 1995.

Gordon, Lewis R. *Existentia Africana: Understanding African Existential Thought*. New York: Routledge, 2000.

Mika, Carl. "Body-Snatching": Changes to Coroners' Legislation and Possible Māori Responses." *AlterNative: An International Journal of Indigenous Peoples* 5, no. 1 (2009): 27–41.

Sartre, Jean-Paul. *Being and Nothingness: A Phenomenological Essay on Ontology*. New York: Washington Square Press, 1956.

3

Whose Tradition? Which Practices?

Sor-hoon Tan

If being parochial means valuing only the knowledge of one's tradition, then many Asian universities are not parochial; their students study western political theory, sometimes, but not always, together with Asian political thought; and more often than not, it is not Asian traditions that take precedence. This is hardly surprising given that many Asian universities have adopted western models of education and employ faculty members from Europe and North America; even local faculty members probably have received their graduate training in the west. Furthermore, tertiary education is seen as a stepping stone to profitable careers—universities are therefore expected to equip students with western-centric knowledge and skills that will make them competitive in the global economy.

What should one do when faced with Asian students who accept western political theory as universal knowledge, excel in such education, and resent or would resent being required to study Asian political thought? Not only do these students feel little sense of ownership for Asian traditions, if they think about it at all, but they also assume that these are obsolete premodern ways of thought and living that their parents have already rejected, and that they are better off without. Paternalistically imposing curricula including Asian political thought could do more harm than good insofar as one's objective is to help them appreciate Asian traditions, whether as their own or as (by now) an alien tradition. Telling them they should study those texts and value their teachings because their ancestors created them is not likely to work. Attempting to present those traditions as valuable by the epistemic (and other) standards such students are familiar with would perpetuate the epistemic injustice highlighted in works arguing for decolonizing and de-imperializing political theory and other western-as-universal knowledge, which are in many ways similar to the de-parochializing project (Tully 13).

The article suggests that before introducing students to comparative political thought, including texts from Asian traditions in Political Theory or Philosophy courses, their education needs to first engage in the critical practice of questioning their own "background horizon of disclosure" (Tully 4). Were the students completely westernized, the approach to de-parochializing or decolonizing their study of politics might not differ from teaching students in western societies insofar as their "horizon of disclosure" is similarly western. However, the situation is often more complicated. Even when they think of themselves as no different from their American or British counterparts, these students are not as westernized as they think and they live in societies that are still Asian, from daily habits and social practices, traditional beliefs and values, to religions, however westernized in their adoption of modern technology, consumption of western cultural products, such as fashion or movies, and participation in the global capitalist economy. The background horizon of disclosure that needs questioning certainly is not simply constituted by Asian traditions; but despite the westernized education, it is also not entirely western, insofar as the society they live in continues to be Asian in various ways, and the adopted western institutions and modes of thought have been modified in practice and interaction with local traditions. For example, in Singapore, laws inherited from the British colonial government governed the validity of marriages and the legal rights of parties involved, but young Chinese couples getting married often solemnize and celebrate their marriages with traditional Chinese marriage ceremonies (and sometimes together with a Christian church ceremony). Furthermore, their married life would likely be governed by expectations and values derived from traditional Chinese thinking, and not just western ideas of marital relations. Whereas it is normal for western societies to be western (whatever that means in particular terms depending on specific localities, for example, American or Scottish), the western aspects of Asian societies are often the result of colonialism, and if the background horizon of disclosure for students has been westernized, its legitimacy is questionable.

Acknowledging the continued presence of Asian traditions despite westernization, and viewing the "meeting of east and west" positively, do not mean that one therefore understands both traditions or the products of their encounter; the problem of projecting over or interpreting one in terms of the other does not disappear just because both traditions contribute to the current way of life of a society. Assuming that one already inhabits both traditions, where relatively westernized formal education has been combined with participation in traditional practices and informal learning of one's ancestral culture, or could move uninhibitedly between them, could prove to be an obstacle to understanding, including self-understanding. The virtue of humility that aids learning points instead to the need to carry out genuine dialogue twofold, one with western traditions as an Asian trying to understand better western political thought, even after years of study, because it is embedded in traditions that do not have their roots in the society one currently resides in, another with Asian traditions as the recipient of a westernized education who has participated in practices that still bear the legacy of Asian traditions but who no longer experiences them in the same way they were experienced traditionally.

The above generalization of "Asian societies" and "Asian traditions" is justified to the extent that westernization has been a common experience (despite diversity in actual forms and degree) that has caused varied disruptions to traditions in various societies in this extensive region. Closer scrutiny of the encounter between Chinese traditions—Confucianism in particular—and western political thought could further reveal the complexity of decentering western political theory in China and the Chinese diaspora. China's modernization had caused so much damage to Confucianism, which was once definitive of the Chinese way of life, from personal cultivation to political institutions, that some have declared Confucianism dead, reduced to a "wandering spirit."[1] This obituary may seem too hasty in view of the revivals of interest in Confucianism, including its political thought, both in and outside China—but the fact that we speak of "revivals" testifies to how much has been lost. While much of Chinese family and social life may still bear the marks of Confucian influence to different extents, the political institutions that purported to realize Confucian political thought have been dismantled and rejected as relics of imperial autocracy. This disruption raises questions about whether Confucian political thought is still embedded in political practice in Chinese societies, or whether we could only seek it in Confucian texts.

Current contending interpretations of Confucian political thought bring the tradition in which it is embedded into the foreground, even as societies that could claim a Confucian legacy reflect on its value and relevance to their future. Recent theories of "Confucian constitutional order" and "Confucian meritocracy" challenge western theories of democracy and attempt to decenter western theory both by introducing Confucian thought into the discourse of which models of governance are best for contemporary societies, the scope ranging from all societies to only China itself, and by rejecting the superiority of western political ideals and values.[2] They reverse the previous modernization discourse that vilified Confucianism as an obstacle to good government, which was understood as liberal democracy. That such interpretations contradict western understanding and judgment is however no guarantee that they understand or present Confucian thought without the distorting influence of western thought, if the rejection is premised on western terms and definitions of problems. For example, the concepts of meritocracy and constitutional order are as western as concepts such as democracy. Interpretations of how the Confucian model of government is superior to democracy may be still measured through criteria from the western political discourse.

As members of the tradition "accept, question, negotiate, and modify" (Tully 11) Confucianism, whether in carrying on or reviving the Confucian tradition, genuine dialogues among members of the tradition, whose interpretations of the tradition disagree, are as important as they are between them and members of other traditions. It would perhaps be easier to engage in genuine dialogues of reciprocal elucidation if one's motivation were purely a scholarly pursuit of understanding (or truth). However, insofar as the discourse of comparative political theory is relevant to solving real problems today, the conversations cannot be unaffected by participants' experiences and diagnoses of problems that most demand the attention of engaged political theory. Those who are more impressed by the problems besieging countries that claim to be liberal democracies understandably would strongly resist any attempt to reinterpret or modify the Confucian tradition in a democratic direction; instead they would seek alternatives in the tradition that would better serve Confucian societies. In contrast, those who are more worried by oppressive political practices historically associated with Confucianism, even if cultural pride favors revival of the tradition, would be more anxious to ensure more liberal, more democratic understandings of the tradition, on the assumption that these are less likely to be oppressive.

Could the interpretive issues be settled by refocusing on the insight that "traditions are grounded in practices and places"? (Tully 12, section 5). Due to the cultural disruptions of their political history during the twentieth century, among Asian societies that have at various times been labeled "Confucian"—the People's Republic of China, Taiwan, Hong Kong, Singapore, Japan, even South Korea—it is debatable if their political institutions and practices could be considered "Confucian." One criterion is continuity with past institutions and practices from a time when a society was Confucian (that is, before western influence); another is the presence of Confucian features in existing institutions and practices even if these have been modeled after western political systems.

In the latter case, whether an institution is Confucian would depend on one's interpretation of Confucianism. In the former case, few can claim continuity with the society's Confucian past (perhaps only South Korea has a strong claim). Even if such continuity is present, the weight to be given to such institutions and practices in interpreting the tradition will still be contested due to the critical attitudes many present members of these societies have toward past political institutions and practices, which they would argue are in various aspects distortions and malpractices rather than embodiments of Confucianism.

While I find the article extremely enlightening and even inspiring, I am still struggling to understand how genuine dialogues might be carried out in the above circumstances. There is no doubt that practices and attitudes recommended in the sections on deep listening and non-attachment, empathy and interdependency, reciprocal elucidation and transformation are edifying whenever one seeks to understand another—be it someone from within one's tradition (tenuous as it might be to identify that) or someone from another tradition. However, it seems that the practices and places, the lifeworld, that one might assume some tradition to be grounded in might not be easily identifiable, and any grounding might prove to be less firm than supposed.

Notes

1 In the 1980s, Yu Yingshi used this metaphor of *youhun* 游魂 to describe the fate of Confucianism: no longer relevant to lives of ordinary Chinese people, and separated from the obsolete imperial political system that was once seen as its vehicle of actualization, it existed only in intellectual discourses, a disembodied soul without a body. See Yu, "Predicament of Modern Confucianism (*Xiandai Ruxue de Kunjing* 现代儒学的困境)," 32.
2 Qing et al., *A Confucian Constitutional Order*; Bell and Li, *The East Asian Challenge for Democracy*.

References

Bell, Daniel and Chenyang Li, eds. *The East Asian Challenge for Democracy: Political Meritocracy in Comparative Perspective*. New York: Cambridge University Press, 2013.

Qing, Jiang and Daniel Bell et al. *A Confucian Constitutional Order*. Princeton: Princeton University Press, 2003.

Tully, James. "Deparochializing Political Theory and Beyond: A Dialogue Approach to Comparative Political Thought." *Journal of World Philosophies* 1, no. 1 (2016): 51–74.

Yu Yingshi. "Predicament of Modern Confucianism (*Xiandai Ruxue de Kunjing* 现代儒学的困境)." In *Macro-perspectives on the Development of Confucianism (Ruxue Fazhan de Hongguan Toushi* 儒学发展的宏观透视). Edited by Du Weiming. 95–102. Taipei: Zhengzhong, 1997.

4

Historicizing Political Theory

Sudipta Kaviraj

James Tully's paper is a pioneering attempt at thinking seriously about a central feature of the field that is slowly coming into relief as scholars open up comparative analyses of political theory. It is a feature that is often noted casually, but rarely seriously examined. Because it is an invitation to think about the nature of political theory as a discipline, this exercise can be open-ended and endless. I shall focus on some aspects that seem to me, because of the peculiar historicity of my position, to be of critical significance in this collective enterprise. My differences with Tully are of two kinds—which we can call disagreements proper and divergence. In the first case, we think about the same issue, but disagree as to how it should be analyzed. In the second case, I believe that in addition to the issues that he takes up, we should also consider some others.

Critical Practice

There is no doubt that serious rethinking about the discipline must be an *askesis*—acting upon the self while engaging in the activity that the self does routinely. Ordinarily, engagement with a subject in academic writing leads to posing and answering of questions, but as a standard practice, this rarely leads to an experience of the kind that Gadamer reviewed—an "experience" that does not leave the self what it was before.[1] Tully quotes Foucault's observation that this can be done through a practice of knowledge that is *foreign* to the knowing self. The only problem with Foucault's statement is the ease that is suggested in this exercise—of a practice of knowledge that is—not unknown, but foreign.[2] To accept, own, and practice what is really foreign in any cognitive practice is particularly hard. Precisely because knowledge exists in systems, or regimes, it is not so easy to simply lift elements from another form of thinking overcoming its foreignness/unfamiliarity. But that is what Tully correctly characterizes as real acts of deparochializing political thought. It is interesting to note the explicit references in Tully's thinking to three forms of historical thinking—Cambridge history, a radical and thoroughgoing practice of historicity from Gadamer, and Foucault's methodological reflections—which might be hard to characterize or systematize, but there is no doubt they are idiosyncratic moves in historicity—bold experiments in thinking historically. I have no doubt that that is the right way to go—to think more deeply about the historical character of political theory as a practice. I shall call this general methodological orientation "historicist." All these forms of thought share a common origin in German historicism.[3]

It is important to ask what can form a foothold for self-critical thinking: How can we begin to see faults in the way we think ourselves? An obvious strategy for this kind of self-criticism can begin with an elementary historicist admission of finitude: the recognition that despite all our efforts, we think in historically deeply limited ways: to state this in a Hegelian language, to be determinate is to acknowledge finiteness.[4] Instead of an abstract call for self-reflection, it is better to begin with a more concrete gesture of recognizing historicity. Tully's first philosophic move I recognize as a historicist one: first "parochializing" political theory, and recognizing its western character and even more its western roots, is a classic historicist step.[5]

Western Origins of Political Theory

Political theory as a recognizable intellectual discipline is of course western in an easily recognizable general sense: But what does that characterization precisely mean? Clearly, the west possesses a long historical tradition of philosophical reflection characterized as "political theory" or "political philosophy" which was marked by the feature that philosophical thinking—which asked relentlessly what was the "true nature" of an object or a practice—was applied to questions of political power. This field included questions like: What structure of political power was just? How could organization of political power be analyzed and morally evaluated? It analyzed political power from the point of view of the subject in both senses of the term: subjects who wielded it and subjects who were subjected to it. From ancient Greece—on Tully's reading from the time of Plato's dramatization of Socratic dialogues—an uninterrupted line of thinking on these matters—named political theory—has existed in the west. Longevity and uninterrupted continuity are the sources of its power. This tradition continued through Roman deliberations on law and political order and medieval Christian reflections on the relation between domains of the sacred and the profane. Italian city states of the renaissance drew upon this tradition and continued it—keeping it alive and active—by focusing on internal questions of the city republics and their mutual relations. From the sixteenth and seventeenth centuries, with the rise of the modern state, political theory as an indispensable discipline for imagining, conceiving, explaining, and evaluating political order under the rapidly changing conditions of modernity came to occupy a central place in European culture. Of course, remarks like Hobbes' statement that "before him civil philosophy was a dream" serve to show that this long and apparently continuous tradition contained internal "ruptures"—the central questions and the predominant nature of thinking in this field underwent substantial change which should be registered historically. Yet, there is no doubt about the sheer presence of this astonishingly long tradition.[6] Political theorists from the west are constituted intellectually by this long historical tradition—consolidated and institutionalized by modern academic training. When an intellectual discipline becomes a part of modern academia, that results in profound alterations in the nature and character of its intellectual practice. Academic training imparts a deep standardization which earlier intellectual cultures lacked. Obviously, intellectuals received rigorous training in earlier periods, but academic training imparts to its language—vocabulary, standard arguments, criteria for making judgments—an unprecedented breadth of reach and influence. It is shared by a much larger body of intellectuals who not merely do work inside the academia but disseminate forms of thinking incubated in these esoteric institutions across vast expanses of a society's intellectual culture. Languages of political theory, sometimes formed inside academic institutions, splash across vast expanses of the public sphere and determine the way ordinary political discourse works. Political theorists in the west are pre-formed by the pre-academic levels of this permeating discourse in their schooling before they step inside universities; once inside, they are rigorously trained in its intricacies as a "normal science." Tully's paper asks the question: How does this form of thinking encounter "other" forms of thought?

Encountering "Other" Forms of Thought: Political Theory in the Non-Western World

Western political theory encounters other forms of thought in at least two ways: it encounters "other" forms of thinking inside its own societies as "remainders" or "surprises" or "minority discourses." To take an example of North America: it might encounter arguments from American indigenous peoples about their claims to land, resources, and "life" in the fundamental sense of the ability to live a life unconstrained by modern abutments into the prior condition of nature.[7] Political theory also encounters other forms of thinking from people who migrate into these societies with some profoundly different core beliefs, as thinkers like Habermas have recognized in relation to Europe's Muslims.[8] Hostile politicians emphasize this through their never-ending calls to "others" to go back where they came from. These examples show that questions raised by Tully's paper are important not merely for academic political theory; they are highly significant for modern western societies. But there is a second sense in which western political theorists might encounter thinking in other forms. Tully's observations start with the recognition that modern culture across the world is irreversibly globalized in a fundamental sense. As a political theorist surveys the world, she would inevitably encounter the existence of forms of thinking about real political power and imaginative possibilities that are profoundly divergent from modern western perspectives; at times, the discussions will center on the question whether modern western political forms like "democracy" or cultural arrangements/configurations like "secularism" should come to dominate and re-order other societies or not. These are also controversies regarding western political theory.

Political Theory and Philosophic Thinking

Before we turn to other questions, let us consider Tully's characterization of the specific character of western political theory as a *form* of thinking. Its defining character is seen to consist in two features: its focus on the "moral bases of political relationships," and its attempt to "universalize" these moral principles (Tully 2).[9] We should not presume, Tully suggests, that all intellectual cultures think about political questions in an identical way. This opens up a very interesting subsidiary question. Political activity is universal, but thinking about that activity through "techniques of universalizing philosophy" is a specific cultural habit. This presumes that other traditions have not thought about questions of politics in similar or comparable ways. But to get to that discussion, we need to explicate another issue first—what makes these other traditions "other" to modern western political theory? It would be risky to assume, on the contrary, that such "universalizing" conversations are altogether unintelligible to other traditions: these questions, or rather this way of asking questions about political life, are necessarily unintelligible to non-westerners; or that we can simply take it for granted that these individuals, groups, or societies are incapable of thinking on the basis of such methodological principles. We can find in the Indian philosophical tradition an intriguing contrast.

On the Historical Career of Western Political Theory

On the next step, I seem to have some differences with Tully's claim that "these moral principles have been and continue to be used to justify the greatest inequalities in human history" (Tully 3). As this judgment stands at the core of the critical debate, we should examine this statement carefully. Is this a wholly correct capture of what was wrong about western political theory and practice? There can be no doubt that some of the greatest wrongs in human history were carried out, and, probably more troubling for intellectuals, justified in the name of principles that were central to western political theory. But the question is: Did these clusters of actions, or historical processes—namely, colonialism, racism, slavery, misogyny—*necessarily* flow from the *philosophical* nature of those principles themselves? Or rather were these patterns of action entirely in contravention of those principles? Certainly, this discrepancy between high principles and mundane acts has been an inescapable feature of modernity's worldwide history. But it is not evident that these courses of action necessarily flowed from the principles themselves. A principle like the moral equality of all human beings had been proclaimed in the US-American constitution, but ignored in long stretches of US-American legal and social history. Legal rules that were entirely discriminatory remained parts of the institutions of US-American liberalism for much of its history. Even after such rules were formally altered, social experience in large measure remained at odds with these principles. A crucial aspect of this discussion is to ascertain correctly the relation between those abstract principles and these historical forms of social injustice—usually endowed with state-legal sanction. Samuel Moyn, in his history of the idea of human rights, offers a characterization of such liberal principles as "truncated universals."[10] That shifts the blame for these terrible histories to the tendency of political societies to ignore and tolerate massive defacing exceptions to their own self-proclaimed ideals. On this reading, the trouble seems to be political or sociological, not philosophical. What was wrong was not that there was something lodged inside these principles themselves which invited this conduct but rather *akrasia*—that these societies and political groups did not have the will and moral ability to follow the rules they proclaimed.[11] A striking example of this fault can be taken from modern Indian history. This can also illustrate the observation Tully is making about political theory in general.

Political Theory and Colonialism

Almost the entire nineteenth century presented an unsettling, puzzling spectacle of two parallel processes unfolding in colonizing European societies. On one side, this was a time of insistent demands for the greatest expansion of political freedom. Political initiatives in the fields of theory and practice demanded and forced the acceptance of more expansive definitions of liberal freedoms—from the right to vote to forming workers' unions. These developments, without doubt, established the bases of institutional structures of modern capitalist democracy. Yet, this was also the period of high imperialism—the greatest and often most brutal military expansion of colonial domains in other parts of the world. As socialist critiques later demonstrated, the working classes in these metropolitan countries were enthusiastic about the expansion of their own freedoms and equally enthusiastic supporters of empires.[12] Ironically, in the domain of political theory, Mill's three interconnected pieces of reasoning which supported and philosophically justified this vast expansion of liberty in Europe—*On Liberty* (1859), *Considerations on Representative Government* (1861), and *On the Subjection of Women* (1869)—came out at the high point of this double movement—of assertion of liberty inside the west, and its denial outside. "Despotism," Mill was convinced, "is a legitimate mode of government in dealing with barbarians."[13] Understandably, Indians found this argument less than persuasive, and began agitation for moderate forms of self-government.[14] However, Indians themselves, when they deliberated about democratic institutions in their own country, often displayed similar convictions about marginalized sections of their own society.[15] I do not think we should conclude that this gap between assertion of universal principles and utter practical disregard of their moral demands followed necessarily either from the nature of the principles themselves or from the underlying form of *philosophical* thinking that produced them. States of affairs in the real world rationalized either by fading or finessing specific moral principles cannot be blamed on the universality of the moral declaration, or the form of philosophical thinking that systematically presents its conclusions in that form. In an intriguing twist produced by our contradictory world, it is right for Tully to emphasize the violations of these rules and for me—an Indian living in postcolonial times—to stress their abstract promise.

There is, however, an interesting ancillary question. How should we respond to the claim that this kind of "universalization" is a defining, and therefore differentiating feature of western political thought? There is no doubt that this is a primary feature of western philosophical thinking, and consequently, such philosophical techniques are applied to questions of political life, creating the field of political philosophy. I believe two observations are relevant here in partial modification of this idea. This claim could be seen to have two parts: an assertion about a general quality characterizing western political thought, and a separable assertion that this feature separates western thinking off from thinking about politics in all other cultures. While the first is generally true, the second cannot be accepted without qualification. Despite the fact that western political theory generally uses modes of universalizing philosophical thought, forceful dissenting traditions emerged in western philosophy itself. Plato's intervention at a decisive originary point in European philosophy did not go unchallenged—at two distinct levels. Aristotle's work the *Politics* and the *Constitution of Athens* contested the Platonic view both at the level of deciding on the "best form of government" and the underlying idea that the best form of thinking is the universalizing mode demonstrated by Plato.[16] By recommending *phronesis* as central to political life and advancing a theory of practical "judgment," Aristotle clearly dissented from a "universalizing" philosophy—at least for analyzing political life. Throughout the long history of European philosophy, a dissenting, alternative strand of thinking can be discerned—that consistently resisted such universalizing temptations.[17] The rise of historicist forms of reflection partly in reaction against the "view from nowhere" version of thinking in the Enlightenment demonstrates that this dichotomy between a universalizing and a "particularizing" strand continued into modern times. In modern philosophy, particularly after Hegel and the rise of German historicism, this mode of thinking has exercised at least equal attraction in social thought.

Are Universalizing Philosophical Methods Present in Other Cultures?

Are other cultures entirely unfamiliar with philosophy's universalizing methods? It seems hard to generalize. Some philosophical traditions certainly evolved theoretical systems based on quite similar universalizing techniques. Philosophy in this mode was certainly known and influential in ancient and medieval India. Islamic thought, after it absorbed enormous Greek influence from the eighth century, was definitely fluent in this style of philosophic reasoning. East Asian thought cultures also display similar forms. However, here again it is interesting to note historical peculiarities of separate cultures. Although ancient Indian culture developed a high philosophic tradition, for some strange reason, political life was not among the object fields it considered a legitimate domain of analysis. Indian philosophy showed exactly similar universalizing or abstract modes of thinking in fields ranging from ontology, epistemology, logic to aesthetics, but in the field of reflection on *political* life, Indian thought restricted itself to mundane digests of rules of conduct, or elementary enumeration of components of the state and their proper functioning, rather than an application of its formidable apparatus of philosophical examination to moral bases of political power.[18]

Historicism and Critique of Universals

"Universalizing" thinking, however, encountered a qualitatively different kind of challenge with the arrival of modernity in Europe. To me the rise of historicism—starting from Hegel, but more clearly from Dilthey and the German Neo-Kantians—seems to be a robust, consistent anti-universalizing form of reflection that has followed the universalizing strands in the Enlightenment like its shadow. Some major thinkers—like both Hegel and Marx—display a mixture, not always consistent, of both strands. To take Marx's example, his analysis of capitalist economic structures reveals two clear lines of analysis placed side by side. *Capital I* spends much of its initial analytics seeking to understand the *invariant* structures of a capitalist economy and its "logic of functioning": yet its final chapters[19] veer toward an historical form of enquiry, taking note of the specificities of capitalist accumulation in each major European economy. Eventually it advances the historicizing formulation that capitalism's history already showed two "trajectories"—with vastly different effects on political outcomes and institutions.[20] The Marxian theoretical project incorporates within itself, from Marx's own works, the idea that what we require is not a history of capitalism but of capitalisms. From the time the difference between natural and historical sciences was unforgettably underscored by historicists, this theoretical mode has remained equally powerful in political reflection. Clearly, from the nineteenth century, the conception of "political theory" as a knowledge domain also changed singularly. To the earlier mode of political theory—practiced by

Hobbes, Locke, and others as a branch of philosophical reflection on political processes, institutions, and events that was distinctly non-historical—is now added a new form of reflection in historical sociology.[21] While the earlier form of thinking started with the question "what is the nature of man?," the new form began with "what were the conditions under which a modern state began to emerge?" The first deliberately erases space and time; the latter equally deliberately remembers them. Again, Marx, Weber, and Tocqueville engage in a form of enquiry in which abstract moral philosophizing is less important than a far more historical and therefore specificity-recognizing mode of theoretical thinking. Yet, it is also emphatically theoretical. The definition of the domain of political theory itself is thus altered profoundly. Since then these two modes of "doing theory" have remained parallel strands. Examining present writing on democracy, for example, shows the parallel presence of both strands. One views democracy as a set of abstract institutional or formal features, and seeks to understand the democratic process worldwide comparatively—often applying quantitative techniques. The other strand views the rise and fall of democracy as historical and seeks to produce explanations chronotopically—*inside* specific histories and cultures. To return to the question of "universalizing" as a technique or feature of thinking, this addition induces us to refine the meaning of "universal"—to insert a distinction when we use this term in the domain of social science. Universal in some instances does mean an invariant conception: like the universality of the skeletal structure of humans. But, clearly, when we assert that language is a human universal, we use it in a second, but intelligible sense—as a variant presence of an indispensable feature. This historical view suggests that the question of "universalizing" modes of thinking in western political theory is a matter of considerable complexity.

Political theory today is part of the historical constellation of modernity itself. As modernity reconfigures different world societies inexorably—globalization is merely a simplistic registration of this complex historical process—it carries political theory along with it. All societies in the world, whether we like it or not, are affected by a process in which political power is restructured from premodern to a generally modern form. Institutions are transformed unevenly, and at times with unpredictable effects, but they cannot escape an alteration toward modern state power.[22] The language of modern political theory is written into such institutional transformation. As institutions "speak" this language, all political agents coming into its orbit, or field of force, have to "use" them too. Today the world is full of states carrying democratic names—though with intriguing adjectival permutations. Parties carry in their titles appellations like "liberal," "socialist," "popular," "communist"—though recently the last one has seen some loss of popularity. Evidently, such names do not indicate that these institutions or groups behave in ways similar to what is found in western history. Some western users of political theory simply go about their analytical task taking these "appellations" at face value, that is, treating these as democratic systems at one level, but showing their "failings" on another.[23] Reasoning of this kind—which Tully legitimately rejects—simply avoids the historicist responsibility of social analysis: ignoring the elementary historical move of that begins by examining the state of affairs from which the emergence of modernity begins—which stamps its character on the nature of modernity itself. It is impossible to hide from modernity, and so from the language of political theory. The sensible approach appears to be to ask what this language is doing in these contexts—the meanings these concepts acquire because of their adaptation to local context.

Colonialism, justifiably, lies at the heart of Tully's critique of modern political theory. But colonialism is not a uniform process or an invariant structure. European states colonized different parts of the world at distinct points in their own history, and the societies which felt the effects of colonization responded divergently according to the character of their own history at that temporal juncture. All parts of the world were affected by the force of European colonial power, but in significantly different ways. Settler colonialism in America and Australia, conquest of Latin American societies, direct colonial sovereignty in India and Africa, the vast mosaic of semi-colonial arrangements in the Middle East and East Asia, and the sheer threat of European power toward countries like Japan were all instances of a vast global change, with different chronotopic results. A history of modernity is not complete without a history of colonialism. And a history of colonialism is not complete without registration of this "strange multiplicity" of its consequences. Alongside Tully's effort, a welcome development in the history of political theory is a turn toward the exploration of liberalism's relation to empire.[24]

Tully's analysis seems to me to fit closely cases of settler colonialism like the United States, Canada, and Australia, where European colonization corralled indigenous populations into a progressively shrinking space, invading and destroying their whole ways of life. However, by constantly retreating in the face of this invasion, and refusing to collaborate, these civilizations maintained the coherence and integrity of their ways of life more successfully—though at a terrifying cost.[25] Colonization of the world was an immense, unprecedented intellectual procedure of "othering"—regarding modern European civilization alone as "civilized," and withdrawing that description from all others, reducing the rest of the world to a strange tapestry of "rudeness."[26] Of course, all other cultures, newly uncivilized, were dotted along the steep slopes running down from the pinnacles in Paris and London. Aligned to the construction of a new hierarchy of cultures were internal hierarchies of social groups produced necessarily by this grid of thinking—from women belonging to the same social class, to proletarians, to slaves. Curiously, a perverse effect of this kind of narrow Enlightenment thought resulted in a compulsively hierarchical conception of the internal social world. This classification downward was produced precisely by the qualities and values that were placed at the center of this civilizing process. We should not underestimate the comprehensiveness and the inexorable hierarchic effect it had—not merely outside European societies but also inside them. This way of thinking may have had many faults, but not inconsistency. The insistent and implicit hierarchies that Tully discovers in modern "conversations" are due to this procedure. Even when modern Europe develops a public sphere, it is marked by not merely exclusions but steep slopes.[27] The question of universalizing thought bears a complex relation with this hierarchical discursive universe. It does produce a "public sphere"—a single discursive universe in which groups "speak" to each other, but the barriers are obvious. In some cases, groups are not allowed to speak at all: women, slaves, later a racial hierarchy of non-whites. As critiques of Habermas' initial work demonstrated, when there were no exclusions, there were slopes along which it was hard for "others" who spoke to gather attention. Moyn's suggestion of persistent "truncation" of liberal universals has the great advantage of separating the sociological-political from the philosophical. In fact, the universal enunciation of principles made it hard for the protectors of these hierarchies to defend them indefinitely—leading to slow, often reluctant, but definite institutional change—a long-term, inexorable pressure from history for practice to conform to principles. Arguments by feminist or African American thinkers that undermined such hierarchies came from within the same philosophic discourse. Thus a first additional point to Tully's call for deparochialization involves a rearrangement of the values and significance of different segments of western political theory itself.

"Western" Political Theory in India

Let me turn now to the strange career western political theory has had "outside" the west. Clearly, in one sense, it is misleading to use the characterization "outside" to the scene of colonial territories brought under European control by imperial expansion.[28] Colonial domination meant precisely that these societies, which were outside the domain of control of modern European states earlier, now fell inside the orbits of their direct sovereignty.[29] Consideration of some texts which bore historical witness to this massive transformation in India—like the *Seir ul Mutaqherin*[30] by a Mughal political chronicler—reveals the simultaneous crumbling of an institutional and a discursive world which co-constituted each other. What followed in the domain of political thinking—the ways in which people made sense of what was happening in their social lifeworld—was apocalyptic. A relative short period of a century—not a very long span in historical time—witnessed not merely the transformation of the Mughal imperial order into the colonial version of the modern state but also—in some ways more curiously—an erasure of the older vocabulary and conceptual language through which political objects were recognized. The nature of this language of political order in North India was peculiarly complex: the language of statecraft and transactions over land, the primary source of wealth, had become predominantly a Persianate vocabulary. In the 1820s, in the writings of Ram Mohan Roy, features of conventional Hindu and Muslim religious dialectics can be seen at work alongside ideas drawn from modern western philosophic thinking.[31] A few decades later, these older languages—of statecraft and of religious disputation—had fallen silent. In English, and even in vernacular writings on political life, descriptive, analytic, or evaluative categories from premodern languages were almost totally erased. By the middle of the nineteenth century, the language of European liberalism had become the dominant language of Indian political expression. Assisted by the power of political imperialism, the language of western political theory had conquered the world.

Ever since, through the embedding of modern western-style representative institutions, a liberal legal system, and the unseen but insistent power of a transformed education system, the language of political theory in India has become in some ways the same as in the west. Undoubtedly, this was assisted by the expansion of colonial cultural institutions—like the profound linking of Indian education to the vast structure of Anglo-American academia. But precisely because of the colonial character of this connection, the intellectual center was simply taken to lie in the western centers—initially in Britain—Oxford, Cambridge, London, and not least, Edinburgh—and this condemned Indian academic thinking to a perpetual self-inflicted posture of "derivativeness." If Indian political theory means simply more of western theory—with a change of locale—what can there be of real interest?

Two distinguished political theorists have commented on the "derivative" character of Indian political thought—though from quite different angles. Bhikhu Parekh noted the "poverty of Indian political theory" in a paper that primarily assessed contributions by academic Indian scholars to the contemporary corpus of serious political theory.[32] Moved by very different concerns, Partha Chatterjee also concluded, in a study of three "moments" of nationalist thinking, that, with the exception of Gandhi, and with the exception of the question of sovereignty and political subjection, much of Indian "nationalist" thought was heteronomous in philosophic terms.[33] Lack of originality or derivativeness had long been a major theme in the self-assessment of Indian intellectuals critically examining this question.[34] Does Indian political thought, then, deserve deep listening?

In a longer historical perspective, it seems to me now, this assessment was flawed. Is there any "otherness" in modern Indian political thought in Tully's sense which makes it interesting and deserves more attention? I shall invoke an argument made earlier regarding feminist and Afro-American political theory. If we judge these forms of thought simply by the "language" they deploy, they would fall entirely within the confines of "western political theory."[35] Critical thinking about race, again, came from a vocabulary and language that was unmistakably "western" in the wider, vaguer sense. Yet, both feminism and anti-racist theoretical critiques came out of an *experiential* "place of otherness."[36] Here, a Marxist addition to the tradition of historicism has played an essential role. Against the Hegelian idea that societies were united in an underlying intelligible grid by an "objective mind," a common consciousness, like the way Greek society was marked by beauty, the Roman by order, and modern Europe by freedom,[37] Marx offered the crucial skeptical insight that societal experience was insurmountably fragmentary and incommensurable. One part of a society had no access to the experience of another.[38] From that point, it is hardly surprising to assert that what feminist and anti-racist critical theory brought to philosophic expression was an entire "experience" that was disregarded and silenced, because these were inaccessible. What made these philosophical articulations of an "other" was not a different language but the nature and structure of "experience" they brought to disclosure through that language.

I would link this argument with another in Tully's paper: in learning about how people think about politics, we must remember that political theory is a compositional "form" (Tully 7–10, Section 3). Serious thinking about political life can be carried on without obeying the *formal* features of this mode of presentation. Not surprisingly, since this is a distinctive form, and has to be learned through a process of instruction, often remarkably, even explosively, original political ideas reveal themselves in other forms—sometimes as literature, and in languages unrecognizable as political theory.[39] Think of the recalcitrant language in which some feminist and anti-racist thinking is expressed, particularly when they intersect.[40]

I suggest that sometimes Indian political thinking has appeared derivative because observers have looked at it in a wrong way: with an optics calculated to fade what was noteworthy and highlight what was uninteresting. Even if Indian authors generally deployed a language of western political theory, from the mid-nineteenth century, they were analyzing and commenting on a history of modernity that was entirely different from the European.[41] Colonial modernity was a fundamentally different trajectory of the modern, and consequently, the conceptual tools of western political theory were made to work upon vastly divergent historical and cultural material. Like the "otherness" of the experience expressed by feminism and anti-racist theory, Indian political thinking also thought its way through an "experience" totally unlike what political theory had encountered in Europe. Its dignity and its claim to separate attention came from this distinction.[42] I shall repeat an assertion from my earlier note:[43] there are two entirely different reasons for which Indian political thought can be distinctively "Indian," and it is essential for clarity to hold them apart. Both forms of Indianness differentiate Indian thought from western political theory—make it distinct and particular—but the grounds in the two instances are quite separate. Certainly, Indian political thought would have been quite different from western theory had it been woven out of the vocabulary and philosophic resources of premodern Indian philosophic systems. Its fundamental concepts, and presumably some of its basic values, would have been different. Politics is presumed to be an activity that belongs only to a small circle of royal advisers and functionaries. Implicitly, the subjects' politics consists primarily of being 'lowlier than the grass, and more tolerant than trees'[44]—perhaps good advice in those circumstances, but totally unsuited to institutions of modern representative politics. But the fact that Indian politicians and thinkers are using the principles learned from Locke[45] does not erase the other historical fact that they are thinking about a different experiential universe, and responding to the need to adapt them to their own experienced reality. Use of vocabularies, principles, and arguments from Utilitarians, liberals, socialists, even nationalists did not turn what the Indians debated equivalent to or simply derivative of European debates of the time. Questions Indian writers tackled, using those languages, belonged to the colonial world. Caste hierarchies were distinctive, utterly different from the stratifications of classes in capitalist economic systems. A major intellectual drawback of Indian communism was its failure to take this difference sufficiently seriously. Mazzini's writings and Garibaldi's exploits were followed with intense interest in the early stages of evolution of anti-imperialist "nationalism." Yet, two major figures of the national movement—Tagore and Gandhi—concluded by the 1930s that the form of nationalism Indians so admired in Italy and Germany was inappropriate for imagining a unity-principle for the deeply diverse Indian "people." Either India should not be conceived as a nation[46] or its 'nation-ness' should be anchored in a different criterion of singularity. Gandhi's skepticism went further—opposing a placid submission of Indian political thinking to contemporary European arguments about the relation between the state and society, on liberal principles of representation, juridical systems based on rights, not to speak of larger questions like the proper human comportment toward nature and its bounties. Tagore and other nationalists too pressed arguments critical of some aspects of European modernity. All these criticisms and rejections, however, worked within a profound affirmation of modernity. None of these thinkers adopted a seriously conservative or historically recidivist politics—seeking the re-establishment of a Hindu monarchy observing the procedures of *Manusmrti*, or restoration of the Mughal emperor. Iqbal, seeking a state for Muslims, urged that the power should come out of the people as the ultimate constitutive source of authority. Skepticism and passionate rejection of elements of European modernity, or demands for a powerfully divergent re-imagination of the political present, did not signal a return to premodern forms of thought or an obedient assimilation into dominant strands of western political thought of the time. In my reading this represented something parallel to what feminist and anti-racist theory brought to expression—a different historical experience of the modern which exceeded the standard vocabularies and arguments of western political thought. It would be erroneous to consider this body of political reflection as derivative in the usual sense.

It is here that Tully's argument about the distinction between political theory and political thought is very helpful. Because the most productive Indian thinkers were active political leaders, application of criteria of theoretical writing can easily result in an impression of an absence of theoretical thought. If we remember the caution that political theory is a form of reflection, it becomes possible to excavate the basic issues/problems about which these thinkers argued and to explore them in a more theoretical mode. The justifiability of imperial power itself was an interesting question. Bankimchandra, an early nationalist thinker and satirist, asked, "if there is a *right*[47] of conquest why not a right of theft?"[48] Clothed in irony, this went to the heart of the imperialist contortions in using a language of "rights" to rationalize results of military force. Indian writers produced a vast body of observation, commentary, explanation, and evaluation that went to examine some of the most profound political questions in their colonial modern world. This body of writing—both in English and in India's numerous vernaculars—represents a *separate* world of political thinking which, if we accept Tully's interpretative principles, has to be incorporated into serious academic exploration of political theory.

The Western/Non-Western Divide *inside* Non-Western Cultures

Strangely, the binary of western/non-western thinking has come to play a peculiar role *inside* non-western cultures. In the course of heated debates on social and political questions, some thinkers attacked arguments on the ground that these showed forms of western thinking. Interestingly, early conservative thinkers did not claim that ideas should be rejected simply because they were western. Bhudev Mukhopadhyay, a conservative Hindu thinker who sought to extract principles of Hindu political life and judge them against the competing ones of "westernness,"[49] argued nonetheless that social institutions had to be grounded in rational principles, not on the simple fact of their being Hindu. Oddly, at times more recent Hindu conservatives in India—and there are parallels in the Islamic world—have sought to pre-emptively damn certain ideas as of "western" origin.

This is not a concern for Tully, but perhaps in all non-western societies, there is an "internal" instantiation of the western/non-western binary. In the Indian context, this binary works in two forms—the first is spurious, the second fundamental. For reasons I have mentioned, after the mid-nineteenth century, a genuinely non-western, which was by definition premodern, view of politics became increasingly hard to articulate. With the entrenchment of the colonial state and its institutions, premodern forms of politics crumbled and decayed. Consequently, the practical orientations which those institutions elicited and encouraged became redundant, and in proportion the textual corpus which commented on that world and advised ordinary people on how to deal with those forms of power correspondingly lost their currency.[50] Different segments of Indian intelligentsia responded in variant ways on this matter: some parts of the Islamic literati, through their scholastic organizations, continued to articulate a conservative opposition to the whole apparatus of modern power.[51] Mainly, Indian Islamic thinkers too, exactly like their Hindu counterparts, responded in innovative, nonconservative ways seeking techniques by which they could take control of the modern state apparatus. At times, Hindu nationalist writers used the epithet "non-western" to characterize ideas and arguments they opposed, but that is in essence a rhetorical device—to damn an idea without having to argue against it. For most part, this is a spurious invocation of the binary. Authors who selectively reject opposing arguments as "western" are themselves entirely rooted in modern historicity and modern thought, and their understanding of the world is totally horizoned within the terms and limits of modern western theory.[52] They have no doubt that the modern state should be based on a nation's identity—they only want that identity to be exclusively "Hindu." This simply attempts to polemically mobilize the surviving fund of historical resentment against colonial domination, but not to make any serious argument dissenting from modernity.

Inaccessibility of Past Thinking

There is, however, another form of the western/non-western binary that raises unsettling questions—where, paradoxically, some of the Tully's reflections on deep listening apply with considerable force. To continue with the example of the nation-state, Tagore and Gandhi, in fact, drew upon premodern traditions of collective belonging—a precolonial idea of a *samaja* based on neighborliness—sharing the earth—rather than the elusive notion of "common blood."[53] On religious accommodation, parallelly, both favored an argument based on ideas of toleration found inside religious doctrines, rather than basing good treatment of others on the modern idea of isolating the state from religious life.[54] The actual historical reception of these suggestions—never made in the recognizable form of political theory—reveals how hard it is for the modern Indian intellectual culture to engage in a dialogue with these dissenting insights. These ideas were mostly dismissed as fads of a religious crank, or a mystical poet. Today, these deep critiques[55] of the nation-state are read with renewed respect, ironically, partly because western political theory has begun to appreciate some of the profound difficulties of the modern model of the nation-state as the pre-emptive form of political community.

Beyond pure and narrow political questions, premodern Indian philosophic traditions, particularly its religious doctrines, offer a wide variety of significant arguments about fundamental aspects of human life which modernists ought to listen to with unprecedented openness. Religious thought had formidable resources to think about the relation between man and nature, the presence of nature and its attunement with the affective life of humanity, and also a much deeper intertwining of the mundane and the aesthetic. Traditional thought proposed an inseverable intertwining of art and craft—objecting to the treatment of everyday things as merely utilitarian shorn of aesthetic import. Music and poetic art, some religious doctrines suggest, should be a part of the taken-for-granted experience of the everyday,[56] rather than a separate, ennobled, visit to the concert hall a few times a year.[57] Implicit in these ideas are very different proposals for the basic arrangements for humanizing a human life which are opposed or angular to mandatory life-forms of modernity. The comprehensive victory of the colonial modern culture has resulted in a strange inaccessibility of such ideas, though these are "our own." They survive in endangered enclaves of religious, popular culture scorned and imperiled by the invading forces of an unrelenting, heedless, un-self-critical modern civilization. Paradoxically, modern cultures marshal against these thought forms exactly the same arguments that Europeans deployed against "others." Many religious leaders have defected to the politically empowered theater of de-sacralized religion, leaving behind the exotic corners of musical and aesthetic solace that premodern religion offered to the unfortunate, lonely, friendless, destitute, and diseased. Religious music itself is experienced less as a calming interlude at every sunset, rather as a bash of a bhakti-utsav, which does not consume too many busy evenings of productive professional lives. Ironically, therefore, in some ways modern Indian society and culture is like a simulacrum of the disjointed lifeworlds Tully analyzes so thoughtfully. Engaging with these thought-forms—because the life-forms that vivified them have shrunk and decayed—requires all elements of the demanding conversational ethic that Tully carefully elaborates from Gadamer. In fact, this shows some of the conundrums of self-understanding in our times. In some ways, this is a conversation between the self of the modern Indian intellectual with the *non-self* of its abandoned past. In others, it could be asked, in what kind of perverse universe of relationships can this be a non-self? Are modern Indian intellectuals not half immersed in a pre-intellectual world of experience that has intimate ties with this culture which we have now learnt to designate as non-self?[58] I suspect that this represents a general problem of postcolonial cultures, and must be shared to some extent by Islamic and African societies.

Structure and Contradiction in a Globalizing World

How seriously should the academic discipline of political theory take such arguments about "dialogue" and their implications? Is this a serious problem in the real world of relations between actually existing states, political forces, individuals, and groups? I believe that if we accept a particular world-picture of modernity, this goes to the heart of the hardships of a globalizing world. Obviously, there can be two variant pictures of the historical process of modernity starting from the times that marked the beginnings of modern social theory. One distinct picture considers the modern world as a complex of structures which emerged in the west, and slowly spread across the world. Modernization of the world meant, to these theorists, a constant similarization—if we can use an awkward term—of structures, institutions, experience, and behavior. Globalization is an accelerated stage of this process. Individuals, groups, and political players will have divergent and specific interests created by their transient circumstances, but the world would be drawn together through constantly tightening bonds into similarity—which would imply that the world would be drawn toward consensus. At least from the mid-nineteenth century this world picture has been opposed by another that views "contradiction" as central to the creation of a modern world. Modernity, on this second opinion, is a complex of "contradictory" processes, in the sense that modernizing change immediately sets up a profound division between those who are for and against—as in case of secularization. Second, often modern structures are in Marx's sense "contradictory": these structures are singular because they cannot go on functioning without distinctive "inputs" from divergent groups—like the bourgeoisie and the proletariat, Marx's classic example. These groups, however, are held in an indelibly/incorrigibly contrary relation in terms of their interests, and more significantly, their experience of the world. So, the world functions as a single whole, but does not produce a singularity of experience. Marx's single instance has, in fact, been "generalized" by successive waves of theorists examining the questions of patriarchy, race, colonialism: in each case the singularity of the structure is marked by the presence of a profound lack of similarity—contradiction. Of course, disparate groups can and do to some extent live out their lives in the separation of resentment, but Marx stresses the structural singularity of the "system" as well.[59] Crucially, all such groups, alienated by resentments, are thrown together into a single world—where the effect of actions of one is felt, usually negatively, by others. Agreement among them cannot be produced by appealing to a singularity of experience. Today, groups like the economically sliding white working class and the successful "cosmopolitan" upper classes, or the Chinese working class that now produces "their" goods are held in this kind of generic relationships within a single structure.

It is interesting to examine the immediate postcolonial[60] age to explore this problem. The UN was created deliberately, specifically, as a "scene" of dialogue. Decolonization began in the late 1940s with Indian independence, and in a more recondite fashion, after the Chinese revolution. The Chinese could retreat into an entirely separate politico-economic "system" with other communist states. After independence, India remained within the "system" of the capitalist world economy. Reflection on their circumstances forced Indian political elites—who worked through modes of political thought, not theory—to recognize that colonialism was more global in its effect than the colonial European powers realized. End of British sovereignty was hardly the end of colonialism. The Indian political leadership under Nehru slowly worked out a fairly consistent "theory" of the global politico-economic order—which emphasized precisely the "effective history" of colonialism, especially in the sphere of international political economy. Reading through the Indian state's interventions in the UN in the 1950s and 1960s, it becomes apparent that they stressed two distinct arguments about injustices in the contradictory world structure—ending direct colonial rule and counteracting long effects of imperial domination. Presentations by western states conceded the demand for ending colonial sovereignty, though with reluctance,[61] but persistently resisted any suggestion of an expanded historical view of colonialism, justifying policies like apartheid.[62] Central to Indian interventions was a claim that instead of hiding behind the flimsy façade of sovereignty of equal states, states should recognize that the world system was contradictory. Global economic processes produced different outcomes and experiences at its different poles, and divergent parts. Ordinarily these conflicts of interest and experience would be acted out in adversarial forms of action. But it was better for all sides to engage in conversation, genuine dialogue. Diplomats did not use a philosophical vocabulary of true conversation, and deep listening. But, at bottom, the issues and suggestions were similar. Through these early decades of the UN, these calls were met by the devices and maneuvers of false dialogue. Globalization has continued to tighten the noose around contradictory/antagonistic agents—to make such enmity more intense and intimate. It has also shown with increasing clarity that the way to avoid violent resolution of conflicts is through conversation. Any serious analysis of numerous dialogues on various themes shows precisely the features of false dialogue Tully has painstakingly identified. Efforts at true conversation lie at the center not merely of an academic enterprise of making political theory less parochial but are demanded by much larger and practically significant global conflicts. Efforts at true conversation are essential not merely for deparochializing political theory but for settling tensions stemming from globalization.

Deep Listening

Gadamer offered a particularly clear understanding of the real obstacles to genuine conversation. Philosophical argumentation is an activity directed toward establishing conclusions, getting others to agree to one's point of view. To start that activity with openness, that is, to acknowledge that one's own deep convictions, however genuine, are fallible, is hard, but, on reflection, nothing is more persuasive—and it can function both as a starting point and endpoint of true conversation. Philosophical traditions have been aware of this problem since ancient times. A play by a distinguished tenth-century Kashmiri philosopher Jayanta Bhaṭṭa—the Āgamaḍambara[63]—outlines the great difficulty, especially for philosophers, of judging between the conflicting "goods" of truth and peace—between seeking to establish a particular religious doctrine because of its truth and allowing divergent opinions to flourish in favor of social peace. Acknowledgment of finiteness—the first and minimal historicist step—allows an escape from the conundrums created by an unrelenting search for truth. Political theory after all is the common, all-embracing name of the language in which humanity acts out its conflicts and agreements. In its best construction, it requires a wide definition. It should include in its scope the vastly different ways in which political experience in the human world is articulated in all its divergent, often contradictory forms. It is of course possible, as part of technical academic practice, to continue to specialize in one of its particular dialects. But even the most specialized practice should be informed by a general awareness of the vast diversity of languages and voices. The best way to practice political theory is to cultivate the difficult art of true conversation, and deep listening. True conversation, as Tully suggests, is exceptionally hard, but also exceptionally rewarding.

Notes

1 Routine academic practice usually stays within the boundaries of "normal science."
2 I use this distinction to indicate a significant difference. Even within normal science of a discipline, there are subjects that are unknown—presumably, these can become

known by careful exercise of its methods. 'Foreign' seems to indicate something more radically distinct—a different mode of approaching knowledge.

3 I use "historicism" in the classical sense. It refers to the line of thinking starting with Hegel, but primarily the one associated with Dilthey and Graf Yorck, and continuing down to authors like Gadamer.

4 Hegel, *Logic*, Chapter 3.

5 Though it seems to me that there is a difference between identification of western roots, i.e., origins, and western character, its characteristics mainly are tied to those roots.

6 It continued in the sense in which Sanskrit philosophers speak of a *parampara*.

7 This raises the interesting, awkward question: Can we ask for an earlier time to be "given back"?

8 A long line of political thinkers has thought about this problem of otherness in the west. Consider, for instance, Habermas' writing of post-secularism, Taylor's on secularism, Balibar's work on race and identity, the intense British debates about "multiculturalism," and continuing discussions on "rights of communities."

9 Tully clearly explains this meaning of "universalizing" thought with an example from Socrates in Plato's dialogues.

10 Moyn, *The Last Utopia*.

11 Gandhi is highly instructive on this question for his insistence that all ethical principles demand a literalist reading; otherwise, no moral rule would have the power to bind people in their conduct. A nonviolent movement meant literally that: murder of a few policemen by a small mob altered the nature of his movement and made its moral claim untenable.

12 Of course, this is a broad statement. Marx and Engels dissented from such colonial enthusiasm, and communists were more critical of straightforward colonial rule.

13 *On Liberty*.

14 The Indian National Congress was founded by colonial liberals in 1885.

15 Implicit caste bias permeated nationalist thinking. Even Ambedkar, the great advocate for rights of untouchable castes, regarded tribals with a Millian condescension.

16 Particularly, if we see the two texts as connected parts of a distinct way of thinking.

17 Since Tully's main example is from Plato, Aristotle can be seen as a counterpoint. But similar trends can be found at the start of modernity: Stephen Toulmin, *Cosmopolis*, offers an interesting list. Gadamer treats the rise of historicism as a dissent from mainstream Enlightenment thought. See his *Truth and Method*.

18 Texts like *Manusmṛti*, *Arthaśāstra*, or *Śukranīti* certainly dealt with questions of political power and state authority, but their mode of thinking was not *philosophical* in the "universalizing" or "fundamental questioning" sense.

19 After Chapter 30, *Capital I*.

20 A prior statement of this analysis can be found in Karl Marx, *Revolution and Counter-Revolution*.
21 Or in the mode of "political economy."
22 For a particularly forceful assertion of this argument about Islamic societies, see Hallaq, *Impossible State*.
23 Think of the title of Farid Zakaria's book, *The Future of Freedom: Illiberal Democracy at Home and Abroad*, and how that conceptual move allows a lot of regimes to pass through the eye of the definitional needle. The actual analysis offered, however, captures the contradictory character of the spread of democracy: a number of regimes desire to qualify as democracies. At the same time, besides elections, they seem to regard all other institutional demands as expendable—making it hard to judge whether the world as a whole was becoming more democratic or less.
24 Mehta's *Liberalism and Empire* was a pioneering work in this field. Recent studies by Keene, Muthu, Mantena, and others have opened up this field. Yet, even this field is marked by a notable asymmetry. Study of the political theory of imperialism should analyze not merely western writers who wrote for or against colonial rule but others from the colonies themselves. Little of that side of this "conversation" has been examined. A rare example is Andrew Sartori, *Liberalism in Empire*.
25 Tully's *Strange Multiplicity* is a remarkable exploration of aspects of this history.
26 Interestingly, authors like Voltaire and Montesquieu treat China, India, and the Islamic world as different "civilizations"; under high imperialism, only the European deserves that name, all others reduced to rudeness. Voltaire, *Philosophical Dictionary*, or his comic story "The Huron"; Montesquieu, *The Persian Letters*. A classic example of the kind of argumentation which accomplished this redescription is Mill, *History of British India*.
27 Shown by the criticisms directed at Habermas' initial statement. See Calhoun, *Habermas and the Public Sphere*.
28 In my short response I had tried to show these effects with brevity focusing on the question: "What is my tradition?" This section merely presents that same argument in a more historically elaborate form. See Kaviraj, "Responses," 173–4.
29 There was considerable variation in the manner in which this sovereignty was exercised. See, for instance, Mantena, *Alibis of Empire* about Henry Maine's "theory" of indirect rule.
30 Khan Tabatabai, *Seir ul Mutaqherin*, provides a panoramic account of transformations in political life from the death of Aurangzeb to the governorship of Warren Hastings—precisely this decisive period of colonization.
31 Hay, *Dialogue*.
32 Parekh, "Poverty of Indian Political Theory." This volume contains essays by Indian philosophers responding to Parekh's original statement.

33 Chatterjee, *Nationalist Thought and the Colonial World*. Note, however, the interrogation mark in the title, though the burden of the argument seems clear. In a paper examining the thinking of the early communist writer M. N. Roy, I too concluded that in fundamental ways, though he was certainly politically radical, his thinking was "heteronomous." See Kaviraj, "A Heteronomous Radicalism."

34 For a famous indictment from a leading philosopher, see Bhattacharyya, "Svaraj in Ideas," later published in a journal appropriately based at Tagore's institution Shantiniketan, which had this question as its central pedagogic concern.

35 True, feminist thought has later emphasized the Eurocentrism of initial stages of feminist thinking, but it cannot be said that feminism as a major new strand of political theory emerged from "the outside," or from a place of "otherness." Rather, after it emerged as a powerful intellectual movement, its internal critics discerned in its initial mainstream arguments the presence of the hierarchies we have discussed earlier.

36 A question raised by this thought, though this cannot be pursued here, relates to the concept of pre-understandings that stand behind world-disclosures mentioned in Tully's essay. Pre-understanding as a concept might not be entirely free of ambiguity: does the "pre-" refer to language or to experience?

37 The basic design of *The Philosophy of History*.

38 To me this seems a more fundamental insight into Marx's thinking about class than the economic implications of the idea.

39 Indian novels on social questions often are heavy with dialogues between characters: for example, Tagore's novel on religious and national identity, *Gora*.

40 For instance, the work of writers like Audre Lorde.

41 Though the commonest device to assimilate it into a history of the west was to view it as a lag, or a slow "transition."

42 Tully's paper is particularly rich in exploring the need for such attention.

43 Kaviraj, "Responses," 174.

44 "tṛṇād api sunīcena: taror api sahiṣṇunā: amāninā mānadena: kīrtanīyaḥ sadā hariḥ"—the saying attributed to the Bhakti saint Caitanya. Kaviraj, *Caitanya-caritāmṛta*, chapter 17; sloka 4, 99.

45 For an admirable account of the uses of Lockean ideas by peasant leaders of rural Bengal, see Sartori, *Liberalism in Empire*.

46 Tagore, *Nationalism*, but his most elaborate argument is presented in Bengali in *Swadeshi Samaj*. See, for its implications, Chatterjee, "Tagore's Non-Nation," and Kaviraj, "Tagore and the Conception of Critical Nationalism," and "Democracy and the Non-Nation State."

47 My emphasis.

48 Chattopadhyay, "Kamalakanter Jobanbandi."

49 Mukhopadhyay, "Samajik Prabandha."

50 A crucial consideration here is the level of literacy. Textual thought reached a very small circle of highly specialized intellectual with command of intricate Sanskrit.
51 See, for example, Ali Nadvi, *Saviours of Islamic Spirit*.
52 For example, Savarkar's *Essentials of Hindutva* seeks to establish an emphatically modern Hindu nation.
53 For the first argument on this question in recent times, see Nandy, *The Illegitimacy of Nationalism*, and Tagore's *Swadeshi Samaj*.
54 Nandy, "Politics of Secularism."
55 These are *deep* critiques, because they do not simply consider how to make the nation-state non-oppressive but whether it is possible to conceive of a sense of belonging that is different from the nation-state.
56 "*sāhityasaṅgītakalāvihīna sakṣat paśu pucchaviṣaṇahīna*"—those without literature, music, art are really beasts without tails and horns—says the *Sāhityadarpaṇa* of Visvanātha, an eleventh-century text.
57 Quite distinct arguments in the Sufi and Bhakti traditions make similar suggestions—encouraging interchange between Hindu and Islamic artistic forms.
58 This is urgent and hard conversation that Indian culture needs to begin: it is likely to be very difficult, but also likely to be very meaningful.
59 This is why "system" and lifeworld are antipodal conceptual descriptions.
60 True, China was not a colony but its revolution powerfully assisted the decolonization process.
61 France, Holland, Belgium engaged in bitter colonial wars to preserve empires.
62 It is fascinating to read UN debates to explore forms of false and genuine dialogues.
63 Translated as *Much Ado about Religion*.

References

Ali Nadvi, Abuhasan. *Saviours of Islamic Spirit*. Lucknow: Academy of Islamic Research and Publication, 1971.

Bhaṭṭa, Jayanta. The *Much Ado about Religion (Āgamaḍambara)*. Clay Sanskrit Series, New York: New York University Press, 2005.

Bhattacharyya, Krishna Chandra. "Svaraj in Ideas." In *Visvabharati Quarterly*, Vol. 20, 1954 [1928], 103–14, reprinted in *Indian Philosophy in English: From Renaissance to Independence*. Edited by Nalini Bhushan and Jay Garfield. 103–11. Delhi: Oxford University Press, 2011.

Calhoun, Craig, ed. *Habermas and the Public Sphere*. Cambridge: MIT Press, 1993.

Chatterjee, Partha. *Nationalist Thought and the Colonial World: A Derivative Discourse?* London: Zed Press, 1986.

Chatterjee, Partha. "Tagore's Non-Nation." In *Lineages of Political Society*. 94–126. New York: Columbia University Press, 2011.

Chattopadhyay, Bankimchandra. "Kamalakanter Jobanbandi." In *Bankim Rachanabali, Volume 2*. 101–12. Kolkata: Sahitya Samsad, 1964.
Cooper, Garrick, Charles Mills, Sudipta Kaviraj, and Sor-hoon Tan. "Responses to James Tully's 'Deparochializing Political Theory and Beyond.'" *Journal of World Philosophies* 2 (2017): 156–73. https://scholarworks.iu.edu/iupjournals/index.php/jwp/article/view/929.
Gadamer, Hans-Georg. *Truth and Method*. London: Sheed and Ward, 1979.
Hallaq, Wael. *The Impossible State*. New York: Columbia University Press, 2013.
Hay, Stephen. *Dialogue between a Theist and an Idolator [Bramna—Pauttalik Samvad]*. Kolkata: Firma K L Mukhopadhyay, 1974.
Hegel, Georg Wilhelm Friedrich. *The Philosophy of History*. New York: Dover Publications, 1956.
Hegel, Georg Wilhelm Friedrich. *Science of Logic*. New York: Routledge, 2002.
Keene, Edward. *Beyond the Anarchical Society: Grotius, Colonialism and Order in World Politics*. Cambridge: Cambridge University Press, 2002.
Khan Tabatabai, Ghulam Hussein. *Seir ul Mutaqherin*. Lahore: Sang-e-Meel Publishers, 2006.
Kaviraj, Krnsadas. *Caitanyacaritamrta*. Edited by Sukumar Sen and Tarapada Chakrabarti. Kolkata: Ananda Publishers, 1985.
Kaviraj, Sudipta. "A Heteronomous Radicalism." In *Political Thought in Modern India*. Edited by Thomas Pantham and, Kenneth L. Deutsch. 209–35. New Delhi: Sage, 1981.
Kaviraj, Sudipta. "Tagore and the Conception of Critical Nationalism." In *Religion and Nationalism in Asia*. Edited by Giorgio Shani and Takashi Kibe. 11–31. London: Routledge, 2019.
Kaviraj, Sudipta. "Democracy and the Non-Nation State." In *Thinking Democracy Now: Between Innovation*. Edited by Nadia Urbinati. 251–67. Milan: Feltrinelli, 2020.
Mantena, Karuna. *Alibis of Empire: Henry Maine and the Ends of Liberal Imperialism*. Princeton: Princeton University Press, 2010.
Marx, Karl. *Revolution and Counter-revolution: Or Germany in 1848*. London: G. Allen, 1896.
Mehta, Uday Singh. *Liberalism and Empire: A Study in Nineteenth-Century British Liberal Thought*. Chicago: Chicago University Press, 1999.
Mill, James. *History of British India*. London: Baldwick, Craddock and Joy, 1826.
Mill, John Stuart. *On Liberty and Other Writings*. Cambridge: Cambridge University Press, 1989.
Montesquieu. *The Persian Letters*. Translated by Margaret Mauldon. Oxford: Oxford World's Classics, Oxford University Press, 2008.
Moyn, Samuel. *The Last Utopia: Human Rights in History*. Cambridge, MA: Belknap Press, Harvard University Press, 2010.
Mukhopadhyay, Bhudev. "Samajik Prabandha." In *Prabandhasamgraha*. Kolkata: Carcapad, 2010.

Muthu, Sankar. *Enlightenment against Empire*. Princeton: Princeton University Press, 2003.
Nandy, Ashis. *The Illegitimacy of Nationalism*. Delhi: Oxford University Press, 1994.
Nandy, Ashis. "Politics of Secularism and the Recovery of Religious Tolerance." In *Secularism and Its Critics*. Edited by Rajeev Bhargava. 321–44. Delhi: Oxford University Press, 1998.
Parekh, Bhikhu. "The Poverty of Indian Political Theory." In *Reasoning Indian Politics*. Edited by Narinder Pani. 25–55. Delhi: Oxford University Press, 2018.
Sartori, Andrew. *Liberalism in Empire*. Berkeley: University of California Press, 2014.
Savarkar, Veer Damodar. *Hindutva: Who Is a Hindu?* New Delhi: Hindi Sanhiya Sadan, 2005.
Tagore, Rabindranath. *Nationalism*. London: Macmillan, 1921.
Tagore, Rabindranath. *Swadeshi Samaj*. Kolkata: Viswabharati, 1964.
Toulmin, Stephen. *Cosmopolis: The Hidden Agenda of Modernity*. New York: Free Press, 1990.
Tully, James. *Strange Multiplicity: Constitutionalism in an Age of Diversity*. Cambridge: Cambridge University Press, 1995.
Zakaria, Farid. *The Future of Freedom: Illiberal Democracy at Home and Abroad*. New York: W. W. Norton, 2007.

5

Dialogues in Black and White

Charles W. Mills

James Tully's essay is a very rich and thoughtful contribution to the project systematically initiated in recent decades of developing a comparative approach to political thought. He lists six obstacles likely to be encountered by such an enterprise and then sketches some ways that a dialogical approach may be able to overcome them. In these comments, that can be read in part as my own thinking out loud about these issues, I want to raise the question of how, if at all, his analyses of obstacles and his suggestions for solutions would need modification for the special "comparative" case of a "white" dialogue with what is increasingly coming to be called the "Afro-modern political tradition" (what would previously have been designated as "black," or, before that, "Negro" political thought).[1]

I

Afro-modern political thought fits awkwardly—when indeed it is noticed at all—into the standard taxonomies of mainstream ("white"/"western") political theory.[2] But this very awkwardness is what motivates my question. The way to think of this tradition is as the political theorizing of blacks in modernity (arguably these populations would not have *been* black before modernity), both in Africa and in the black diaspora (to the Caribbean, the Americas, and Europe), grappling with systems of white domination, first in the forms of Atlantic racial slavery and European colonialism, and then in the forms of post-Emancipation and post-colonial/neo-colonial regimes of continuing structural racial disadvantage. If this characterization seems unhelpfully abstract, try the ostensive route instead: just think of representative eighteenth—and nineteenth-century figures, such as Olaudah Equiano ("Gustavus Vassa"), Quobna Ottobah Cugoano ("John Stuart"), David Walker, Martin Delany, and Frederick Douglass (abolitionists), or representative twentieth-century figures, such as Ida B. Wells, W. E. B. Du Bois, Marcus Garvey, C. L. R. James, James Baldwin, Aimé Césaire, Frantz Fanon, Kwame Nkrumah, Malcolm X, and Steve Biko (anti-colonialists, anti-imperialists, anti-white-supremacists).

How should we conceive of this tradition in relation to Tully's categories? It is certainly non-western and "Other" insofar as it arises out of "practices and places," a "lifeworld," that is very alien to the white experience of modernity. And this "otherness" is manifested in the general exclusion of such texts from the western political canon, as established by histories, anthologies, introductory textbooks, and defining book series of western political thought.[3] Yet in other respects it is not non-western at all, and its alterity/"Otherness" is far more unsettlingly and uncomfortably close to the white western Self—perhaps even contributing to the constitution of that Self—than most or all of the other candidates from the rest of the world's peoples. I do not, of course, mean that African civilizations before Atlantic slavery and the later imposition of European colonial rule over the continent were themselves "western," but that the self-image of the west—more precisely, what we have come to think of as "the west"—was already being shaped even in the premodern period by images of blacks and Africa. And correspondingly, from the modern period onward, Afro-modern political theory is in large measure defined precisely by its opposition to western political ideologies of racial subordination, in the process often seeking to retrieve and rewrite those ideologies for emancipatory purposes.[4]

Consider the list I just gave above. In his *Culture and Imperialism*, Edward Said characterizes as "contrapuntal ensembles" the interrelation between western and non-western identities.[5] Even for the African Afro-moderns, born in the non-west—the abolitionist ex-slaves Equiano and Cugoano, the anti-colonial/anti-neo-colonial and anti-apartheid thinkers Nkrumah and Biko—the "contrapuntal" relation between their theorizing and western ethico-political frameworks is clear. And for the African Americans (Walker, Delany, Douglass, Wells, Du Bois, Baldwin, Malcolm X) and Afro-Caribbeans (Garvey, James, Césaire, Fanon), unequivocally products of western "civilization," western educational systems, western values and norms, albeit in the racially dimorphized forms requisite for establishing and maintaining white settler, slave, and colonial societies, it is incontrovertible.[6] For it is in the name of Christianity, or liberalism, or democracy, or socialism, or nationalism, that the politico-ideological struggle against these systems of domination has been waged, in terms that—even when they have been infused with a content deriving from indigenous perspectives and axiologies—should have been completely recognizable to their oppressors, given their own supposed commitments (to Christianity, liberalism, democracy, socialism, nationalism). So the alterity of these black voices is, in a sense, superficial, the making of demands readily understandable—not "Other" at all—to their white interlocutors if they were genuinely prepared to listen.

But were they and are they? For in another sense, of course, black demands have been quite unfathomable, in that they have insisted on the extension across the color line of values and norms really intended only for white men. The white male attainment in modernity of individuality and equal moral status was restricted to themselves, and never meant to apply to others—not even to white women, let alone people of color. The racialization of western ethico-political theory introduces a set of conceptual barriers of its own. In the classic diagnosis of James Baldwin: "*Negroes want to be treated like men*—a perfectly straightforward statement containing only seven words. People who have mastered Kant, Hegel, Shakespeare, Marx, Freud, and the Bible find this statement utterly impenetrable."[7]

So the question, then, is how Tully's identification of obstacles and strategies for deparochialization translate for this peculiar variety of "comparative" political dialogue, a dialogue with interlocutors simultaneously closer to home (or even at home!) and farther away, familiar yet utterly strange, speaking one's own language but in a tongue that is incomprehensible.

Consider, in this light, the six factors Tully lists as likely to interfere with genuine dialogue: pretense for strategic reasons, self-deception, projection of one's own tradition on to others, the silencing of critical elements within the tradition, secondary explanations that justify western superiority, and fast-time pre-scripted processes. Nowhere on this listing does Tully highlight racism as an obstacle—perhaps he means it to be subsumed in one way or another under these other factors. But I will suggest, as indicated, that an understanding of racism in general, and anti-black racism in particular, will be crucial to a realistic mapping of obstacles to a Euro-modern/Afro-modern conversation. For it is clearly going to affect all of them deeply given the enduringly degraded position blacks have occupied and continue to occupy in western thought, linked (unlike any other group) to racial slavery in modernity, tied in their origins to a continent traditionally "Dark" and without any contemporary national success stories comparable to, say, Asia, and inheriting a stigmatized iconic status that some researchers have contended goes all the way back to the classical world.[8]

II

Let us begin with racism in general. Traditional biological understandings of race, even if not themselves racist, saw races as natural subsections of the human race that, in coming into contact with one another, would "naturally" develop feelings of rivalry and antipathy. So just as race was a socio-independent biological identity, racial antagonisms and hostilities were trans-historical. The discrediting of "scientific"/biological racism by Nazism and the Holocaust, not to mention the anti-colonial struggles that triumphed (insofar as they did) in the postwar period, also undermined the foundations of such explanations. It was not merely that the equality of the human races was resolutely affirmed but, more radically, that the very reality of races as discrete existents was challenged. Traditional racist hierarchies (cognitive, characterological, spiritual, etc.) were not merely wrong (there was no such hierarchy) but conceptually incoherent, predicated on a category mistake. (There was no set of entities available to arrange in a hierarchy in the first place.) In the words of one classic paper of the time, "There are no races, there are only clines [gradients of continuously-varying phenotypical traits, with no 'natural' divisions, no 'joints' at which to cut]."[9] So if, as a growing biological and anthropological consensus seemed to agree, there were not any races to begin with, and so no natural "racial" antipathies to explain racism, then where did the category and the related feelings and/or belief-sets come from?

Given the anti-colonial ferment of the period, it was unsurprising that the most popular account attributed them to the establishment and growth of the very European empires then being challenged. Since it was undeniable that racism had been central to the justification of colonial rule—the superiority of the civilized over the barbaric and primitive—the development of colonialism likewise seemed the simplest and most obvious explanation of its origins. Whether in liberal versions (racism as a moral rationale for the illiberal exclusions of putatively liberal states) or in Marxist versions (racism as the "superstructural" ideology of expansionist colonial capitalism and racial slavery), a straightforward and prima facie plausible case for racism as modern appeared self-evident. Similarly, Caribbean historian Eric Williams in his pathbreaking *Capitalism and Slavery* contended that Atlantic slavery preceded anti-black racism, not the other way around, echoing in this judgment, whether he had read him or not, Du Bois' earlier claim, in his 1915 *The Negro*, that blacks had been regarded as equals in the ancient Mediterranean world, whereas "The modern world, in contrast, knows the Negro chiefly as a bond slave in the West

Indies and America."[10] Reinforced by growing postwar dubiousness about the very concept of race, a widespread conviction began to crystallize that anti-black racism, and indeed racism more generally, was distinctively modern. The black classicist Frank M. Snowden, Jr., for example, wrote two well-received books, *Blacks in Antiquity* and *Before Color Prejudice*, denying that classical civilization viewed blacks in racial and prejudicial terms.[11] And this view has continued to be very influential till today. Thus, Nell Painter's recent *The History of White People* begins with the declaration that neither whites nor blacks existed as "races" in antiquity, since the concept did not exist, and "people's skin color did not carry useful meaning."[12]

These theorists, and other like-minded commentators, can be categorized as proponents of the "short periodization" of race and racism that locates the emergence of racial thinking in early modernity. It is an optimistic periodization in its implications, for it suggests that racial differentiation and discrimination occupy only a few hundred years of the history of humanity, and, as a presumed corollary, can be readily expunged with the right kind of education and social engineering. We recently lived in a pre-racial world and can, with appropriate strategies, eventually bring such a world back into existence.

But there is a competing periodization, the "long periodization," that suggests a darker and more pessimistic picture, especially perhaps for anti-black racism. In his widely-assigned text, *Racism: A Short History*, George Fredrickson begins by observing that discussions of anti-Semitism and colonial white racism have historically gone their separate ways and argues that we should try to unite them.[13] But Fredrickson himself is a "short periodization" scholar, contending that premodern examples of ethnocentrism and religious bigotry should not be mis-categorized as racism. And it could be that his theoretical goal would be more convincingly achieved with the longer periodization that he rejects. David Nirenberg's *Anti-Judaism: The Western Tradition*, for example, points to the origins of anti-Judaism in ancient Egypt, long before the birth of Christ, invoking what he calls a "three-thousand-year history" that constitutes the west through prejudicial exclusion.[14] With the advent of the Christian epoch, and a gradually Christianizing Europe, Jews would become a central locus of reference, defining by their identity what a Christian was *not*, and thereby constituting a generic signifier of *wrongness*, the ontological antipode not merely to human virtue but indeed to humanity itself.

For Fredrickson, such beliefs—though of course to be condemned—would not count as *racism*. But a book from fifteen years ago that would establish itself as one of the strongest supports for the revisionist long periodization, Benjamin

Isaac's *The Invention of Racism in Classical Antiquity*, contends that the standard analysis simply begs the question by operating with a tendentious conception of racism.[15] Racism is conceived of as presupposing innate biological differences (tied to cognitive and characterological hierarchies) between color-coded continental populations. But this conception, Isaac argues, conflates racism as a general concept with one specific variety, its modern exemplar. In other words, you define racism in such a way that only modern incarnations qualify, and then declare, "Look—racism is distinctively modern!" A non-question-begging conception would drop biology, color variation, and geographical origins and just make racism the positing of hierarchical differences that cannot be altered between superior and inferior subsets of human beings.

Likewise, Isaac insists, the genealogy of these differences should be left open, thereby accommodating not just biological but also cultural and supernatural causation, as well as—Isaac's own diagnosis of the most important classical candidate—a weird combination in which environmental influences (geographical, climatic, cultural, even stellar) so shape our bodies that acquired traits are then reproductively transmitted to our descendants. So rather than the familiar environmentalist/hereditarian opposition, we would have a kind of ur-Lamarckian fusion of both. By this non-tendentious definition, Isaac concludes, racism can indeed be found in the ancient world, and in fact the pioneering racist theorist turns out to be none other than Aristotle. Insofar as he assumes an innate distinction between naturally free Greeks and naturally servile Persians, his "natural slave" conception, linked as it is to ethnicity, is a racist one. (Isaac originally spoke of "proto-racism" but came to believe that the prefix was misleading, and so dropped it in later work.) A conference volume bringing together Isaac and other like-minded ("long periodization") scholars, *The Origins of Racism in the West*, would follow, and further contributions, such as Denise McCoskey's *Race: Antiquity and Its Legacy*, have subsequently appeared.[16]

The point is, then, that if this analysis is vindicated, racism is much older and much more deeply entrenched in the western tradition than assumed by an explanation attributing it to modern European expansionism. Moreover, a template inherited from the classical world passed down in the Middle Ages is not merely an abstract possibility but an actuality. Pliny the Elder's *Natural History* would become a central resource for medieval Christendom's concept of "monstrous races." In the Christian iconography of the period, we find a panoply of grotesques, creatures of myth and imagination: the headless (Blemmyae), the one-legged (Sciopods), and the dog-headed (Cynocephali). Their literally fabulous nature might seem to definitively remove them from taxonomies of the human, locating them instead in a different species ontology altogether. But in her study of the art of the period, *Saracens, Demons, and Jews*, Debra Higgs Strickland emphasizes that *real-life humans* are also numbered among the "monstrous races," specifically "Ethiopians" (standing in for Africans in general), Jews, "Saracens," and Mongols.[17] And it turns out that "they share many of the same physical, moral, and behavioral characteristics," having "deformed bodies, strange dwellings, barbaric habits, and sinful behavior."[18] So the enemies of Christendom, whether infidels or heretics, those who never accepted Christianity in the first place or those who are now apostates from their former beliefs, are already being identified in racial terms, part of an eschatological demonology. More recently, Geraldine Heng's *The Invention of Race in the European Middle Ages* contends, as her title declares, that race is indeed premodern (though medieval rather than ancient), and her book accordingly includes chapters on Jews, Saracens, blacks, Native Americans, Mongols, and Gypsies.[19] And for Heng Christianity's causal reach is far more impressively ecumenical than standardly presupposed: "*religion* ... could function both socioculturally and biopolitically: subjecting peoples of a detested faith, for instance, to a political theology that could biologize, define, and essentialize an entire community as fundamentally and absolutely different in an interknotted cluster of ways."[20]

So far as I am aware, even critical philosophy of race has not kept up with this recent revisionist literature in classical and medieval studies, let alone mainstream political philosophy and political science. But its implications for our standard scholarly periodizations (ancient, medieval, modern), both of political systems and political ideologies, are quite dramatic. It would mean that the concept of a racial state, far from being distinctively modern—see, for example, David Theo Goldberg's *The Racial State*[21]—may be applicable from western antiquity onward, whether based on pagan or Christian normative exclusions. The ethnoracial Other—Jew, Persian, Ethiopian originally, later Saracen and Mongol—would then have to be politically reconceived as not incidental and marginal to the constitution of the polity but rather as serving by its presence to define, through reciprocal identitarian opposition ("we are the not-they"), the western tradition from the start. In the ominous conclusion of Michael Hanchard's recent book, *The Spectre of Race*, inclusionary democratic citizenship is achieved through exclusion from the time of ancient Athens, so, contra the conventional scholarly wisdom in political theory, there is in principle nothing new about modernity's ethnoracial polities.[22] What has until recently been very much a peripheral topic in the discipline (race and political theory/political philosophy) would actually need to be moved toward its center. And because of the link between the racialized polity and racialized political ideology, resistance to any genuinely transformative dialogue with its "Others" would presumably then be far more deep-rooted and intransigent, since the very identity of the polity is under threat.

III

And that brings us back to blacks in particular, who—contra Du Bois, Williams, Snowden, Fredrickson, Painter, and others—would indeed then need to be understood as racialized and stigmatized from the time of their initial encounter with the west. David Goldenberg, one of the contributors to the *Origins of Racism in the West* volume, argues that anti-black sentiment in antiquity predates Christianity, shaped by the significance of the Ethiopian's darkness in Greco-Roman color symbolism, associated with death and the underworld. But it is then greatly reinforced by a Christian iconography that links Ethiopians not merely with demons but with the Devil himself.[23] Similarly, Strickland emphasizes that "it was blackness that served as the point of departure for the Church Fathers who routinely compared Ethiopians and Ethiopia to the Devil, vice, and sin."[24] And as if this were not bad enough, the Old Testament story of the Curse of Ham began at some point (sources differ as to when, and which group is primarily responsible) to be interpreted as referring to blacks. According to Genesis (9:18-27), after the Ark's descent on Mount Ararat, Ham had looked at his father Noah in his drunken nakedness, thereby provoking a paternal curse on Ham's child Canaan, all of whose progeny would be condemned to be slaves. Neither blackness nor Africa were mentioned in the text, but since the Biblical Table of Nations attributed the origins of the continental populations of Europe, Asia, and Africa to their founding respectively by Japheth, Shem, and Ham, it began to be read as meaning that Africans were destined to be slaves, a "slave race."

Goldenberg suggests that the Curse of Ham "has been the single greatest justification for Black slavery for more than a thousand years."[25] It was still being invoked in the United States, for example, as late as the nineteenth century. Unlike polygenetic theories (positing multiple origins for humanity), which—though enjoying an episodic vogue (and endorsed, at different times, by Hume and Voltaire, not to mention the American School of Ethnology)—were obviously in tension with Christian orthodoxy, the Ham Curse was itself biblically authorized. Humanity did indeed have a single origin, but the radically different nature of its various branches could nonetheless be accounted for in a way consistent with monogenesis. Moreover, the several hundred years of Atlantic slavery would, of course, deeply imprint this association upon western (indeed global) consciousness—so much so, in fact, that "negro" became virtually synonymous with "slave." And even after nineteenth-century emancipation, the rise to eventual hegemony of "scientific" racism, for example in social Darwinism, once again singled out blacks as belonging to a special derogated category of their own. Less advanced on the evolutionary ladder, they were seen as closer to apes than Europeans, a connection enduring to this day with innumerable manifestations: King Kong imagery in popular culture; the hugely successful twentieth-century creation of the Tarzan of the Apes character, a white jungle king ruling over African humans not that different from his simian subjects; the findings of IAT (Implicit Association Test) research on unconscious white bias and black/ape associations; and widespread representations on racist media of former president Obama and the former first lady as a simian couple.[26]

Even on the shorter periodization, then, blacks are singled out by their role in the Atlantic slave economies as constituting "a slave race" in modernity, precisely the period in which western normative theory is proclaiming the general equality of "men." So their legitimate belonging as fully-fledged and paid-up members of the human race would on those grounds alone come into question. But if the shaping role of precursor premodern sources, Christian and secular, is confirmed, then it means that prejudicial representations of blacks, albeit with a fine disregard for consistency (*both* demonic/diabolical *and* servile!), are far more deeply entrenched in western culture than acknowledged in conventional left-wing explanations of racism. Consolidated with differential impact by "material" factors (slavery, the later conquest, and partitioning of Africa)— after all, neither Jews, Muslims, nor Mongols would be identified with racial chattel slavery in modernity—the inherited classical/medieval iconography of inferiority would, in its deep embedding in the literature and imagery of the west, become intimately imbricated with conceptions of the "white" self and related normative identity.

IV

I suggest that this history, premodern and modern, will have implications for all of Tully's listed obstacles, not just exacerbating their deleterious power individually but creating a negative synergy among them, a collective field of psychic and interlocutory resistance to genuine dialogue, more formidable in its effect than for other colonial subjects. Blacks have been so categorized in the western imaginary that "epistemic injustice" against whatever they may say (to cite Miranda Fricker's very influential work) is guaranteed in advance.[27] Their moral and ontological inferiority carries over, in a natural sequence, to their cognitive inferiority.

Remember that the black speaker in the Americas in particular is either the slave or the descendant of slaves, and thus arguably even today "speaking property." Moreover, because *racial* slavery is a matter of one's intrinsic inferiority, the fact that particular individual representatives may through contingent circumstances be currently free does not affect their essential status. In his second autobiography, *My Bondage and My Freedom* (1855), Frederick Douglass describes how he was treated, after he had ..., having had escaped from slavery to the north and was giving abolitionist speeches "I was generally introduced as a '*chattel*'—a '*thing*'—a piece of southern '*property*'—the chairman assuring the audience that *it* could speak."[28] But even if *it* could, would it be worth listening to? Gayatri C. Spivak famously asks the question of whether the subaltern can speak, suggesting a general deafness on the part of the hegemonic. Yet differences need to be marked even within the category of the subaltern, and I would claim that the lack of receptivity to, say, the South Asian colonial subject (member, after all, of a recognizable if "backward" and "stagnant" civilization) is different in kind from the deafness to one's property, whether current, escaped, or (putatively) emancipated. (Perhaps an essay needs to be written on the subject: "Can human property ever be freed?") Cheryl Harris' "Whiteness as Property" argues that de facto (if not always de jure) relations of differential white property rights in the United States continue into the postbellum period, maintaining asymmetries of racial entitlement and exclusion whatever the actual law may say (e.g., supposed Constitutional "equal protection").[29] And likewise, it could be contended, for political voice, insofar as the polity is originally conceived of as a polity of property owners, self-owning men of substance who are the ones with the real say.

So it will be less a matter of "pretense for strategic reasons" or even "self-deception" undermining sincere dialogue than *genuine* belief in black inferiority, whether biologically or culturally determined, that is likely to foreclose any equitable exchange of views. This is not the Other one does not know and (in these relatively more enlightened times) is self-consciously aware one does not know but the Other white westerners are already confident that they *do* know, and have known for (at least) hundreds or (possibly) thousands of years, with the categories and sense-making narratives to prove it. Insofar as "projection" is the apposite term, it is not a matter of "sense-making" through assimilating the non-western Other to the western Self—I can only make you and your actions intelligible within my framework of understanding by representing your tradition in my terms—but of "recognizing" you in the terms you have *always* occupied in my tradition. The "pre-scripted" "secondary explanations" will, as emphasized, vary over time, from the theological to the biological to the cultural. But there will be no change in the essential assumption of western/"white" cognitive superiority, and the corollary skepticism about the alternative "testimony" and subversive "hermeneutics" offered by the black voice.[30]

For (to further complicate things) an additional obstacle to reciprocal communication is the risk of hearing what one's present/past property might *say*. It is not merely that one's present/past property does not know how to speak but that—in a seeming paradox that will surprise only those unfamiliar with the contradictory logics of domination—it might reveal a knowledge too threatening if it does. Unlike the colonial subject of the European sojourner colony (India), or even the indigenous subject of the white settler state (the United States, Australia), the Other here is domestic rather than foreign *through that very proprietarian relationship*. So there is an intimacy here that is far closer and more threateningly revealing in its reciprocally constitutive relationship than that between the colonial rulers and the native masses, or the white settlers and indigenous peoples in the United States and Australia (where the Other is somewhere over in Indian Country and the Outback, or, later, the reservation). Here, the Other is simultaneously *physically right at hand* (in the slave quarters, in the white household, across the street that demarcates the beginnings of Darktown) and *psychically unintelligibly remote*, inhabiting a strange tabooed inverted black world that must be policed but need not and must not be truly understood, for the price of such knowledge would be too costly for a white world resting on its exploitation. To cite another classic line from Baldwin: "[E]ven if I should speak, no one would believe me," and "they would not believe me precisely because they would know that what I said was true."[31]

Tully's point about "the silencing of critical elements within the tradition" thus takes on particular significance within this context, both because of what is at stake, materially and psychologically, and because of the ambiguity of the borders of the "traditions" in question. A dialogue between "traditions" clearly separated historically in both the politico-economic and the discursive spheres does not entail the same risks as a dialogue between "traditions" possibly not merely linked but in part overlapping, or even locatable as strains within the *same* tradition. If the African American ex-slave abolitionist and anti-racist activist/ theorist Frederick Douglass, shaped by US slavery and subsequent US Jim Crow, educates himself in western texts and proceeds to indict the racism of his US oppressors by reference to the US Constitution, in which tradition is he working? What about the African American scholar and anti-racist activist/theorist Du Bois, educated at Harvard University and the University of Berlin (today Humboldt University), engaged at one point in dialogue with Max Weber?[32] How much more respectably "western" could one be?! Yet despite the fact that these are unequivocally *American* political theorists, long recognized as such by black Americans, we do not hear their voices in the canonical halls of "American" political theory. Only recently have they begun to gain some acknowledgment in the larger "white" mainstream intellectual community.[33] And the reason for this historic exclusion is surely at least in part that—in addition to aprioristic intellectual dismissal—their admission would so dramatically undermine the official story told by the "white" tradition, the sanitized political representation both of the United States as a nation and the actual workings of its institutions.

By contrast with the case of the "silencing" of elements in the western tradition auto-critical of the west for its deprecation or complete ignoring of a clearly external political tradition, then, the "silencing" here is a suppression of what is at least in some cases an internal but denied element of the western tradition *itself*. As noted at the start, Afro-modern political thought, if not under that particular designation, has been around for at least 250 years. But— to focus just on the black Americans—when have Walker, Delany, Douglass, Wells, Du Bois, Ellison, Baldwin, and others ever been included in the American political canon? It is a familiar fact about the United States that it was once formally segregated, and that though literal "White" and "Colored" signs no longer regulate the geography and norms of daily interaction, de facto segregation persists, not just residentially and educationally but in patterns of everyday socializing: who hangs out with whom in the most general sense. The metaphor—if it is a metaphor—of a "color line" can very easily be applied to a great deal of American intellectual life also, both in the selection of canonical disciplinary figures and the choice and treatment of what are deemed to be essential disciplinary themes. Reproduced through socialization (doubly) in the norms of the subject in question, a lifeworld is constituted in this way that will, for most whites, be a segregated, Jim-Crowed lifeworld, both experiential and intellectual.

Consider the following example. As we all know, John Rawls is standardly given the credit for the revival of Anglo-American political philosophy, the judgment being that it was on its deathbed in the mid-1950s. Philip Pettit, in his contribution to the Blackwell *Companion to Contemporary Political Philosophy*, matter-of-factly asserts that from the late nineteenth century to the mid-twentieth century, "political philosophy ceased to be an area of active exploration.... [T]here was little or nothing of significance published in political philosophy."[34] I am sure that in making this judgment—explicitly or implicitly addressing his fellow white mainstream colleagues—he did not think that he was asserting a claim in any way controversial. Yet the work of most of the theorists listed above falls precisely, of course, into this very time period. Might it not be surmised that for a liberalism predicated on the importance of a universal individual equality and freedom that breaks with the ascriptive hierarchy of the premodern epoch, or a republicanism concerned about domination, the situation and writings of those systematically denied equality, freedom, and liberation from domination because of their race might just conceivably have some political interest? But if you have been educated in the exclusionary Euro-conception of what constitutes the "western" political philosophical tradition, it will not even *occur* to you to seek out and include the voices of people of color. It is not that the Afro-modern tradition is analyzed and rejected but that the Afro-modern tradition *is not even acknowledged to exist*. The "silencing" is carried out through a set of testimonial and hermeneutical injustices so effective in their shaping power (the pre-emptively derogatory conception of blacks as incompetent knowers, the aprioristic dismissal of alternative "black" conceptual frameworks as unworthy of being taken seriously) that—as with the best and most efficient forms of hegemonic domination—their influence is ubiquitous and ineluctable while being quite invisible, certainly not overtly proclaimed in the framing of the texts themselves.

Moreover, these epistemic injustices extend to both the characterization of the polity and its normative evaluation, the themes respectively of political science and (post-Rawls) political philosophy. Rogers Smith's massive *Civic Ideals* from twenty-five years ago documented how—despite the country's long unambiguously racist character, encompassing de jure as well as de facto white racial domination—the United States is still standardly conceptualized by American political theorists as having an essentially inclusive political culture.[35] Race and racism have been represented as marginal rather than—as they have been—integral to the political order. A nation so racist in its "basic structure" that in the early 1930s—as the pre-eminent "racial state" on the planet—it would serve as a juridical role model for the Nazis when they were drawing up the anti-Semitic Nuremberg Laws[36] has been depicted as basically liberal-democratic. The longtime competing oppositional black American political conceptualization of "white supremacy" has been ignored.

And likewise, of course, for its complementary Afro-modern normative evaluation. Along with the revival of Anglo-American political philosophy in general and social contract theory in particular, Rawls is routinely praised for his (alleged) innovation of reorienting the normative concerns of the field away from political obligation to social justice. But ask yourself the following question: Once the conceptual blinders preventing the recognition of the work of Walker, Delany, Douglass, Du Bois, and others *as* political theory/political philosophy have been removed, isn't it obvious that social justice has been their theme from the start? Certainly, for the black citizens of an oppressive white supremacist state, especially during the periods first of slavery and then of postbellum disenfranchisement, the idea that the government had been established on a consensual basis would have been dismissed out of hand as absurd. One obeyed because one had no realistic alternative, not because of normative legitimacy. The real issue would be the wrongness of these systems, racial slavery and then continuing postbellum racial subordination. So even if the phrase *social justice* is not used, that is the overwhelming and pre-eminent concern of these texts. A case can be made, then, for rewriting the standard periodization of "western" political philosophy so as to acknowledge that the critical thematization of social justice was by no means introduced for the first time by John Rawls but rather by the Afro-modern victims of the west. But as I have repeatedly pointed out in my work, racial justice as a theme has been almost completely ignored over the past half-century of resurrected (for whites) Anglo-American political philosophy.[37] Indeed the very phrase appears nowhere in the 2000 pages of Rawls' five books. Neither the historically white-supremacist character of the polity nor the imperative of its dikailogical condemnation can be admitted. "Silence" reigns in both spheres. The racial state denies its racial makeup and pre-empts by its conceptualization of social justice its normative critique.

So the "interests" at stake are multiple. From the black/Afro-modern perspective, the fundamental political goal motivating the demand for such dialogue (and resisted by whites accordingly) has always been racial justice and an end to white oppression, whether in the form of racial slavery, colonial rule, Jim Crow/apartheid, or a merely formal juridical equality disconnected from material equality (indeed, used to obfuscate and/or rationalize continuing material racial inequality). So, as mentioned earlier, the oppositional black narrative—certainly in the west (the Americas), but to a significant extent even in Africa—is not an "external" political tradition but a radical contestation *within* the white tradition of the story it is telling itself and others. Michael Hanchard suggests that a key goal of the Afro-modern tradition is exploring "the implications of racial domination for the epistemic frames, definitions, and modes of classification for politics, polity, and society in the vocabulary and lexicon of the western political tradition."[38] But why would the west be open to such an exploration when those "epistemic frames, definitions, and modes of classification" have historically sanitized the history of indigenous expropriation and genocide, African slavery and post-bellum subordination? A genuine dialogue with such interlocutors would require an admission of the truth of this past, and an end to the claimed white "innocence" that thinkers like James Baldwin have diagnosed as so crucial to the white American character.[39] It would, in a sense, require the death of the "tradition" itself, insofar as it has been constituted on this foundation of moral evasion. And finally, apart from the moral and conceptual revolutions, the psychic transformation, the radical disciplinary reconceptualization, the vertiginous turning upside-down of the familiar world, that a thoroughgoing Self- and Other-revisioning of this kind would mandate, old-fashioned material interests of formidable dimensions are involved also. For example, the black American case for reparations for slavery (originally) and Jim Crow (later), first put forward after the Civil War and resurfacing repeatedly since then, would by some estimates carry a price tag of *trillions* of dollars.[40]

Tully's recommendation for overcoming these obstacles—deparochializing western political theory through (first) reparochializing it in its local context—thus metamorphoses far more threateningly for the specific case of the white/black dialogue. Here, the "parochialization," the self-conscious "grounding of tradition in practices and places," for which he calls, would of necessity translate into an investigation of the extent to which the western political tradition has historically been constructed on the derogation of blacks, and thus *already* has a set of racially dichotomized rules and norms for (mis)understanding their political demands. It is not at all that dialogue is being initiated for the first time but that patterns of discourse have long been established in which structures of epistemic injustice are already integral to the architecture of western modernity's political outlook.

In sum, the laudable goal Tully describes of "trying to understand the other in the terms and ways of their own tradition" is reflexively complicated here by the fact that this (Afro-modern) tradition is in large measure *itself part of* the western tradition, seeking to use western values and ideals of freedom and equality, of liberal modernity, to condemn their racially restricted incarnations—and in that way forcing an unwelcome transparency and self-knowledge about how that white tradition has historically actually been constructed. To recognize in its full implications that "traditions are grounded in practices" would mean acknowledging the set of racist practices and structures that have shaped the white west and the "lifeworld" of its white citizens, and that in a sense have from the start ruled out on principle "deep listening, openness, receptivity, empathy" and any genuine desire for "dialogues of reciprocal elucidation" with the black population. The problem is not a "translation" from a different language or, even more demandingly, a set of political "texts" not recognizable as such by the western canon. Rather the problem is an unwillingness to read texts written in straightforward English (and the other colonially inculcated languages of the mother country), adopting formats and using a political vocabulary generally *completely* recognizable from the European originals on which they are often modeled, but that are saying things whose truth cannot be admitted.

In sum, a deparochializing political dialogue with the stranger across the ocean to find out what they know is demanding enough. But a deparochializing political dialogue with the black stranger (and simultaneous familiar) who is the neighbor next door may be too terrifying to undertake because you already know that they know what you don't want to know.

Notes

1 See, for example (moving successively backward in time), Gooding-Williams, *Shadow of Du Bois*; Dawson, *Black Visions*; Brotz, *Negro Social and Political Thought*.
2 Hanchard, "Contours of Black Political Thought."
3 For documentation, see my "Decolonizing Western Political Philosophy."
4 Bogues, *Black Heretics, Black Prophets*.
5 Said, *Culture and Imperialism*, 52.
6 See Rogers and Turner, *African American Political Thought*.
7 Baldwin, *Nobody Knows My Name*, 96.
8 Nederveen Pieterse, *White on Black*; Goldenberg, *The Curse of Ham*; Jordan, *White over Black*.
9 Livingstone, "On the Nonexistence of Human Races," 133.
10 Williams, *Capitalism and Slavery*; Du Bois, *The Negro*, 2.
11 Snowden, *Blacks in Antiquity* and *Before Color Prejudice*.
12 Painter, *History of White People*, 1.
13 Fredrickson, *Racism*.
14 Nirenberg, *Anti-Judaism*.

15 Isaac, *Invention of Racism in Classical Antiquity*.
16 Eliav-Feldon, Isaac, and Ziegler, *The Origins of Racism in the West*; McCoskey, *Race: Antiquity and Its Legacy*.
17 Higgs Strickland, *Saracens, Demons, & Jews*.
18 Ibid., 59.
19 Heng, *Invention of Race in the European Middle Ages*, 3.
20 Ibid., 3.
21 See, for example, Goldberg, *The Racial State*.
22 Hanchard, *Spectre of Race*.
23 Goldenberg, "Racism, Color Symbolism, and Color Prejudice."
24 Higgs Strickland, *Saracens, Demons, & Jews*, 84.
25 Goldenberg, *Curse of Ham*, 1.
26 Hund, Mills, and Sebastiani, *Simianization*. For a popular piece on the issue, with various useful hyperlinks, see my online essay with Hund "Comparing Black People."
27 Fricker, *Epistemic Injustice*.
28 Douglass, *My Bondage and My Freedom*, 213.
29 Harris, "Whiteness as Property."
30 Fricker, *Epistemic Injustice*.
31 Baldwin, *Fire Next Time*, 53–4.
32 Morris, *Scholar Denied*.
33 See the two recent important entries in the University Press of Kentucky's "Political Companions" series: Bromell, *Political Companion to W. E. B. Du Bois* and Roberts, *Political Companion to Frederick Douglass*.
34 Pettit, "Analytical Philosophy." Vol. 1, 6.
35 Smith, *Civic Ideals*.
36 Whitman, *Hitler's American Model*.
37 Mills, *Black Rights/White Wrongs*.
38 Hanchard, "Contours of Black Political Thought," 512.
39 Baldwin, *Collected Essays*.
40 Martin and Yaquinto, *Redress for Historical Injustices in the United States*.

References

Baldwin, James. *The Fire Next Time*. New York: Vintage International, 1993.
Baldwin, James. *Nobody Knows My Name: More Notes of a Native Son*. New York: Vintage International, 1993.
Baldwin, James. *Collected Essays*. New York: Library of America, 1998.
Bogues, Anthony. *Black Heretics, Black Prophets: Radical Political Intellectuals*. New York: Routledge, 2003.

Bromell, Nick, ed. *A Political Companion to W. E. B. Du Bois*. Lexington, Kentucky: University Press of Kentucky, 2018.

Brotz, Howard M., ed. *Negro Social and Political Thought, 1850–1920*. New York: Basic Books, 1996.

Dawson, Michael. *Black Visions: The Roots of Contemporary African-American Political Thought*. Chicago: University of Chicago Press, 2003.

Douglass, Frederick. *My Bondage and My Freedom*. In *The Oxford Frederick Douglass Reader*. Edited by William L. Andrews. 164–222. New York: Oxford University Press, 1996.

Du Bois, W. E. B. *The Negro*. New York: Oxford University Press, 2007.

Eliav-Feldon, Miriam, Benjamin Isaac, and Joseph Ziegler, eds. *The Origins of Racism in the West*. New York: Cambridge University Press, 2009.

Fredrickson, George M. *Racism: A Short History*. Princeton, NJ: Princeton Classics, 2015.

Fricker, Miranda. *Epistemic Injustice: Power and the Ethics of Knowing*. New York: Oxford University Press, 2007.

Goldberg, David, Theo. *The Racial State*. Malden, MA: Blackwell, 2002.

Goldenberg, David M. *The Curse of Ham: Race and Slavery in Early Judaism, Christianity and Islam*. Princeton, NJ: Princeton University Press, 2003.

Goldenberg, David M. "Racism, Color Symbolism, and Color Prejudice." In *The Origins of Racism in the West*. Edited by Eliav-Feldon, Isaac, and Ziegler. 88–108. New York: Cambridge University Press, 2009.

Gooding-Williams, Robert. *In the Shadow of Du Bois: Afro-Modern Political Thought in America*. Cambridge, MA: Harvard University Press, 2009.

Hanchard, Michael. G. "Contours of Black Political Thought: An Introduction and Perspective." *Political Theory* 38, no. 4 (2010): 510–36.

Hanchard, Michael. G. *The Spectre of Race: How Discrimination Haunts Western Democracy*. Princeton, NJ: Princeton University Press, 2018.

Harris, Cheryl I. "Whiteness as Property." *Harvard Law Review* 106, no. 8 (1993): 1709–91.

Heng, Geraldine. *The Invention of Race in the European Middle Ages*. New York: Cambridge University Press, 2018.

Higgs Strickland, Debra. *Saracens, Demons, & Jews: Making Monsters in Medieval Art*. Princeton, NJ: Princeton University Press, 2003.

Hund, Wulf D., Charles W. Mills, and Silvia Sebastiani, eds. *Simianization: Apes, Gender, Class, and Race*. Berlin: LIT Verlag, 2015.

Isaac, Benjamin. *The Invention of Racism in Classical Antiquity*. Princeton, NJ: Princeton University Press, 2004.

Jordan, Winthrop D. *White over Black: American Attitudes toward the Negro, 1550–1812*. Second Edition. Chapel Hill, North Carolina: Omohundro Institute of Early American History and Culture/University of North Carolina Press, 2012.

Livingstone, Frank B. "On the Nonexistence of Human Races" (1962). In *The "Racial" Economy of Science: Toward a Democratic Future*. Edited by Sandra Harding. 133–41. Indianapolis, Indiana: Indiana University Press, 1993.

Martin, Michael and Marilyn Yaquinto, eds. *Redress for Historical Injustices in the United States: On Reparations for Slavery, Jim Crow, and Their Legacies*. Durham, NC: Duke University Press, 2007.

McCoskey, Denise Eileen. *Race: Antiquity and Its Legacy*. New York: Oxford University Press, 2012.

Mills, Charles W. "Decolonizing Western Political Philosophy." *New Political Science* 37, no. 1 (2015): 1–24.

Mills, Charles W. *Black Rights/White Wrongs: The Critique of Racial Liberalism*. New York: Oxford University Press, 2017.

Mills, Charles W. and Wulf D. Hund. "Comparing Black People to Monkeys Has a Long, Dark Simian History." *The Conversation*. February 29, 2016, https://theconversation.com/comparing-black-people-to-monkeys-has-a-long-dark-simian-history-55102.

Morris, Aldon D. *The Scholar Denied: W. E. B. Du Bois and the Birth of Modern Sociology*. Oakland, CA: University of California Press, 2015.

Nederveen Pieterse, Jan. *White on Black: Images of Africa and Blacks in Western Popular Culture*. New Haven, Connecticut: Yale University Press, 1995.

Nirenberg, David. *Anti-Judaism: The Western Tradition*. New York: W. W. Norton, 2013.

Painter, Nell Irvin. *The History of White People*. New York: W. W. Norton, 2010.

Philip, Pettit. "Analytical Philosophy." In *A Companion to Contemporary Political Philosophy*. Edited by Robert E. Goodin, Philip Pettit, and Thomas Pogge. Second Edition. 2 volumes. 5–35. Malden, MA: Blackwell, 2007, Volume 1.

Roberts, Neil, ed. *A Political Companion to Frederick Douglass*. Lexington, Kentucky: University Press of Kentucky, 2018.

Rogers, Melvin L. and Jack Turner, eds. *African American Political Thought: A Collected History*. Chicago: University of Chicago Press, 2020.

Said, Edward W. *Culture and Imperialism*. New York: Knopf, 1993.

Smith, Rogers M. *Civic Ideals: Conflicting Visions of Citizenship in U.S. History*. New Haven, CT: Yale University Press, 1997.

Snowden, Jr., Frank M. *Blacks in Antiquity: Ethiopians in the Greco-Roman Experience*. Cambridge, MA: Harvard University Press, 1970.

Snowden, Jr., Frank M. *Before Color Prejudice: The Ancient View of Blacks*. Cambridge, MA: Harvard University Press, 1991.

Whitman, James Q. *Hitler's American Model: The United States and the Making of Nazi Race Law*. Princeton, NJ: Princeton University Press, 2017.

Williams, Eric. *Capitalism and Slavery*. With a New Introduction. Chapel Hill, North Carolina: University of North Carolina Press, 1994.

6

Continuing the Dialogue

James Tully

Introduction

I would like to thank Monika Kirloskar-Steinbach, Garrick Cooper, Sor-hoon Tan, Sudipta Kaviraj, and Charles Mills for reading my initial provisional sketch of a transformative deparochializing dialogue so carefully and for presenting such insightful responses in a shared spirit of working with each other on this difficult problem. I am especially grateful to Sudipta Kaviraj and Charles Mills for writing new chapters for this volume. These dialogue partners have brought to light modifications to my sketch of obstacles and genuine dialogue that have to be made to free it from the prejudices and limitations of my partial perspective. I am immensely grateful for and humbled by these gifts of critical reciprocity. I will try to respond in the same generous spirit of reciprocal elucidation by accepting the modifications, showing how they modify the initial sketch, and reciprocating in turn.

To do so I begin in *Dialogue and Decolonization* by situating our dialogue of contemporary political traditions more clearly and concretely in the contemporary global context of unequal discursive and nondiscursive relationships than in "Deparochializing Political Theory and Beyond" (DPTB). I do this by drawing on the work of Mills and Edward Said. I address two questions aptly formulated by Edward Said and raised in DPTB and the four responses: What is this global "contrapuntal ensemble" of culture *and imperialism* we inhabit, and how can we academics help in decolonizing it? I suggest that the answers to both are disclosed to us through participation in democratic dialogues of reciprocal elucidation with their diverse inhabitants. When dialogues of reciprocal elucidation are situated in this neocolonial field, we can see that they are not only a way to understand each other but also to decolonize the relationships we bear as subjects and agents.

In the following four sections I respond to the issues my dialogue partners raise in light of this interpretation of the field in which we are situated. My responses to Kaviraj and Mills are considerably longer than to Cooper and Tan because they wrote longer and more demanding engagements with DPTB. One of my central aims is to show that multi-traditional and multiracial local and global dialogues of reciprocal elucidation, oriented to decolonization, already exist in practice and theory. Our modest dialogue is a contribution to them.

Dialogue and Decolonization

Steps Toward a Dialogue of Equals

I begin with a quotation from Charles Mills that I read after writing DPTB. He concludes his article entitled "Decolonizing Western Political Philosophy" with the following depiction of the obstacles that need to be overcome to achieve a "dialogue of equals" that co-cultivates "*genuine* self-knowledge"[1]:

> What is called for, then, is a rethinking of Western political philosophy which will, in Dipesh Chakrabarty's famous phrase, "provincialize Europe," locating it as a particular part of the globe rather than the center of the globe, whose dialogue with the rest of the world has, however, as a result of imperial hegemony, been more like a monologue, drowning out the voices of others. A revisionist history needs to be undertaken, which will not only recognize alternative non-Western political traditions, both outside and inside the West (thus redrawing the "West"), but make central how the non-recognition of the equality of others has, from modernity onwards, distorted the West's own descriptive mapping of and prescriptive recommendations for the local and incipiently global polities it has constructed. Such a history would, *inter alia*, seek to recover and conscientiously engage with the epistemological and normative resistance, both internal and external, that the project of Euro-domination has always encountered. The rethinking of familiar categories in the light of their imperial genealogy, the admission of new categories that illuminate structures of domination not registered in the official lexicon, the complicating of standard narratives, would open up the cognitive field of the discipline's current self-conception so as to make possible a *genuine* self-knowledge that current orthodoxies—given the need to evade the past—preclude. In this revised framework, a real dialogue of equals could take place that would better be able to address and begin the remedying of the legacy of the Euro-polity, thereby giving the appropriate respect and justice to the "non-political" Others upon whom for hundreds of years it has historically been imposed.

This is a superb synopsis of obstacles we are working to identify and overcome and of the dialogue of equals we hope to bring into being, each from our own perspective. In relation to it, my initial, modifiable sketch of a dialogue of reciprocal elucidation is best seen as a *way* to such a "dialogue of equals" that brings about "genuine self-knowledge" among participants. This is the meaning of my subtitle: "a dialogue approach to comparative political thought." The reason I devoted Sections 6–8 of DPTB to the main features of such a dialogue is that, in human communication and interaction, the *way* (or means) prefigures and characterizes the end. The way is *autotelic*. The dialogues of comparative political thought will become genuine dialogues of equals if and only if we enact the virtues and ethos of egalitarian dialogue as the way, and, in so doing, persuade our partners to do the same.

As I suggest in DPTB, the exchange of modifications over each other's proposals is the first step in a dialogue of reciprocal elucidation. The participants "provincialize" each other's normal disposition to take their presumptive structure of background judgments and foreground inferences that disclose the field as *the* comprehensive view, rather than as one partial and limited perspective from their tradition and *standpoint* within it that reveals some aspects while concealing others. In Cooper's nice phrase, the exchange of modifications "frees" each other from "bad faith"—the unwillingness or failure to bring their socialized prejudgments into question. If successful, this step enables them to see the field from others' perspectives and to begin to modify and transform their views. The dialogue thus begins as a cooperative struggle against dogmatism.[2]

This first step of exchanging proposed modifications requires the virtue of epistemic humility: to always try to provincialize our own view as we present it as truthfully as possible, when asked to speak, and thereby open ourselves to deep listening. If, in contrast, we assert our view and prepare to defend it against responses, others will tend to retaliate in kind. Each justifies their own view and refutes others by arguments that rest on and reinforce the background, intersubjective criteria of justification of their tradition. The vicious monological clashes of unequal theories, traditions, and civilizations that Mills mentions continue and escalate. This is one of the fundamental problems of the present.[3]

Epistemic humility and receptivity are often seen as weakness, yet they are the *way* of the strong. It takes enormous courage and persistence to uphold this nonviolent ethos, as Martin Luther King, Jr. demonstrated.[4] The exemplary enactment of this demanding ethos over time is the nonviolent power that can move others to feel secure and trusting enough to present their own views in the same way. This "moral jiu-jitsu," as Richard Gregg famously called it, begins to free us from our prejudgments and, *eo ipso*, opens us to experience and take interlocutions *as* proposed modifications, rather than as attacks to be refuted or minor adjustments to be assimilated. This is thus the first step of trust building, mutual provincializing, and cooperation.[5]

As such dialogues develop, participants show each other the limitations and partiality of each other's background assumptions from their different perspectives and suggest and discuss modifications, as my dialogue partners have done. As we begin to "integrate" (not assimilate) modifications into our heterogeneous understandings of the complex relationships we bear with each other as dialogue partners, we gradually create new and previously unimaginable ways of seeing the field, our partial subject positions and self-understandings within it, and our unequal relationships with others. This is the "creative event" or interchange. It is the only democratic way to understand each other, work out our differences, and find ways to live together in peace and equality in this diverse, interrelated, and interdependent world. The American philosopher of dialogue Henry Wieman argued that this creative and mutually self-transformative interchange is the great epistemic gift of dialogues of comparative and critical reciprocal elucidation, yet only if we are willing to take this ethical step of freeing our present self-understandings to its transformative powers.[6] The primary ethical responsibility to take this first step surely belongs to critical members of hegemonic traditions, even though, historically, it is the oppressed who have had the courage to do so more often than not.

In DPTB, the steps that follow provincializing exchanges are to disclose, understand, and critique the roles that political traditions (languages, genres) play in the local and global unequal power relations, social systems, and political struggles in which we live (Step 2). Next, to do so we need to situate political philosophies and theories in the underlying and much broader contexts of everyday "political thought" and practice (Step 3). The reason for this is that political theories and philosophies, as a condition of intelligibility, are extensions and clarifications of ordinary language use and reasoning. Moreover, there are important and complex relationships between philosophical dialogues and the situated dialogues of political thought going on in practice. Philosophical dialogues are most often reflections on and reformulations of political dialogues and struggles in practice (Tully 8–13).

Thus, dialogues of reciprocal elucidation are not only oriented to mutual understanding and the generation of dialogues of equals. As in Mills' quotation, they are also oriented to exposing and decolonizing the unequal and unjust social relationships that political traditions legitimate or contest. I mention several critical traditions engaged in these types of dialogue in DPTB, as does Mills' in "Decolonizing Western Political Philosophy." Modernity/coloniality, epistemologies of the global south, critical race theory, settler-colonial studies, Indigenous studies, postcolonialism, colored cosmopolitanism, critical feminist theory, subaltern studies, and Afro-American political theory are well-known examples. These approaches employ family resemblance concepts with crisscrossing and overlapping criteria, references, and complex genealogies that disclose different aspects of the field of comparative political thought and practice in their distinctive ways.

A Decolonizing Dialogue

"Deparochializing" is simply one approach within this broad field.[7] To bring it into conversation with other decolonizing approaches, I will now show how it contributes to decolonizing comparative political thought and practice through engagement in the contemporary global contexts of unequal discursive and nondiscursive relationships. Like many of these critical and constructive approaches, this democratic dialogue tradition uses Edward Said's interpretation of the present as a "contrapuntal ensemble" of neocolonial relationships and decolonizing practices of freedom.

A Contrapuntal Ensemble

The first question is how initially to interpret the global labyrinth of political traditions in order to understand them in relation to the problematic of colonization/decolonization shared by the traditions mentioned above. One way to do this is to begin with the work of Edward Said. In *Orientalism* he shows how the major modern western traditions have conceptualized the non-west as subjects of western processes of colonization.[8] There is room for a certain amount of unevenness in these processes, but the overall perspective is one of western theorists understanding and interpreting world-historical processes of development, especially since the immensely influential stages of view of historical development of the Scottish, French, English, and German Enlightenment. With this parochial perspective firmly in place as the meta-narrative of world history, all other peoples and their cultures and traditions of thought could be colonized by placing them at some lower stage of development in relation to the west.

Then, in *Culture and Imperialism*, Said moved around and examined western colonization from perspectives of some colonized peoples.[9] The western political traditions, relations of power, and modes of subjectification remain hegemonic, yet they are seen as confronted and shaped by a multiplicity of kinds of practices of contestation by colonized peoples, and then counterinsurgency by the colonizing powers and their intellectuals. These contestatory practices of freedom range from cooperation and compliance while following the rules differently, non-cooperation and acting otherwise, to insubordination, violent and nonviolent resistance and revolution, writing and arguing back, and so on. These counter-practices of freedom take place by the colonized from within modified western traditions, as in some Indian traditions, as Kaviraj illustrates; by some critical western members of western traditions, as Mills exemplifies; and by colonized peoples contesting from within their own political traditions, as with Gandhi in India, and Indigenous peoples in settler colonial states in the Americas, Australia, and New Zealand-Aotearoa, as Cooper illustrates.[10]

From these perspectives, the global labyrinth does not appear as a set of inevitable global processes emanating from Europe and its white settler colonial states, but a much more complex, interactive, interdependent, and indeterminate imperial "contrapuntal ensemble," as Said described it, or, perhaps, "multipuntal" ensemble. Even what counts as the "west" varies.[11] Mills' quotation describes this interactive ensemble. All peoples and their traditions are situated inhabitants in this labyrinth. None has the comprehensive view of the whole, although most traditions have the tendency to project theirs as more comprehensive than it is. Thus, global political thought has to be seen and studied dialogically from these different perspectives to provincialize, understand, and decolonize its complex modes of knowledge, power, subjectification, and counter-practices of contestation and acting otherwise (desubjectification). From this revolutionary multi-perspectival view *of* and *in* the ensemble of global political traditions, most of the Eurocentric western traditions appear as a family of parochial perspectives masquerading as universals, albeit with critics within them. This presumptively transcendent orientation causes their subjects not only to misunderstand the world they inhabit but also to overlook the global injustice of colonization that their perspectives characterize as development and progress. This is a monumental epistemic injustice.[12]

Hegemon-Subaltern Relationships

The question this multi-perspectival view of the world of political traditions and practices raises is how best to characterize the plenitude of colonial/decolonial relationships of contestation. As Mills' quote illustrates, the response by many approaches is to use the language of "hegemon-subaltern" discursive and nondiscursive relationships. Hegemon-subaltern does not refer to a specific theory of hegemony. Rather, it just disposes us to look for the hegemonic and subaltern traditions of political thought at play, the hegemonic and subaltern relationships of power in the practices, systems and global networks in which these regimes of knowledge are employed, the modes of relational subjectification and self-awareness of the unequal and interdependent participants, the ongoing practices of contestation and counter-contestation of the participants, and our own places within them. This orientation is indebted to the pioneering work of Michel Foucault, Homi Bhabha, and Gayatri Chakravorty Spivak. It is now widely used in the critical traditions mentioned above.[13]

Of course, not all hegemon-subaltern relationships are relationships of colonization/decolonization in the traditional sense of formal colonization. The ways that the global contrapuntal ensemble evolved over the last one hundred years have transformed systems and practices of hegemon/subaltern and colonization/decolonization. Simultaneously, people engaged in decolonial and other subaltern struggles have extended the criteria and range of reference of "colonial" and "decolonial" and "free" and "unfree" to understand and challenge these changes. Like all essentially contested concepts, their meanings (criteria, reference, and evaluative force) are fought over in the struggles in which they are used to describe and evaluate, and redescribe and re-evaluate, the relationships being contested. Accordingly, it is difficult, if not impossible, to understand the complex current uses and meanings of hegemon/subaltern and colonial/decolonial without understanding these changes.[14] Here is a brief and incomplete genealogy of some of the major changes in vocabulary.

From Formal Decolonization to Neocolonialism

The first major change came with Third World formal decolonization, by violent and nonviolent struggles and the achievement of statehood. These hard-won victories were recolonized by the hegemony of the imperial "great powers," their multinational corporations, institutions of global governance, and the global military network of the United States. By a multitude of informal means and relationships, they continue to govern indirectly the political and economic development of these new states, including their struggles against this new, neocolonial phase of imperialism. This global contrapuntal ensemble is the prototype of new uses of the language of hegemony/subaltern and colonial/decolonial after formal decolonization.[15]

The formally decolonized Third World colonies won powers of self-government, formal recognition of equal sovereignty and statehood under international law, and seats at the United Nations and institutions of global governance. Yet, they remained dependent on the unequal relationships between them and the great powers constructed by centuries of western imperialism. Thus, as Adom Getachew shows, black leaders tried to address these relationships of international inequality through a pan-African federation of states, exercising their right of self-determination in independent ways, and the great struggle for a New International Economic Order at the United Nations (1974).[16] Founded in 1961, the Non-Aligned Movement of former colonies also attempted to free themselves from dependency on the United States and Soviet Union and renegotiate the global order.[17] These were world-making attempts beyond state building because their leaders realized that, without major changes, they would remain de facto subaltern and exploited states. The United States and its European allies gained hegemony over these movements during the Cold War.

Due to the informal hegemony of the great powers over the global infrastructure shaped by centuries of inequality, dependency, exploitation, and racism, subalternization continues into the present. In contrast to the period of formal colonies, the peoples of the now-called global south are governed through the indirect control of their subaltern powers of self-government by economic, scientific, technological, educational, and military means of the hegemonic states. This interactive form of power, in which hegemons govern the conduct of individual and collective subalterns by allowing and constraining their exercise of powers of self-government and interaction, is characteristic of a whole range of distinctly modern forms of hegemon-subaltern power in the network age. It is important to note that hegemons are within the field of power, knowledge, and subjectification, not above it, and often subaltern relative to other actors in some respects, whether they are states, multinationals, or military complexes. It has historical roots in practices of indirect rule and free trade imperialism in the nineteenth and early twentieth centuries by the United Kingdom in India and Africa and the United States in Latin America.[18]

Kwame Nkrumah, W.E.B. Du Bois, C.L.R. James, and King called this new mode of informal imperialism "neocolonialism" and the continuation of the global color line. Nkrumah saw that it enables a more ruthlessly exploitive phase of imperialism than formal colonization:

> For those who practice it, it means power without responsibility, and for those who suffer from it, it means exploitation without redress. In the days of the old-

fashioned colonialism, the imperial power had at least to explain and justify at home the actions it was taking abroad. In the colony, those who served the ruling imperial power could at least look to its protection against any violent move by their oppressors. With neo-colonialism neither is the case.[19]

Nkrumah perceived that, with the end of "old-fashioned colonialism," the imperial powers do not have to explain and justify to their publics what they are doing in the global south. The continuity and transformation of the global imperial system is hidden from view. For the publics of the global north, international law, mainstream international relations, and liberal political philosophy, colonialism ended in 1960 with decolonization Article 1514. From this international perspective, the global colonial system was replaced by the "rules-based" global system of free and equal sovereign states under international law as the new basic structure. Although legally equal, states are socially and economically unequal. The massive inequality is said to be the result of being at a lower stage of development, not the result of the underlying global imperial system. They may require some assistance from the developed states. The fact that the United States has a global economic and military empire with eight hundred bases abroad, imposes authoritarian capitalist systems on states of the global south, overthrows governments that resist, and profits from reconstruction and rearmament afterward either goes without saying or is redescribed as necessary for modernization, marketization, globalization, and democratization.[20]

Thus, when actors and academics speak of the "neocolonial present" today, they are referring to this more complex neocolonial contrapuntal ensemble of hegemon/subaltern relationships and struggles within and against it. In bringing this unequal ensemble to light they are provincializing and challenging the hegemonic traditions that disclose it as a rules-based international liberal system of free and equal sovereign states, oriented toward future peace and democracy, as well as showing how they serve to occlude the neocolonial present.[21]

Neocolonialism

During this period subalternized peoples of color within white settler colonial states extended the meaning and use of "colonial" and "anti-colonial" to their situations of "internal colonization." From the 1920s on, African Americans, such as Du Bois, A Philip Randolph, James Farmer, and Bayard Rustin, described their struggles for justice within the United States as integral partners with the global struggles against colonialism and neocolonialism, racism, poverty, and militarism. In 1957, after meeting with C.L.R. James in London, en route to meet Nkrumah in decolonized Ghana, King succinctly summarized this anti-imperial tradition:[22]

> The determination of Negro Americans to win freedom from all forms of oppression springs from the same deep longing that motivates oppressed peoples all over the world. The rumblings of discontent in Asia and Africa are expressions of a quest for freedom and human dignity by people who had long been the victims of colonialism and imperialism. So in a real sense the racial crisis in America is a part of a larger world crisis.

This global network includes Indigenous peoples colonized within white settler colonial states in North America-Turtle Island, South America, Australia, and New Zealand-Aotearoa, as well as Indigenous peoples colonized within the newly decolonized Third World states. In 1955, Indigenous peoples attended the Bandung Conference of the Non-Aligned Movement and described their struggles as complementary "Fourth World decolonization" movements for self-determination and Indigenous sovereignty. This global network gave rise to red power movements and red and white alliances in practice and a variety of academic fields.[23] Many other oppressed peoples within states, such as the Dalit in India, also described their struggles in terms of decolonization.[24]

These internal colonization movements were blocked from decolonization by UN Resolution 637 VII (1952), the "blue water" resolution, and the decolonization Resolution 1514 (1960). Only overseas colonies could decolonize. Peoples oppressed within existing states, including settler colonial states throughout North and South America, could not because this would disrupt the "integrity" of the existing UN system of sovereign states. Nevertheless, decades of contrapuntal contestation against this neocolonial limit gave rise to a right to internal self-determination.[25] Indigenous peoples gained recognition of their right to self-determination under international law in the *UN Declaration on the Rights of Indigenous Peoples* in 2007. Many Indigenous peoples see this as a step in a double decolonization strategy. The first consists in the resurgence of their Indigenous relational ways of life with each other and the living earth—Indigenous counter-modernities. The second consists in the transformative reconciliation of the maze of neocolonial, hegemon-subaltern relationships with settler peoples into co-created relationships of interdependent freedom and equality by treaty and treaty-like dialogues and negotiations.[26]

As these struggles are going on, sympathetic academics disclose and criticize the features of western political and legal traditions that have justified the subjugation of colored peoples for so long. That is, they are "decolonizing" western political and legal traditions, as Mills puts it. In the eighteenth and nineteenth centuries, "decolonization" was restricted to the liberation of white settler colonies from their "mother" countries and the formation of replication, European-style states. They inherited and continued the dispossession, extermination, slavery, and subjugation of internally colonized colored peoples. This was legitimated by the Enlightenment doctrine that colored people were at a lower stage of cognitive development. The scientific racism of social Darwinists reinforced this prejudice with its view of human evolution as a struggle for existence among races and the natural extermination of the less fit.[27]

As decolonization struggles increased and racist theories were refuted by Franz Boas, W. E. B. Du Bois, and others, members of western political traditions responded by recolonizing them under new, neocolonial developmental theories of decolonization.[28] They argued that many colonized peoples could move up through the stages of development to eventual self-government and European-style statehood under the guidance and tutelage of the advanced western powers. The Mandate System of the League of Nations drew up schemes of development for three different types of colonized peoples and applied them throughout the decolonizing world. These processes continue under the auspices of the United Nations Trustee System and the Constitutional Assistance Program today. The colonial terms "civilizing" and "civilization" were removed from the documents of the United Nations and replaced by the terminology of the western social and political science, theory, and philosophy: modernization, globalization, democratization, constitutional assistance, human rights, marketization, and liberalization.[29]

In these processes and languages of neocolonialism, decolonization, development, and the achievement of freedom and equality are conceptualized as "inclusion" into processes of western modernization, as these are interpreted in the modern western political traditions. Inclusion consists in a range of strategies, from complete assimilation to the western models to inclusion plus various degrees of recognition of subaltern difference.[30] For example, there are distinctive modern traditions of Indian liberalism, Marxism, and nationalism. They share the modern/modernizing framework yet express Indian theoretical and historical distinctiveness within it, as Kaviraj explains. These modern political traditions also coexist with a variety of vernacular Indian traditions that predate them and continue today, such as the Gandhian and sarvodaya tradition.³¹ Sor-hoon Tan provides an example of the hegemony of the western liberal tradition in Singapore and the subalternization of Confucian traditions. Mills exposes a trend within contemporary liberal political philosophy to "foreclose" recognition of Afro-modern political traditions.

Many ongoing struggles against neocolonial inclusion and subalternization have achieved significant degrees of recognition and accommodation in various forms of human rights, multiculturalism, multinationalism, affirmative action, collective rights, and immigration of displaced peoples, both within states and among states in the UN and the institutions of global governance. Nevertheless, these seeds of equality and diversity remain subject to assimilation into liberal and neoliberal modernization on the one hand, or to roll back, internal colonization, and assimilation under white supremacist and authoritarian forms of populism, on the other.³²

Contesting Neocolonialism

Consequently, as many scholars have argued, the languages of formal decolonization, inclusion, and formal equality occlude the new neocolonial colonization of the included and subalternized peoples.³³ David Scott argues that the west has colonized not only non-western peoples but also their imaginaries of postcolonial futures.³⁴ Accordingly, the work of many postcolonial activists and academics is to contest and decolonize this complex neocolonial formation. New languages and traditions of decolonizing have developed. Sometimes, as Mills notes, these new languages are developed by subalterns within the dominant traditions. For example, Mills works to decolonize liberal political philosophy by exposing its exclusion of Afro-modern Political Theory and trying to bring it into dialogue with this rich tradition without subordination.³⁵ However, as Mills points out in "Decolonizing Western Political Philosophy," the major academic challenges have come from scholars outside of the liberal philosophical tradition.

Moreover, these complex processes of imperialism, colonization, decolonization, and neocolonization of human beings and their labor power have always included the colonization of the living earth through the commodification of land as natural resources. These processes of "earth colonization" are the major causes of climate change, mass extinction of biodiversity, and the complex ecosocial crises they are causing. That is, the colonizers dominate, exploit, and destroy the colonized living earth on which they depend, as if they were independent, in ways similar to other modes of colonization. The great struggles in response to these ecosocial crises are thus often conceived as "decolonizing" the living earth.[36]

Finally, another crucially important site of colonial/decolonial contests came into prominence in the midst of these contestations. This is the use of colonization and decolonial praxes to redescribe and seek to transform specific types of individual and collective hegemony-subaltern relationships, such as patriarchy. Feminism, critical race theory, economic class, gender studies, sexual orientation, two-spirited, and LGBTQ are well-known examples. As Kimberly Crenshaw and her associates have shown, these "intersectional" hegemon-subaltern relationships exist within and across every other colonial-decolonial system and their respective traditions of political thought.[37] "Decolonial praxis" and decolonial pedagogies exist within all of these diverse and overlapping relationships.[38] They bring to self-awareness the similarity of these forms of hegemon/subaltern relationships to others and thus the need to include them in the field of decolonial studies and practice.

Thus, the crucial feature of this extension of the criteria and reference of "colonial" and "decolonial" to everyday hegemon-subaltern relationships is that, for any project to be genuinely decolonizing, it has to be grounded in practices of decolonizing the dispositional relationships of self-formation and self-awareness (subject formation) each person bears in such relations. Decolonization begins with practices of decolonial ethics of self-transformation in relations with others. One branch of decolonial ethics began with Gandhi, Mirabehn, and Kamaladevi Chattopadhyay in the Indian decolonization movement.[39] A complementary branch grew in the African American church-based decolonization movement with the Harlem Ashram, Jo Ann Gibson Robinson, and Ella Baker, and another with Malcolm X.[40] The Ubuntu movements took this turn in Africa and the community-based women's organization throughout the global south. Carol Gilligan, Cressida Heyes, bell hooks, and other feminist philosophers brought decolonizing ethics into western philosophy. In the last four years of his life, Foucault turned to ancient Greek ethics to ground contemporary decolonizing political philosophy and practice. Along with Pierre Hadot, he revived the Socratic idea of philosophy as a way of life grounded in the ethics of the care of the soul (*psyche*) as the preparation for politics.[41] These movements have joined hands with the engaged Buddhist tradition of Thích Nhất Hạnh.[42] They include not only meditation and dialogue but also physical, mental, and spiritual work on every aspect of the self and its relations with others, as Wendy Palmer illustrates.[43] There are now practices of ethical decolonization and self-transformation in most decolonization movements.

The upshot of this remarkable revolution in reconceiving and enacting decolonization is that all our practices of freedom need to be grounded in the critical dialogical relationship one has with oneself (de facto form of subjectivity), others, the living earth, and the spiritual dimension of life. Furthermore, given the unequal and unjust hegemon-subaltern relationships we all inhabit, decolonization has to be democratic all the way down. It needs to be with, by, and for all affected in their subject positions in the contrapuntal ensemble. This is the only way to avoid speaking over others, and either entrenching existing unequal relationships or generating new ones, as Albert Camus forewarned.[44] Thus, democratic dialogues of reciprocal elucidation, or some better version of comparative and critical dialogue, are the revolutionary way of decolonization—of being the change.

Discovering the Decolonizing Power of Nonviolence

The question that this democratic and dialogical way of decolonization raises is: How do subalterns, engaged in their practices of freedom, move hegemons to enter into dialogues of negotiation and transformation of the unjust relationships they bear? Revolution cannot consist in overthrowing hegemons and seizing power or founding an independent structure of power. In both cases, the power-over organizations and strategies of revolution reproduce power-over relationships, and cycles of violence and counter-violence. One answer to this question is the power of integral nonviolence initiated by Gandhi. On this view, the relationships of cooperation, contestation, and conflict resolution that exist in democratic relationships of dialogues of reciprocal elucidation involve a nonviolent mode of power, power-with (or with-and-for) that is different in kind from hegemon-subaltern power-over. This is the power of nonviolence. It expresses the original meaning of participatory democracy. The people (*demos*) exercise power (*kratos*) **with** each other: demos+kratos. There is no relationship of ruler and ruled (*arche*), governor and governed, or hegemon and subaltern.[45]

The argument of the nonviolent tradition is that decolonizing movements can organize counter-communities of practice in nonviolent, participatory democratic ways and learn how to exercise this unique form of power-with, freedom-with, and equality-with. On this basis, they can contest the hegemon-subaltern relationships they bear by means of power-with campaigns of various kinds in which they assert truthfully the injustice of the relationship, non-cooperate with its activities, disrupt the status quo, and destabilize powers-that-be. At the same time, they display their nonviolent, democratic way of life for hegemons and bystanders to see, and trustfully offer to enter into free and equal dialogues and negotiations with them to transform the unjust relationship. That is, they always treat their opponents with respect and nonviolent persuasion, as free and equal partners capable of changing their minds. Hegemons habitually respond with violence and their repertoire of power-over countermoves. Nonviolent campaigners suffer. Nevertheless, over time the persistent, public contest over two very different ways of life and of conflict resolution gradually persuades and moves bystanders and hegemons to trust the campaigners and enter into nonviolent dialogues with them. In these power-with relationships, they begin to compare and contrast the existing hegemon-subaltern relationship with the equal-with-equal relationship on offer. As they move along, they enter into transformative negotiations. That is, these dialogues and negotiations can become "dialogues of equals."[46]

In *The Power of Nonviolence*, Gregg called this revolutionary movement moral jiu-jitsu because its persuasive physical, reasonable, rhetorical, and moral aspects are analogous to the ways jiu-jitsu and Aikido disarm and befriend an opponent.[47] It does not end conflict. It makes the world safe for disagreement, contestation, and conflict resolution. It has the capacity to transform violence and replace war and violent revolution as the effective and lasting means of social change. During and after Gandhi, this approach to dialogue and decolonization spread rapidly around the world. As King put it in 1958, with the invention of atomic weapons and other weapons of mass destruction, the choice is not between nonviolence and violence but between nonviolence and nonexistence.[48] I have tried to indicate briefly that it answers our question by linking together, as tightly as possible, decolonizing dialogues of reciprocal elucidation, practices of freedom, and local and global nonviolent, transformative decolonization. I discuss this further in my responses to Kaviraj and Mills.

Global Decolonizing Dialogues

The objective of this brief sketch is to indicate some of the decolonizing roles dialogue plays in the local and global labyrinths we inhabit. In addition, if this sketch of the neocolonial contrapuntal ensemble today is plausible, then it seems to me that complex global, multiracial dialogues of comparative political thought have been constitutive features of it for over a century. These dialogues emerged in practice before they entered into various university disciplines. The relationships between dialogues in practice and universities are now interactive and complex, due especially to community-engaged research. From within certain specialized university disciplines it may appear as if our small dialogue is separate from these broader dialogues, or even that comparative political thought is something that has yet to be developed. However, my further objective is to contextualize our small dialogue: to enable us to see it as a partner in this much larger contrapuntal world of dialogues of comparative and critical political thought. In the responses that follow I try to show some of these connections.

It is helpful to recollect that such dialogues with those who are seen as "others" have been going on since time immemorial. Boas argued that such dialogues are constitutive of the human condition. In our period, at one end of the spectrum of dialogues, they include the analytical and erudite exemplars of Dalton and Santos in DPTB, detailed comparisons of Kant and Du Bois, and multi-traditional engagements with King and Du Bois as political philosophers.[49] There are also the broader global dialogues of political thought, now referred to as "colored cosmopolitanism," "confluence of thought," and "worldmaking after empire."[50] These dialogues are related in various ways to the dialogues of encounter, interchange, and interaction that shaped the modern world, with its unequal interdependent relationships and corresponding forms of relational subjectivity.[51] At the other end of the spectrum, these families of dialogue are also related to the everyday dialogues of dis-inherited, impoverished, and criminalized black, red, brown, yellow, and white prisoners of the incarceration systems of Canada, the United States, and equivalent systems elsewhere. I discuss these dialogues further in my responses to Kaviraj and Mills.

This global concatenation of networks is far from a dialogue of equals. Yet, as Howard Thurman and Barbara Deming argued in the 1960s, there is no excuse for despair. Within the seemingly overpowering darkness of sedimented injustices is always the *luminosity* of the person who has the strength and courage to say "enough" of centuries of conquest, oppression, and counter-conquest, to free herself from her subalternized form of relational subjectivity, and assertively speak truthfully and disruptively in both words and deeds to the hegemon of the unjust relationship she bears along with others. Then, in an ethical act of self-oblative freedom and equilibrium, she turns and offers the open hand of dialogue and negotiation, rather than a closed fist of counterviolence, to the powerful. Occasionally, a hegemon or bystander is disarmed by this unmerited gift of co-creating their shared relationship through free and equal dialogue. Moved by gratitude, the desire not to look bad to others, and the dawning awareness of a qualitatively superior way of resolving disputes, they refuse to take selfish advantage of this trustful offer and begin to reciprocate in kind.

A gift-reciprocity decolonizing relationship thus comes into being and shines its exemplary light on another way of being *with* fellow human beings.[52]

The global nonviolent protests of the police killing of George Floyd *and* the reciprocal nonviolent proposal of reforms to the justice system of May–June 2020 constitute an example of the transformative power of nonviolence. I discuss other examples in my response to Mills. It is important to remember that even Nietzsche, the greatest critic of false promises, saw the historical self-overcoming (*metanoia*) of the power of violence by the superior power of nonviolence as the greatest transformation humans could take. He described it simply as becoming human[53]:

> To finally take all this [deep reflection on the history of violence, domination and counter-violence] in one soul and compress it into one feeling—this would surely have to produce a happiness unknown to humanity so far: a divine happiness full of power and love, full of tears and laughter, a happiness which, like the sun in the evening, continually draws on its inexhaustible riches, giving them away and pouring them into the sea, a happiness which, like the evening sun, feels richest when even the poorest fisherman is rowing with an golden oar! This divine feeling would then be called—humanity!

Like Nietzsche, King also sees the overcoming of violence as the synthesis of the best features of power and love (*agape*):[54]

> And one of the great problems of history is that the concepts of love and power have usually been contrasted as opposites, polar opposites, so that love is identified with a resignation of power, and power with a denial of love .... Now we have to get this thing right. What is needed is a realization that power without love is reckless and abusive, and that love without power is sentimental and anemic. Power at its best is love implementing the demands of justice, and justice at its best is love correcting everything that stands against love.

Response to Garrick Cooper

I agree with Cooper's central observation that such "genuine" dialogues bring into being relationships of openness and reciprocity in which the partners recognize and interact with each other as "fully human." This type of dialogical relationship brings to light the deep attachments (prejudices or comprehensive doctrines), as well as the "bad faith" that conceals them, and opens them to the scrutiny of reciprocal examination. If these dialogues are to be "truly transformative," they "require us to change, and change can be painful and traumatic, for some, more than others" (Cooper 44).

These are central themes of the type of dialogue outlined in Sections 6–8 of DPTB. I refer to this type as "genuine" dialogue and Cooper gives good philological reasons for the use of this adjective. I would just like to add for clarification that I also use "genuine" to refer to other features of reciprocal elucidation dialogues in the course of the chapter: meaningfulness, truthfulness, oriented to mutual understanding, and so on.

The most enlightening feature of Cooper's chapter for me is his explication of a Maori practice of "truth-seeking" *(tono tupapaku)*. He compares this rich practice to the ancient Greek practice of *parrhesia* and Mahatma Gandhi's practice of *satyagraha* (Cooper 42). I refer to these truth-seeking practices as constitutive practices of de-imperializing dialogues of reciprocal elucidation. This complex Maori practice is enlightening in two ways: in its own right and in broadening the field of truth-seeking practices beyond *parrhesia* and *satyagraha*. While *tono tupapaku* shares enough similarities with *parrhesia* and *satyagraha* to be seen as a family member of these truth-seeking practices, it also exhibits enough dissimilarities to be unassimilable to them. In so doing, it broadens the horizon of the field of truth-seeking practices in a way unimaginable without the comparison and contrast. I discuss other examples in my responses to Kaviraj and Mills. We need to extend this dialogue on truth speaking and truth acting practices to dialogues with other Indigenous traditions. This is one of the major de-imperializing roles of dialogues of reciprocal elucidation.

Response to Sor-hoon Tan

Sor-hoon Tan introduces another distinctive way of relating to western political theory traditions. She explains that many Asian students "accept western political theory as universal knowledge, excel in such education, and resent or would resent being required to study Asian political thought." The pedagogical question she raises is how to introduce these students to comparative political thought. I agree that the first step is to encourage students to "engage in the critical practice of questioning their own [western] 'background horizon of disclosure'," and thus to begin a dialogue of reciprocal elucidation. This is possible because the "students are not as westernized as they think." The "background horizon of disclosure that needs questioning certainly is not simply constituted by Asian traditions; but despite the westernized education, it is also not entirely western, insofar as the society they live in continues to be Asian in various ways" (Tan 48). Comparative and critical dialogue has to take into account this complexity. As she nicely puts it, this requires the virtue of humility. She illustrates some difficulties of generating the kind of reciprocal elucidation in which the participants co-cultivate a certain distance from each tradition in turn. She concludes that such dialogues are important and edifying, yet, at the same time, she rightly cautions that "the practices and places, the lifeworld, that one might assume some tradition to be grounded in might not be easily identifiable, and any grounding might prove to be less firm than supposed" (Tan 51).

I could not agree more with her analysis of the difficulties that a dialogical approach to comparative political thought encounters in this context. I have learned a lot from this brief survey of the challenges and thus the epistemic, ethical, and temporal humility with which we have to approach the hard work of engagement and apprenticeship in comparative political thought. As I reflect on this example, it seems to me that similar, yet also dissimilar, difficulties arise in all other contexts with which I am familiar. My hope is that the somewhat elaborate yet incomplete sketch of features of such a dialogue in Sections 6–8 of DPTB might be of some help in understanding how genuine dialogues might be carried out in these and other circumstances. Comparing these specific difficulties with others in different circumstances might enable us to improve our preliminary sketches.[55] I try to begin this by discussing the examples presented by Kaviraj and Mills. I hope to come back to this example in future discussions.

Response to Sudipta Kaviraj

I am grateful to Sudipta Kaviraj for responding by disclosing important aspects of modern western political traditions in both the west and India from his erudite historicist perspective. He shows the distinctively Indian ways in which these modern traditions have been accepted and modified to articulate Indian colonial and postcolonial experience. First, I respond to two questions he raises about my interpretation of western political traditions and say a few words about the dialogue tradition to which I belong. Then, I ask him if the distinctive aspects of Indian modern political theory he brings to our attention can be seen, in turn, as intermediate steps to a more radical comparative and critical dialogue occurring in India and elsewhere throughout the global south and north. I develop this question further in my response to Charles Mills in the following section.

The Roles of Universal Principles

Kaviraj interprets me as claiming that the characteristic form of thinking of western modern political theory consists in two features: its focus on the moral bases of political relationships and its attempt to universalize these moral principles. This is not the claim I am making in this opening section or in the chapter as a whole. My point here is that if we wish to enter into dialogues of equals with other political traditions, then we have to decenter and suspend the prejudgment that the dialogues should be oriented around these two features. These two features are the major concern of contemporary liberal philosophy in relation to other traditions. If this were to be the orientation of comparative political theory dialogues, then other traditions clearly would be colonized within this framework.[56] As I mention, I am not opposed to these questions coming up in comparative dialogues; I just do not think they should set the agenda. Rather, I suggest the way to begin comparative dialogues among political theorists and thinkers from various traditions is to ask each other what sorts of features they wish to discuss, and to ask the participants from subaltern traditions, and subaltern members from hegemonic traditions, first. This helps those who are used to setting the agenda to pause and exercise their listening skills. It builds trust and ensures that the dialogue is created democratically by all affected having a say and a hand in generating the dialogues and its questions, as I mention in "Dialogue and Decolonization" and Section 6 of DPTB.

Next, Kaviraj agrees with me that "there can be no doubt that some of the greatest wrongs in human history were carried out, and, probably more troubling for intellectuals, justified in the name of principles that were central to western political theory." He then asks, "did these clusters of actions, or historical processes—namely, colonialism, racism, slavery, misogyny—*necessarily flow from the philosophical* [my italics] nature of those principles themselves" (Kaviraj 57). The answer is no, these historical processes did not flow from the philosophical nature of those principles. Rather, colonialism and neocolonialism flow from western capitalism, the spread of western law and state formation, imperialism, and militarism.[57] This assemblage of social systems generates specific forms of general injustices: violence, slavery, domination, exploitation, inequality, poverty, and ecocide. It also mobilizes racism, patriarchy, and misogyny. Many of these injustices exist in other civilizations in different forms.

My point here is that "*abstracted* moral principles" have been used to legitimate injustices of imperialism *and* to criticize them. This specific problem is the abstraction from being "grounded in the experiential self-understanding of those to whom they are applied," not the principles themselves, which is a separate issue. I think Kaviraj would agree with this, given his later argument about the need to understand the use of modern political theories by Indian scholars to articulate their distinctive experience of colonization in contrast to the way these political theories are articulated by metropole theorists.

Modern Political Theory and Imperialism

To be clear, the justifications and legitimations of western colonialism and neocolonialism are not primarily this or that moral principle. Rather, they involve the taken-for-granted modern form of representation or worldview of the global field of politics that was called civilization during the colonial period and is called modernization or globalization in the neocolonial (or postcolonial) present. The modern political theories that work within this worldview are also social theories of the actual existing processes and institutions of modernization. Moral principles standardly play their role of legitimation or delegitimation within this larger mode of disclosure of the field of political theory as a whole. For example, it is normally the "stages" view of the history of political, economic, educational, cognitive, and moral development and progress of civilization, modernization, globalization, and constitutionalization that does the heavy lifting.

Since the education and policy institutions of western imperialism have socialized much of the world into this self-understanding of human progress, the legitimation usually goes without saying. The justification and critique dialogues take place within it in its liberal, Marxist, and nationalist forms. For example, Kant, Marx, and Mill acknowledge that they cannot "justify" the injustices of European wars and violent processes of imperial expansion. Nevertheless, these processes are argued to be irresistible and necessary means to move humanity up through the stages of development to a world of Kantian-style states, international law, and perpetual peace, or Marx's violent imposition and development of capitalism, the development of a revolutionary class, grave-digger's dialectic, and communism, in some future generation, always "to come."[58] This "not yet" legitimating mode of representation of world history continues today in endless theories of the spread of western law and capitalism by means of one more war, or one more violent revolution, as the means to peace and democracy.[59]

As Kaviraj phrases it, these modernizing theories come along "with their abstract promise" (Kaviraj 59). There are actually two abstract promises. From the Mandate System to its successor programs today, colonized people are encouraged and induced to move up through the stages of development and so become moderns. They are promised inclusion in the "truncated" universals of modernity from which they were originally excluded (Kaviraj 57). Then, they too can share in the second abstract promise that the modernizing processes they inhabit will carry future generations to world peace and democracy.

However, we can know if this modern way of life is superior to all the other ways of being and knowing on the planet, as it claims, *only* if subjects of them can compare and contrast them with one another. Yet, this kind of dialogue of presumptive equals is foreclosed by the modernist worldview of western political theories. It discloses, prejudges, and ranks them as inferior-lower, less-developed, and premodern, as Kaviraj points out. Indigenous peoples are seen as "remainders" of dispossession and genocide (Kaviraj 63, 55). Traditional Indian political traditions are seen as a "mundane digest of rules of conduct or elementary enumeration of components of the state and their proper functioning, rather than an application of its [western political theory] formidable apparatus of philosophical examination to moral bases of political power" (Kaviraj 60). This is what Boaventura de Sousa Santos calls the "epistemicide" of the ways of being and knowing of the global south by the hegemonic traditions of the global north and their roles in processes of modernization.[60]

A second prejudgment of modern political theories from Kant, Marx, and Mill to their present followers is the premise that the violent imposition and protection of processes of modernization and their master-subject relationships are necessary features of socialization and progress. In Kant's immensely influential formulation, "man is *an animal who needs a master* … to break his self-will and force him to obey a universally valid will under which everyone can be free."[61] This prejudgment rests on another: the state of nature as a state of war, or "rabble hypothesis" that outside of modernity humans are anti-social and antagonistic—incapable of nonviolent self-organization and self-government. These premises are dubious to say the least, yet, within the modern traditions, it is a performative contradiction to call them into question because humans are presumed to become reasonable only through socialization into the processes of modernization, the pacification of the law, the development of civil society, and modern education.

Thus, it is not only moral principles within modern political theory that need to be questioned. It is also these background, constitutive presuppositions that foreclose questioning from within the modern worldview and serve to legitimate the injustices of colonization and neocolonialism. These are the "alibis of Empire," to use Karuna Mantena's apt phrase.[62] This is why we desperately need genuine dialogues of comparative and critical political traditions that reciprocally provincialize these prejudgments and prejudgments that play similar roles in other traditions, and thereby expose the injustices they legitimate. There is no global justice without this epistemic justice.

Universalizing and Historicizing

I agree with Kaviraj that modern political traditions have two strands since the early nineteenth century: universal and historicist. His historicist tradition is rightly famous for its expansion of the historicist strand and his own scholarship is exemplary. My reservation is that this tradition has the tendency to historicize by locating the historicized subject matter in the presumptively universal Eurocentric representation of world historical development of humankind. This limited contextualism thereby reinforces rather than questions one of the most important presumptively universal features of modern political theory that serve to legitimate its hegemony. I think Kaviraj acknowledges this limitation when he writes that this tradition is neo-Kantian and emphatically theoretical (Kaviraj 60). He mentions that critical scholars began the work of calling this mode of representation into question, exposing its racism, and tracking the ways it serves to legitimate the hierarchies of colonial and neocolonial capitalism (Kaviraj 63). They also show that the racial hierarchies of the developmental worldview persist under a patina of color blindness in the hegemonic schools of modern political and legal theory and philosophy.[63]

Practical Political Knowledge in Comparison with Theoretical Political Knowledge

I would like to introduce and compare another western political tradition that is different from Kaviraj's broad two-strand tradition. Like Kaviraj's, it also derives from Socrates and Aristotle. Socrates is one of the founding members of this dialogical tradition. He understood philosophy as a way of life. It consists in engaging in public dialogues with fellow citizens in public places, not only official public spheres. The dialogues are carried on in the vernacular language of politics. Their aims are the ethical care of one's soul (*psyche*), to come to understand the meaning of vernacular concepts of ethics and politics by examining and cross-examining the various ways humans describe and redescribe concrete cases, and to act accordingly (knowledge *is* virtue). It is the search for truth, and one should be willing to die rather than be silenced.

Sometimes Socrates seems to be accepting Plato's view that there are comprehensive definitions or theories of moral and political terms (the forms), but what his questioning shows over and over again is that these terms have "shades of meaning": that is, slightly different yet overlapping criteria (sense, reference, and evaluative force) in different contexts. So, what we need is not a single definition or theory but an exchange of definitions, analogies, and disanalogies that brings to light the distinctions we overlook.[64] As I mention in DPTB, the dialogue tradition is founded on this working hypothesis that most political concepts are family resemblance concepts and, thus, essentially contestable, as Nietzsche and Wittgenstein also argue. Perhaps it is more accurate to say that they are family resemblance concepts with a range of overlapping and crisscrossing senses *because* they are contested in the history of political struggles.

Aristotle inherited this dialogical understanding of political and moral knowledge and provided an account of central features of this practical knowledge. He argued there is no such discipline as political theory because there is theoretical knowledge only of things that do not change. Politics, along with ethics and rhetoric, is in the world of change. Its knowledge holds only "for the most part," and the use and sense of its terms vary in different contexts and from different perspectives (polysemy). Thus, he categorized all political knowledge, as well as ethics and rhetoric, as practical knowledge (political thought), not theoretical knowledge (political theory).[65] Its descriptions and recommendations are generalizations from a limited number of cases, not universalizations. Like all practical knowledge, they need to be tested by trial and error to disclose the limits of their validity.

This practical knowledge is acquired through practice in learning how to use political concepts and to give reasons for using them in such and such a way in various senses and contexts in dialogue with others who use them in slightly different ways and give their reasons for so doing (*paradiastole*). Understanding the meanings of concepts is not to acquire a universal definition. Rather, it is to understand the differing criteria being invoked by the contestants, the reasons they give for them, and, if all goes well, arriving at case-by-case reconciliation of all parties involved. In the best cases, reconciliation involves a dialectic in which the best features of both sides (thesis and antithesis) are preserved in a new set of criteria (synthesis), and this lays the groundwork for future use and contestation (Tully 25). In King's well-known example, the dialectic is capitalism (thesis), communism (antithesis), and beloved community (synthesis).[66] But, in many cases, it consists in recognizing that the parties are invoking slightly different criteria from their different perspectives, standpoints, and traditions, without a definitive resolution, as in most legal and political decisions, and, thus, with the crucial proviso that dissenters can continue to contest the outcome. In both cases, the dialogue never ends.

Aristotle argues that this kind of political understanding requires training in the ethics and rhetoric of dialogical interaction. Rhetoric—the arts of persuasion oriented to truth—requires three dialogue features. These are as follows: arguments (proofs), grounding arguments in some vernacular usages while contesting others (*topoi* or commonplaces) so it is understandable to fellow citizens, and embodying what you argue for in one's conduct ("take care of your soul or aligning bios and logos," as Foucault comments). He borrows Protagoras' term for this unique kind of understanding and judgment in his dialogue with Socrates (*Protagoras*): *phronesis*. My description of the ethics of dialogue in DPTB Sections 6–8 is indebted to this tradition.[67]

Accordingly, the distinctive feature of this dialogue tradition of political thought is that, unlike Kaviraj's modern traditions, it does not have a "universal strand." It is practical knowledge all the way down and self-critical of its generalizations and contextual prejudgments. I think one of the political traditions today with family lineage and resemblance to this Socratic-Aristotelian tradition is contemporary neo-pragmatism or practical holism. It is associated with the (re)turn to ordinary language and Wittgenstein, who studied Socratic dialogue carefully and added new methods of question and answer to it. His style of philosophy is called "polyphonic" dialogue.[68] It is based on the working hypothesis that our language games are not grounded in universal propositions but in ways of acting or forms of life that can be called into the space of questions and changed.[69] In North American political philosophy and theory this broadly pragmatist tradition is associated with people as diverse as William James, John Dewey, Henry Wieman, Richard Rorty, Du Bois, King, Cornel West, Linda Zerilli, bell hooks, Anthony Laden, and Clayton Chin.[70] As Kipton Jensen argues, African American political theorists brought the ethical dimension of being the change to the forefront by combining pragmatism with personalism to ensure it remains grounded in everyday experience.[71] David Hildebrand summarizes it in the following (contestable) way[72]:

> Life, as we live it, is largely beyond our control. It foists upon us the good, the bad, the beautiful, and the ugly. Since we have significantly greater control over theories than over experience, we develop a penchant to have them to limn our wishes. Against this, experience commits pragmatism to radical fallibility; it defies

totalizing appraisals declaring, "it's contexts all the way down" or "all experience is a linguistic affair" or "reweaving a web of beliefs is ... all anybody can do." It forbids neither realism nor legitimation, but insists that they be advocated, as Joseph Margolis puts it, "in a relativistic, historicized, anti-universalistic spirit." If one subscribes to the philosopher-as-gadfly ideal, it follows that she can only fulfill that obligation if she's not tangled in endless scholastic disputes. A gadfly must be free to follow the horse. Experience as method encourages this ideal with the recurring admonition to address social and political issues, helping to ensure that [as John Dewey wrote], "the distinctive office, problems and subject matter of philosophy grow out of stresses and strains in the community life ... and that ... its specific problems vary with the changes in human life that are always going on and that at times constitute a crisis and a turning point in human history."

Articulating Political Experience in Modern Theory Traditions

The most enlightening section of Kaviraj's chapter for me is his characterization of Indian political theory in the colonial and neocolonial periods. He observes that the language of western modern political theories spread around the world with the imperial spread of European and Euro-American political institutions in many different ways. There are two major ways colonized peoples respond. They can articulate their experiences and responses in their traditional languages of politics or they can accept and work within the hegemonic western modern traditions. Setting aside the first path for a moment, he says that Indian political theory overwhelmingly took the latter path. As a result, the language of European liberalism became the dominant language of Indian political expression by the mid-nineteenth century. Western Marxism followed. The older, coexisting Indian languages and traditions of politics were "erased" and classified as "premodern" within the modernist developmental view. "Assisted by the power of western imperialism," the language of western political theory "conquered the world" (Kaviraj 64). Consequently, it seems to some theorists that Indian political theory is simply "derivative" of western political theory, and thus not worth deep listening (Kaviraj 65).

However, this is to overlook what actually happened in India and in other colonized civilizations when theorists work within western political traditions. Indian political theorists use the language of modern political theories in distinctive ways to articulate their unique experiences of modernization in the colonial and neocolonial periods. As a result, Indian modern liberal, Marxist, and nationalist theory is distinct and different from the use of these western languages of political theory by western theorists in the imperial metropole to articulate their experiences. "Indian political thinking ... thought its way through an 'experience' totally unlike what political theory had encountered in Europe" (Kaviraj 66).

I think we can distinguish two different ways of articulating experience in shared hegemonic languages of modern political theory. The first is to accept the institutions, norms, and promises of the western traditions, object to the experience of being excluded from participation in them, and demand inclusion and equality in them. This is what Kaviraj refers to as the promise of overcoming the "truncation" injustice of western imperialism. The Mandate System of the League of Nations and many policies of inclusion of the United Nations after decolonization are of this type: that is, inclusion and assimilation.[73]

A second way is to articulate and demand recognition and accommodation of distinctive experiential ways of inhabiting modern political institutions and using the language of modern political theory. This is what I refer to as practices of freedom vis-à-vis neocolonial liberalism in "Dialogue and Decolonization." It is, as David Scott puts it, the demand to "live modernity differently."[74] India is a prime example of this experiential way of being modern in, for example, its distinctive forms of federalism and religious diversity.

As we have seen, this global phenomenon of sharing the languages of modernization and their various traditions, yet using their vocabulary and grammar in diverse ways, is both possible and actual due to the indeterminacy of meaning and use. This is precisely why we require dialogues of reciprocal elucidation to understand each other and, in so doing, to disclose the limits of our local ways of theorizing our experiences, rather than projecting our use of these shared languages over others.

Kaviraj suggests that these two ways of inhabiting modernity are similar to feminism and African American political theory and practice. Their practitioners have undermined a whole range of "hierarchies" (Kaviraj 63). I agree. Feminists moved very quickly from simply inclusion in the allegedly universal, yet truncated, masculine, heterosexual norms of formal freedom and equality to the right to interpret and inhabit norms differently. They challenged the masculinity, patriarchy, heterosexuality, racism, and classism of the norms of modern societies and their legitimating theories of formal freedom and equality and substantive unfreedom and inequality. These kinds of struggles over the experience, articulation, and institutionalization of modern norms vary across different contexts. Again, this is why we need dialogues of reciprocal elucidation.

However, second- and third-generation feminists and eco-feminists went beyond working differently within the constraints of modern political theory. They replaced the modern principles of independence, self-determination, and justice with interdependence, cooperation, care, and transformative justice. This generated feminist traditions beyond modern political theory. These traditions share more in common with several non-modern traditions, to which we now turn.[75]

Articulating Political Experience in Non-Modern, Vernacular Traditions

In the penultimate section, Kaviraj turns to the first way mentioned above of responding to western imperialism and the hegemony of its modern political theories. This is to articulate the experience of colonization and the struggle for local and global justice in the non-modern, vernacular traditions of the colonized peoples of the planet. This is a huge field of comparative political thought that includes people colonized in all the senses of "colonized."[76] Kaviraj mentions that it includes the five hundred million Indigenous people who ground their resistance to five hundred years of settler colonial dispossession, genocide, marginalization, and epistemicide in their traditional ways of knowing and being. It is important to realize that Indigenous scholars, lawyers, feminists, and activists are also very successful in articulating their experience and concrete aspirations in the concepts of modern political and legal theory, such as prior sovereignty, self-determination, and freedom, when they have to. They have acquired the skills of comparative and critical political dialogue. However, his main example is Gandhi's use of non-modern Indian philosophical and religious traditions and his global influence.

I comment on this important section because it brings to light the global field of dialogues of comparative political traditions beyond dialogues among modernist traditions. These include two broad types of dialogue. The first are dialogues among the multiplicity of contemporary, old and new, living political traditions throughout the world that do not share the prejudgments mentioned above of Kaviraj's modern western political traditions and the non-western variations of them. These are commonly referred to as "non-modern," "non-modernist," or "vernacular" political traditions.[77] The second types of dialogues are among these vernacular political traditions and modern political traditions. As we have seen, to exclude them from a genuinely open and democratic field of comparative political traditions would be a monumental epistemic and democratic injustice, both to them and to those within the modern political traditions. Kaviraj articulates this point succinctly with reference to non-modern Indian philosophical, spiritual, and ecological traditions. He credits them with introducing the idea of *samaja* [belonging] based neighborliness—"sharing the earth" (Kaviraj 69):

> [They] offer a wide variety of significant arguments about fundamental aspects of human life which modernists ought to listen to with unprecedented openness .... Implicit in these ideas are very different proposals for the basic arrangements for humanizing a human life that are opposed or angular to mandatory life-forms of modernity. The comprehensive victory of the colonial modern culture has resulted in a strange inaccessibility of such ideas, though they are "our own."

One of the fundamental roles of comparative political traditions is thus to free colonial and western modern political theory from its deeply ingrained prejudgment that these so-called "premodern" traditions are below and before its superior epistemic stage, and thus inaccessible from the heights of modern theory. The example of Gandhi helps us to see how this deparochializing revolution and renaissance can occur.

The Example of Gandhi

Like Kaviraj's colonial Indian political theorists, Gandhi tried to live up to the truncated standards of western modernity and cross the color line by becoming a common law lawyer, down to details of diet, dress, and comportment. He then entered into the great decolonizing debates of articulating Indian colonial experiences in the traditions and institutions of modern law, liberalism, Marxism, and nationalism. Yet, unlike the majority, he took the transformative, deparochializing step of calling into question the background modern world picture and the civilizing-modernizing processes these traditions share, and subjecting them to critical examination.

Gandhi did this in the following ways. First, he put them to a radical, dialogical test between "editor" (himself) and "reader" (Indian decolonizing modernists) in *Hind Swaraj* (1909). Inspiration for the use of dialogue came from his careful reading of Plato's *Apology*.[78] He argued that if Indian modernists bring about decolonization, they would simply create another, replication modern state, economy, and materialist culture with all the problems of the modern world states system of increasingly vicious cycles of wars, plunder of the planet, and selfish materialist competition for comparative advantage. "It would be called not Hindustan but Englistan. This is not the Swaraj I want."[79] If, on the other hand, Indians turn to their philosophical, spiritual, political, and local vernacular traditions that have sustained a thriving multinational civilization for millennia, they will create a nonviolent counter-modernity oriented to cooperation, well-being, and sustainability. This transformation would overcome the constitutive problems of liberal and Marxist modernization.

Gandhi was able to question and overcome the fundamental prejudgment of modern political traditions (and many other traditions) that violence and the imposition of power-over relationships are the basis of government, economics, and civilization because humans are incapable of nonviolent self-organization and self-government. He was able to do this because he discovered a more powerful and effective substitute for violence: the power of nonviolence, or cooperative power-with, that, he argues, sustains all life (*ahimsa*).

At the same time as he was working out this self-overcoming of modernity's problems, he was also transforming himself. He decolonized his diet, dress, and conduct, established ashrams, began each day with ethical meditative practices of being peace, and turned to nonviolent, self-governing, self-sustaining, and village-scale agriculture and handicrafts (Khaddar). In addition to these constructive programs, he began experimenting with nonviolent contestation and conflict resolution against the injustices of modernity as an effective substitute for both war and violent revolution (*satyagraha*). He entered into dialogues with Indian Dalit peasants and their vernacular traditions to learn about local, self-reliant economics (*swadeshi*) and village-centered, democratic self-government (*swaraj*). *Swaraj* includes ethics (government of the self), as well as the democratic self-government of villages and their eventual global federation (*purna swaraj*). Gandhi also rediscovered the spiritual dimension of politics that the secularization of modernity represses, and, in so doing, generates modernity's reactionary religion-based, ultranationalist other, such as the ultranationalist neoliberalism of Prime Minister Modi (Kaviraj 69).[80] He then set up schools throughout India to teach these practical arts and crafts (*sarvodaya*). All these concepts and practices are in the realm of practical knowledge.

Gandhi also entered into dialogues with modernists and argued for the superiority of these practices of cooperation, contestation, sustainability, and well-being over the processes and institutions of modernization. Moreover, he worked with the proponents of modernization and participated in modern institutions when he thought it was useful to do so. Finally, he drew on the immensely rich, non-modern Indian traditions of philosophy, spirituality, government, ethics and practical knowledge to articulate, develop, test, and teach all aspects of this integral nonviolent counter-modernity.[81] In DPTB I refer to *Sources of Indian Traditions* for the depth and breadth of several of these traditions and Dennis Dalton's contextualization of Gandhi's *swaraj* (free self-rule) in relation to them. Thus, in each step Gandhi was being the change he spoke and wrote about by putting it to the test of trial and error in his own life: integrating bios and logos.[82]

All these features of Gandhian counter-modernity are discussed in the one hundred volumes of Gandhi's writings, republished in many specific selections, and interpreted in countless commentaries. One of the first commentaries to focus on Gandhi's turn to Indian traditions to describe this actually existing vernacular alternative and argue for its superiority relative to modern state-centered capitalist and communist modernity is S.N. Agarwal, *Gandhian Constitution for Free India,* in 1945. Gandhi read the manuscript, suggested some changes, and wrote a Foreword to it in November 1945.[83]

> Let me not be misunderstood. I do not mean to suggest that we should be blind to the experience of other nations and develop a kind of narrow nationalism. Far from it. But it is high time for us to realise that our sense of "inferiority complex" must go, and instead of always looking to the west, we should cultivate the habit of looking within. We have aped the west for long; let us now be proud of our Indian culture and institutions in the right spirit.
>
> I go a step further. The type of decentralised democracy that India had carefully evolved and maintained for centuries in the form of Village Republics was not a relic and survival of tribal communism; it was a product of mature thought and serious experimentation. The kind of local self-government which our country had developed is her numberless Village Communities stood the test of centuries of political storms and is still capable of being organised into an ideal form of democratic administration. I do not suggest that the old system of local administration should be re-introduced exactly in the ancient form. Several modifications will have to be incorporated to suit modern conditions of civic life.

Agarwal goes on to describe the development of Gandhi's ideas from *Hind Swaraj* onward: the constitutional debates in India, and the main features of Gandhian constitution, which he calls "Swadeshi Constitution for Swaraj." He also compares and contrasts it with modern constitutional states and liberal, Marxist, and anarchist theories.

From the perspective of Indian modern political thought, Kaviraj writes, traditional "Indian thought restricted itself to mundane digests of rules of conduct, or elementary enumeration of components of the state and their proper functioning" (9). From the perspective of Gandhi, Agarwal, and their many successors, traditional Indian thought provides an invaluable practical toolkit to build a free and democratic India.

The Example of Richard Gregg

This kind of self-overcoming of the limits of modern political theory and the processes it legitimizes is not restricted to Gandhi or colonized people. Richard Gregg, a Harvard-educated lawyer with a background in the natural sciences and agriculture, engaged in a similar self-overcoming of liberal capitalism. He was a lawyer for the black and white unions in the great railway strikes of the 1920s. The violent suppression of labor persuaded him that capitalism could not be reformed from within. He came across a book on Gandhi in a Chicago bookstore, read it, and decided to move to India to see Gandhi's alternative firsthand. He moved into the Sabarmati ashram in 1925 and began a lifelong conversation and close friendship with Gandhi. He learned Gandhian economics and wrote the first book on it with Maganlal Gandhi. Gandhi sent him to various *swadeshi* schools to teach self-reliant, cyclical economics, agriculture, and handicrafts, and to help establish constructive programs.

When he returned to the United States, Gregg translated and explained Gandhi's projects in the language of the modern human and natural sciences in a series of books and articles from 1930 to 1960. Like Gandhi and Agarwal, he developed the dialogical skills of comparing and contrasting these different traditions of thought and practice, and, in so doing, showing others how they could learn to do so as well. He compared and contrasted Gandhism with capitalism, socialism, and communism.[84] He is most famous for his books and lectures on Gandhi's *satyagraha* techniques of nonviolent contestation, conflict resolution, and transformation of unjust social relations and systems. He argued that it is an effective substitute for war and violent revolution and presented the most comprehensive philosophy of nonviolence as a way of life—a counter-modernity.[85]

In 1950, Bharatan Kumarappa edited an integrated volume of Gandhi's writings on all aspects of his work. His point, like Gregg's, was to remind western readers of the scope and depth of Gandhi's counter-modernity[86]:

> Satyagraha or non-violent resistance, as conceived by Gandhiji, has an important lesson for pacifists and war-resisters of the west. Western pacifists have so far proved ineffective because they have thought that war can be resisted by mere

propaganda, conscientious objection, and organization for settling disputes. Gandhiji's showed that non-violence to be effective requires constructive effort in every sphere of life, individual, social, economic, and political. These spheres have to be organized and refashioned in such a way that the people will have learnt to be non-violent in their daily lives, manage their affairs on a cooperative and non-violent basis, and thus have acquired sufficient strength and resourcefulness to be able to offer non-violent resistance against organized violence. The practice of non-violence in the political sphere is not, therefore, a mere matter of preaching or even establishing arbitration courts or Leagues of Nations, but involves building up brick by brick with patience and industry a new non-violent social and economic order.

A Renaissance of Vernacular Counter-Modernity Traditions

As Gandhi's renaissance spread rapidly in India, it also diffused around the globe.[87] It came into contact in diverse ways with similar vernacular renaissances occurring throughout the colonial world after decolonization. People began to question the hierarchies, grand theories, and abstract promises that accompanied decolonization and state building under neocolonialism, as Gandhi predicted in *Hind Swaraj*. Unlike the spread of modern political theory, the community-based globalization of Gandhi's counter-modernity did not colonize the practitioners that adapted it. Rather, it functions as an exemplar that encourages oppressed people to overcome their inferiority complex, look into their own traditions and practices for analogous alternatives, and articulate their experiences in them. Many are organized by women. Examples are the beloved community tradition of black churches, liberation theology, cooperatives, unions, and nonviolent organizations in African American political thought and practice, Ubuntu in Africa, and food sovereignty in Latin America. Paulo Freire contributed a unique, empowering mode of consciousness-raising dialogue to articulate specific experiences of oppression and ways of overcoming them in vernacular languages and practices.[88]

As Kaviraj mentions, these movements grew quickly in India, often around the ideas of the interdependency or interbeing of all forms of life (*samaja*) (Kaviraj 69). In Gandhi's formulation, the ground of our being is nonviolent relations of love (*ahimsa*). Movements of Sarvodaya, Chikpo, Working Women's Forum, Earth Democracy, Dalit, Ekta Parishad, Jan Satyagraha, Kalpavriksh Environment Action, and Adivasis (Indigenous) began to connect with the rise of alternative economics in Indian universities.[89] Beginning in the 1960s, scientists exposed the limits to growth, the unsustainability of the processes of modernization, climate change, and the sixth mass extinction.[90] New natural and social sciences began to explore this alternative worldview, represented in James Lovelock's Gaia hypothesis and Lyn Margolis' planetary symbiosis.[91] Ecology, life sciences, and earth systems theory joined hands in universities and in community-engaged research with the movements being the change in practice. Students in the global north began to rediscover western traditions of political philosophy that had been classified and dismissed as "premodern" by the modern political traditions.[92]

Practitioners of "think globally act locally," commoning, and participatory democracy entered into networks of dialogue and mutual learning in communities, universities, and World Social Forums. Indigenous peoples' traditional ecosocial traditions of knowledge and practice entered into dialogues with the new ecological, life, and earth scientists at the United Nations, the Intergovernmental Panel on Climate Change, universities, and in global struggles over sustainable practices. Scientists such as David Suzuki, Fritjof Capra, Nancy Turner, and Vandana Shiva showed ways to see the connections among these diverse ways of knowing and to join hands.[93]

The spiritual traditions that secular modern political traditions excluded from politics and the public sphere joined the dialogues and communities of practice. For example, Liberation theology, engaged Buddhism, Pope Francis' encyclical on climate change and social inequality, the African American black church tradition, and Fellowship of Reconciliation brought the interdependent spiritual dimension of all life into dialogues with politics, ethics, and ecology. Charles Taylor argues that modernization and modern political theory "excarnates" modern subjects from interdependent social, ecological and spiritual relationships of belonging together (*samaja*), whereas these movements "reincarnate" or reanimate everyday life.[94] By 2009, Paul Hawken argued that these local and global informal networks and proto-federations of place-based academic and practical movements and dialogues comprise the largest movement on the planet.[95] It constitutes the multiplicity of decolonial practices of freedom that render the present an unpredictable contrapuntal ensemble, rather than a set of universal, necessary and obligatory processes.

Common Threads

Here are some of the common threads of these vernacular traditions of political thought and practice. They are based as much as possible on the articulation of experiences in the languages of everyday use and the activities in which they are woven. They are traditions of practical knowledge, not theoretical, based on generalization, experimentation, and trial and error. This is true even of the life and earth sciences associated with the Gaia hypothesis. They are based on Gandhi's ethos of "be the change" because means prefigure ends. Ethics is thus seen as the ground of politics. They involve ongoing debates over violence and nonviolence. And, within nonviolence, the pros and cons of unarmed friend-enemy struggles (*duragraha*), represented by Gene Sharp, or the transformative power of love (*satyagraha*) tradition, represented by Gandhi, Gregg, King, Deming, and Thích Nhất Hạnh. The Gandhian tradition understands humans to be in life-sustaining relationships of interdependency with all forms of life. Their meta-norm is the sustainability and well-being of all life. The climate crisis, sixth mass extinction, and an uninhabitable earth are not seen as a problem *within* modernization. They constitute a problem or crisis *of* modernization and its modern political traditions.

A final common thread is the toolkit of practices of freedom. First, they engage in practices of freedom in the neocolonial systems of power, knowledge, and subjectification through which they are governed by inclusion, subalternization, and limited participation. These decolonial praxes within modern systems of knowledge and power challenge, test, and go beyond current limits in countless ways, as in Kaviraj's examples. Second, they turn to their own vernacular traditions and engage in constructive programs of counter-modernities, often called "resurgence." Third, they engage in practices of nonviolent confrontation, contestation, and transformation of the systems of knowledge and power that oppress them. While they draw on Gandhi for all three practices of freedom, they have a century of experiments and academic research on these and a large number of new and creative tools.[96]

This is a much broader field of politics and political thought than modern political theories and their corresponding institutions and processes of modernization. It is a field of interdependent relationships of governance and freedom *with:* oneself (ethics), other human beings, all the fellow life forms of the living earth, and the spiritual realm. We are disclosed as citizenships of this four-dimensional world in the first instance, with cooperative responsibilities of sustaining the wellbeing of its members and relationships.

Vandana Shiva describes it in terms of three concentric circles of complex systems.[97] The first and largest is the life system of systems that has sustained life on earth for over 3.8 billion years and through five previous mass extinctions. Within this symbiotic biosphere is the large sphere of informal ecosocial relationships among humans that cooperate and interact in a diversity of ways that mimic the biosphere systems and sustain human life and the ecosystems systems on which it depends. These include the movements mentioned above, as well as informal everyday relations of mutual aid. The third system within these two sustainable systems is the assemblage of destructive and unsustainable social systems and theories of modernization that have developed over the last five hundred years. From this much broader, counter-modernity form of representation of the present, modern political theory is not only a tradition that overlooks the two life systems that sustain all life. It is also one that legitimates the assemblage of systems that is destroying life on earth at an accelerating pace.

From this broader, non-modern perspective genuine comparative dialogue between modern political traditions and vernacular, counter-modernity traditions is not an abstract, scholastic exercise. It is the urgent task of discovering through comparison and criticism, general conditions of a sustainable present and future, and putting them to the test of practice: that is, experiments with truth.

The Inaccessibility of Vernacular Traditions to Indian Political Theorists?

Kaviraj agrees that we need genuine dialogues between Indian modern political traditions and these non-modern traditions (Kaviraj 70). However, he argues that these Gaia-centric or *samaja* practical traditions are "inaccessible" to modern Indian political theorists, even though they are "our own" (Kaviraj 70). As we have seen, this is a striking contrast to the ecological, life, and earth scientists like David Suzuki, who dialogue, work, and often protest with members of non-modern vernacular traditions.[98] He attributes this inaccessibility and estrangement to the "unrelenting, heedless, un-self-critical modern civilization" (Kaviraj 70). Indian modern political theorists use and mimic the same arguments against their non-modern traditions as western modern political theorists deploy against non-western traditions: that is, historicizing them as premodern in the stages view of historical development. Modern political theory effects an "erasure" of these traditions (Kaviraj 64). This other way of seeing ourselves as subjects in the world with others is inaccessible because it is a "non-self" relative to the self-formation and self-understanding that modern political theorists are socialized into through their lengthy education and professional ascesis (23). He concludes that this "represents a general problem of post-colonial cultures" (Kaviraj 70).[99]

I agree with this analysis. It applies, *mutatis mutandis*, to western political theorists as well.[100] As we have seen with the examples of Gandhi and Gregg, the deparochializing and self-overcoming of modernist subjectification is a long and difficult task of decolonial counter-ascesis. Agarwal writes that, in the colonial context, it is the difficult task of overcoming an "inferiority complex" induced by colonization and the modern worldview that legitimates it. Adopting the form of subjectivity of modern political theory and criticizing one's own traditions appears as the means of overcoming this complex, if one can cross the color line and articulate your experience in this hegemonic language.

Furthermore, interpolation into both colonial and western political theory tends to come along with a professional "superiority complex." This is the presumption mentioned by Kaviraj that the longevity, training, analytical rigor, historical depth, and internal contestation characteristic of modern political theory render it epistemically superior to vernacular traditions. While these are important skills, other traditions also have distinctive and demanding training and skills that enable humans to experience and disclose the world of politics and government differently, and so to act differently within it. As Rorty and Iris Marion Young observed, this superiority complex is reinforced by the further presumption that modern political theories, and often the processes they describe, are above the vernacular self-understandings of the demos. They both argued that not only is democracy prior to philosophy but also the way of education in democracy is through participation as equals in ordinary language conversations with fellow citizens.

For these reasons, the inaccessibility of non-modern political traditions to modern political theory is self-imposed. As Wittgenstein puts this problem: "One predicates of the thing what lies in the mode of representation," and a *"picture held us captive. And we couldn't get outside it, for it lay in our language, and language seemed only to repeat it to us inexorably."*[101] It estranges its members from everyday language games and the experiential practices of governance and freedom in which they are used. In *Magister Ludi*, Herman Hesse described how this kind of education alienates the educated elite from life itself. Then, he wrote *Siddhartha*.

Notwithstanding, it has been my experience over forty years of cross appointments in law, philosophy, and political science in three universities— McGill, Toronto, Victoria—that these fields are undergoing a slow yet transformative sea-change. Students and professors set this change in motion by critical practices of freedom that deparochialize and decolonize the modern canon. They treat modern political theory pragmatically, as one complex yet limited tradition of thought among others, as Hildebrand suggests above. Going beyond internal critiques, they initiate comparative and critical dialogues with vernacular traditions to articulate their diverse experiences, expose injustices, and address them together. For example, the transformations that Indigenous students and professors have made to the curricula of law, philosophy, and political science in Canada and other settler colonial countries is an outstanding example.

Kaviraj is correct to say that there are differences between the ways these changes occur in universities of countries like India, which experienced administrative colonialism by a tiny minority, and the settler colonial states of the Americas, Australia, and New Zealand, where the colonizers dispossessed and decimated the native populations, built states on their traditional territories, often with slave labor, and became the majority. Notwithstanding the immense diversity of experience, the curricula of the universities of all modern states share the hegemonic modern political and legal theory tradition. And now, they communicate and share the multiplicity of challenges and changes to it. Kaviraj and many other Indian political theorists have been at the forefront of this renaissance. I would like to ask Kaviraj if these changes are making Indian modern political theory less closed to non-modern political traditions.

Conclusion: Learning from Gandhi and Tagore

In conclusion, Kaviraj mentions the famous dialogue between Gandhi and Rabindranath Tagore as an exemplar of genuine dialogue.[102] I agree. Their "deep critiques of the nation-state are read with renewed respect" because the nation-state model has "profound difficulties." Their critiques are "deep" because "they … [question] whether it is possible to conceive of a sense of belonging that is different from the nation-state" (Kaviraj 77). This is also the central theme of the Indian Sarvodaya, or "gentle anarchist," tradition, as well as of the Indian philosopher Aurobindo Ghose.[103] It is also another common thread and question in the counter-modernity movements. Namely, where are the background, interdependent kinship relations of gift-gratitude-reciprocity that sustain all forms of life on earth (*samaja*) in the assemblage of violent, competitive, hierarchical, us/them, modern/premodern, allegedly universal, and unsustainable relations of modern theory and practice? After his time in India, Edward Goldsmith was among the first westerners to rearticulate this now global dialogue as one between "homeotelic" and "heterotelic" social systems.[104]

At one point, Kaviraj says that the dialogue between Tagore and Gandhi takes place "entirely within a profound affirmation of modernity" (Kaviraj 67). He also says they both draw on "premodern traditions" (Kaviraj 69). If I may, I would interpret it as a dialogue in which both diversity-aware partners have the abilities to access and engage in comparing and contrasting modern and non-modern forms of representation of belonging *in the present*. That is, they provincialize "modernity" as one mode of disclosure of the present among others.

The dialogue is also exemplary for another reason. Although Tagore and Gandhi disagree deeply on this fundamental question, they nevertheless treat each other with profound respect. Such a dialogue requires an ethos of mutual trust and compassion, perhaps even what Gandhi calls love. This shared, intersubjective ground is exhibited in the way they listen and respond to each other. Fortunately, for those of us who are trying to learn this difficult art and craft, Ramachandra Guha gives us a glimpse of their ethos in his moving account of Gandhi's fast while he was imprisoned in September 1932.

Gandhi wrote to ask for Tagore's "blessings" if he approved of the fast; if not, he would "yet prize your criticism, if your heart condemns my action." Before he could post the letter, he was handed a telegram from the prison staff. It was from Tagore, saying he would "follow your sublime presence with reverence and love." Gandhi then added a postscript, saying Tagore's "loving and magnificent wire" would "sustain me in the midst of the storm I am about to enter." Guha then describes the hardship of the journey that Tagore endured from Santiniketan to Poona to be with Gandhi as he broke his fast.[105]

I am sure I have not lived up to the standards Gandhi and Tagore co-achieved. However, I hope I have entered into a dialogue with Sudipta Kaviraj with at least a semblance of their virtues and shown the deep respect I have for his exemplary scholarship.

Response to Charles Mills

Charles Mills presents the most challenging case for genuine dialogue, and so for dialogical comparative political thought. In "Dialogues in Black and White" (DBW) he presents an outstanding critical synopsis of the complex relationship between contemporary liberal political philosophy and Afro-modern political thought (AMPT) and the racist, hegemon/subaltern system in which these two traditions are differently situated. He delineates the unique relationship between these two traditions and the long and short historical periodization of the contrapuntal ensemble they inhabit. He explicates practices of freedom in which African, African diaspora, and African American political thinkers and actors have engaged to try to enter into dialogues with the liberal political tradition. White liberal political philosophers refuse to reciprocate. Dialogue is "foreclosed". The AMPT is "silenced" and suppressed (Mills 92). He then presents the major reasons and material causes for the "unwillingness" (Mills 96) of white liberal political philosophers to engage in dialogue. With this in mind, he turns to my sketch of obstacles to dialogue and asks what modifications need to be made to them to explain this foreclosure. He makes two important modifications to my initial sketch.

Modifications

The first correction is that my sketch does not capture the unique nature of the "unsettlingly intimate" and inside/outside character of the relationship between these hegemonic and subaltern traditions (Mills 82). Second, he politely suggests that the six obstacles to dialogue I present fail to account for the depth of the unwillingness of members of the liberal philosophical tradition to dialogue because they do not focus sufficiently on racism. Racism is the central feature of the hegemon/subaltern discursive and nondiscursive relationship between whites and blacks. Underlying and entrenching all the obstacles I mention is the racist "essential assumption of western/"white" cognitive superiority, and the corollary skepticism about the alternative "testimony" and subversive "hermeneutics" offered by the black voice." This *"genuine* belief in black inferiority, whether biologically or culturally determined, is likely to foreclose any equitable exchange of views" (Mills 90).

I agree with the first correction and the need for modification. What we have seen in each response is that political traditions and their diffuse relationships with each other are unique. No single, universal, or even general description holds in all cases, and each case changes over time. I also agree that the six obstacles to dialogue I mention, which were not meant to be exhaustive, cannot bring out the centrality and characteristics of racism in the depth and detail that Mills does. Also, my one mention of race as a factor in blocking dialogue and my reference to works on race from which I have learned are too brief.[106] I focus on the stages view of historical and cognitive development because it redescribes, disguises, and continues racism in the modern period. I respond to his analysis of racism below.

It is worth noting that some of his obstacles to dialogue are similar to mine. His liberal "unwillingness" to dialogue is similar to my resistance to provincializing, or bad faith, as Cooper calls it. His "moral evasion" is like my "self-deception."

He also agrees that a number of the central features of a dialogue of reciprocal elucidation would bring white liberals around to see the epistemic and social injustices of racism and foreclosure of dialogue (Mills 83, 95–96). I disagree with his claim that the white liberal belief in black inferiority is a "genuine belief" (Mills 90). My understanding of a genuine belief about a racialized people by non-members is a belief arrived at by means of a process of examination that approximates to some degree a "genuine dialogue," as outlined in DPTB, or Mills' similar "dialogue of equals." At the minimum this would involve calling such a habitual belief or prejudgment into the space of questions and examining it, preferably in dialogue with the people the belief is about, and, if not, then through some form of self-examination. The degree of genuineness varies with the degree of examination. A belief in black inferiority according to Mills is, in contrast, a belief that the white person has been socialized into in virtue of his or her hegemonic position in de facto segregation and protected from deparochializing by the refusal to engage in dialogue.

Boas and Secondary Explanations

Mills mentions that "secondary explanations" of black inferiority and white superiority, such as social Darwinism and the stages view of cognitive and political development, vary over time, yet the underlying presupposition of white superiority and black inferiority does not "change" (Mills 91). However, this does not reduce the importance Boas placed on the exposure of how changing secondary explanations serve to render the superior-inferior relationships acceptable, legitimate, and justifiable. The method of secondary explanations developed by Boas is designed specifically to expose the *changing* racist ideologies and traditions of western political thought of colonization of Africans, African Americans, and Native Americans; the ways hegemonic members become socialized into visceral attachment to them; and also to uncover the truth of colonization, slavery, dispossession, exploitation, and "de facto segregation" today that these sedimented secondary explanations conceal. For Boas, the modern political tradition is a classic example of a secondary explanation.

As I mentioned in "Dialogue and Decolonization," these changes over time are in response to the practices of freedom and decolonization of African Americans, Native Americans, and other colonized peoples. Secondary explanations provide genealogies of changes in the contrapuntal ensemble in ways similar to the genealogies of Edward Said, Michel Foucault, W.E.B. Du

Bois, and Christopher Lebron.[107] This critical knowledge of the history of the present is indispensable in freeing ourselves and others from the relational secondary explanations we bear, as Mills argues in "Decolonizing Western Political Philosophy."[108] A decolonizing dialogue is precisely a dialogue that calls reigning secondary explanations into the space of questions and exposes the unjust power relationships they legitimate. This kind of immanent critique is especially important in this case where the subaltern shares the master's political language of freedom and equality after formal emancipation and decolonization. For there is something in this system of thought that makes the master think that he or she is treating the subaltern as *formally* free and equal, so any underlying social inequality must be their fault, as the quotation from Baldwin illustrates.

Boas' anthropological method exposes the underlying basic *equality* of human capabilities of all peoples; the diversity of their expression in different imperial and colonized communities, cultures, and civilizations; and the diffusion of their knowledges, practices, and techniques through interaction over time.[109] In so doing, Boas' anthropological and empirical research undermined explanations of racial hierarchies. It replaced them with a social-scientific hypothesis of equality and diversity that is "closer to the truth." Moreover, he argued that the recognition of this underlying reality of equality and diversity is the only means to world peace and criticized the dominant western view that the imperial spread of western civilization is the means to peace.

Perhaps most important of all for our purposes, Boas carried out his research by means of entering into dialogues with African Americans and Native Americans to try to understand their lifeworlds, traditions, ways of conceiving hegemonic cultures, and ideas of emancipation. This dialogue experience substantiated his human equality/diversity hypothesis. Boas had his own limitations, but he represents an attempt at self-provincializing dialogue of reciprocal elucidation oriented to understanding, decolonization and equality.[110] Many critical dialogue approaches Mills mentions in "Decolonizing Western Political Philosophy" owe a debt to Boas.

Although Boas founded cultural anthropology, he and his followers were criticized for being cultural relativists in challenging the superiority of western civilization. Thus, he was left with a problem similar to Mills. How do we bring the members of the hegemonic culture around to enter into a dialogue based on presumptive equality, rather than presumptive inequality, as in DPTB, and thus open themselves to the injustices that underlie their society, tradition, and position of privilege?

Mills' Explanation of the Obstacles to Dialogue

Mills provides a powerful explanation of why liberal political theory forecloses dialogue with AMPT, despite their shared language of individual freedom and equality, and thereby suppresses it. The western political theory tradition has been based on the contrast and exclusion of an inferior other since Athens. The justifications vary but not the underlying "intrinsic" inferiority (Mills 90). Material factors persist in the modern world from slavery, through Reconstruction, Jim Crow, "differential white property rights" (Mills 90), to the new Jim Crow, de facto segregation and racial discrimination of the present (Mills 90). Yet, there is a rich tradition of African American political theorists, educated in the best American and European universities, using the language of freedom and equality, criticizing white racism, and oriented to emancipation. They show, over and over again, that the liberal ideals are systematically violated in their "racially restricted incarnations" (Mills 95) and the "continuing structural racial disadvantage" of today (Mills 81). It is a "radical contestation within the white tradition of the story it is telling itself and others" for "racial justice and an end to white oppression" (Mills 94). Yet, this close at hand AMPT "is not even acknowledged to exist" (Mills 93).

The reasons for foreclosure are not only the sedimented, dispositional belief in superiority-inferiority. Opening up to AMPT would expose the injustice, both of the whole western tradition and the injustices of the history of the United States: "indigenous expropriation and genocide, African slavery and post-bellum subordination" (Mills 95). Material interests play a role as well, in the refusal to take reparation seriously. The knowledge of the past and present is too costly and too close to home. As Baldwin puts it, "they know what I would say is true" (Mills 96). If they were to engage in the practices of dialogues of reciprocal elucidation, these injustices would come to the fore. These truths thus "cannot be admitted": "a deparochializing political dialogue with the black stranger (and simultaneously familiar) who is the neighbor next door may be too terrifying to undertake because you already know that they know what you don't want to know" (Mills 96).

Response: Introduction

This is a very powerful analysis of the racist reasons and material factors that explain why liberal political philosophers have not entered into deparochializing dialogues with African American political philosophers, even though they are close at hand and have been engaging with liberal political philosophy for generations. The question for those of us who believe in the importance of deparochializing dialogue for decolonization remains: How can such a dialogue be initiated? I believe that the pragmatic AMPT has discovered and tested one answer to this question. I would like to describe its genealogy in the following way.

First, I survey a contemporary school of liberal political philosophy—procedural or deliberative liberalism—that has entered into a type of dialogue with AMPT. It is not a genuine dialogue of equals or even a dialogue of reciprocal elucidation among unequals. Features of the linguistic structure of this contemporary liberal tradition are obstacles to genuine dialogue. The features enable the inclusion of black theorists and traditions in the curriculum and public sphere. However, they are subalternized under the hegemony of the procedural liberal political tradition in various ways that block dialogues of mutual deparochialization. I show how this form of liberalism makes it appear that liberals are treating blacks and AMPT as free and equal when, in fact, their mis-recognition of AMPT and practice perpetuates the racist social system of de facto segregation. I call it neocolonial liberalism. (This is why the critique of secondary explanations is necessary.)

In the second part, I turn to a school of AMPT that exposes the limits and injustices of neocolonial liberalism, on the one hand, and describes an AMPT alternative or counter-modernity: local and global beloved communities of practice. I also show how this pragmatic tradition discovered a mode of integrated nonviolent persuasion that can move the colonizer to dialogue, negotiation, and decolonization. That is, I try to do what Mills asks us to do: to enter into a dialogue with an AMPT. I attempt to understand it and present a provisional first interpretation of it in the hopes that Mills will respond and correct my mis-interpretations, which I am sure are many. Mills knows this field far better than I do. This exchange would continue the black and white dialogue he generously initiated. From the perspective of the dialogical pragmatic tradition I mentioned in response to Kaviraj, nothing could be more important and rewarding.

Neocolonial Liberalism

The historical context in which neocolonial liberalism emerged after formal decolonization is the pre-existence of thriving multi-traditional, multiracial, and multi-continental decolonizing dialogues of reciprocal elucidation that began in the early twentieth century. These contrapuntal, decolonizing dialogues of "colored cosmopolitanism" began in practice, yet they also moved to universities in the interwar years. They have been reconstructed by a wide range of scholars in recent years, such as Robert Young, Cornel West, Bidyut Chakrabarty, Nico Slate, Adom Getachew, Peneil Joseph, Kipton Jensen, Barbara Ransby, Uli Y. Taylor, and many others. In "Decolonizing Western Political Philosophy" Mills mentions the various forms they have taken recently in different disciplines in universities of the global south and north, including political theory within political science. In many cases, the academic wing of them has remained in dialogue with communities of practice through various forms of community-engaged research. In other cases, scholars have traced the complex history of racism and imperialism in western philosophy. Mills also mentions that these dialogues are slowly establishing beachheads in political philosophy texts and courses.[111] From this perspective, the foreclosure of dialogue of mainstream liberal political philosophy appears as an anomaly. However, if we examine its procedural and deliberative features, it also appears as an indirect response to these critical, multiracial, and multi-traditional dialogues in theory and radical politics in practice occurring all around it.

Inclusion and Subalternization

As we have seen, a distinctive feature of neocolonial power, knowledge, and subjectification is that it does not always exclude and foreclose. Rather, it includes, subalternizes, and encourages constrained participation in modern social systems comprised of hegemon-subaltern relations. These are complex, interactive games in which subalterns exercise participatory power within the interactive governance of hegemons. The power of the hegemon to control the rules of the game is often called regulatory capture or constitutional capture (containment). As Kaviraj argued, there are two very general types of game: assimilation to hegemonic norms of conduct and the more contestatory articulation of subaltern experiences in the languages and systems of modernity. This general neocolonial form of hegemon-subaltern relationship is the hard-won result of generations of struggles for recognition, distribution, and participation against more direct and dominative forms of rule under direct colonization, slavery, patriarchy, sexism, and racism. Participants and academics are now well aware of how seemingly free participation brings the subaltern under the interactive governance of the hegemon, and so of the need to refuse and act otherwise in some cases. However, participation also opens up new possibilities of decolonial praxis within and against the limits of the unequal relationships they inhabit and have limited room to maneuver.

Deliberative or procedural liberalism can be interpreted as a response to these demands for recognition and participation. The aim of deliberative liberalism is to replace Kant's monological test of the universality of liberal norms with a deliberative test in which the people subject to the norms participate in testing and agreeing to them. This device is said to respect the equiprimordiality of democracy and constitutionalism, and, in so doing, unite the modern liberal and democratic traditions. It is neocolonial in virtue of the status of liberalism. Liberalism is not seen as one equal tradition among others to which fellow citizens belong. Rather, it unilaterally provides the procedures for deliberation. These procedures "capture" the regulation of deliberation. Political traditions of nonliberal citizens are classified as comprehensive doctrines that are subject to liberal procedures. They become the arbiters. This finesses the first egalitarian step of dialogues of reciprocal elucidation: comparing the different ways political traditions engage in political dialogue and deliberation.[112]

In the first phase, comprehensive doctrines were restricted to the private sphere or somewhere in the nonliberal world. They could not be brought into the public sphere and public reasoning. As liberals realized that this constraint excluded the majority of citizens in modern societies, they revisited public reasoning in public spheres. Citizens were permitted to ground their arguments in their comprehensive doctrines and even bring some nonliberal political and religious arguments into the public sphere. That is, they could articulate their lived experiences in their vernacular languages at the beginning of public reasoning. However, the telos of deliberation is to move from the particular reasons of citizens' comprehensive doctrines up to the articulation of universal norms that transcend the particularities of comprehensive doctrines (vernacular traditions). Deliberators are permitted to check the compatibility of proposed norms with the core features of their comprehensive doctrines as they reason along. Hence, justified norms allow for reasonable pluralism of traditional ways of interpreting and living in accord with them, subject to the burdens of citizenship. The ultimate test is not consensus but that a proposed norm cannot be reasonably rejected relative to the liberal procedures and conceptions of free and equal individuals.

Hence, it is often called inclusive, multicultural, or multi-modernities liberalism. It includes citizens from different traditions, subalternizes them relative to the liberal procedures and norms, yet also allows and encourages them to enact their cultural differences in the way they participate in the subsystems of liberal states and deliberate in official public spheres.

Starting Points of Neocolonial Liberalism and AMPT

One procedural norm is that deliberation begins from the premise of independent individuals who are free from each other, formally equal (equality of opportunity), and subject to the laws that deliberation in accord with procedures of public reason justifies. This is the basic device of representation of the field of politics and law. Liberal political philosophy consists in articulating and debating the conceptual details of competing normative theories of justice from within this background picture. These elaborate theories of justice are then applied to any problem of injustice that arises. The problem with this approach is that its canonical language of disclosure of the field of politics is partial and so overlooks or misinterprets many of the most pressing injustices we face. Just as disclosing the field of global relations as a liberal system of independent states and international law overlooks the continuation of global imperialism and the global color line into the neocolonial present, disclosing the field of politics within states in terms of free and equal independent individuals and state law overlooks underlying, unjust social systems.

In contrast, AMPT and other pragmatist traditions start from sharing comparative experiences of actual existing interdependent individuals and groups within unfree and unequal hegemon-subaltern *social* and legal relationships, with their corresponding secondary explanations and forms of relational subjectivity. Like Socrates and Wittgenstein, they begin from the problem at hand, as in DPTB. They then ask each other how can we work together to transform them. Resolution and reconciliation are worked out democratically by all affected and relative to their multi-perspectival understanding of the problem at hand. Liberal participants provide one limited device of representation among others. Just as you cannot see the global system of imperialism and the color line through the liberal lens of independent states and international law, you cannot see the racial social system of de facto segregation through the liberal lens of free and equal independent individuals within states.

Liberal Norms, Basic Structure, and De Facto Segregation

Neocolonial liberalism also presupposes that the basic structure of a liberal state is its constitutional structure. The liberal norms that are tested and affirmed through liberal deliberation justify this basic, liberal democratic constitutional structure. The structure is not perfect, but it can be perfected by reform within the political and legal institutions of the constitutional order, helped along by political philosophers articulating proper forms of public deliberation. The problem with this relationship between liberal norms and de facto constitutional structures, as Mills points out, is that the constitution of the United Sates is a structure of domination imposed over the dispossession, genocide, and colonization of Indigenous peoples, the enslavement of African Americans, and the Jim Crow and new Jim Crow systems of de facto segregation (Mills 21). Political and economic theorists add primitive accumulation.[113] It conceals and colonizes these underlying unjust social systems. Contemporary liberalism presupposes that this constitutional structure of domination is the imperfect yet perfectible foundation of liberal freedoms and republican freedom as nondomination.[114]

This internal relationship between the normative foundations of modern liberalism and the de facto constitutional order limits the scope of public reason.[115] It forecloses deparochializing this relationship, moving around to see the underlying unjust social systems by means of dialogues with African American and Native American subjects of them, and calling aspects of the normative-constitutional ensemble into the space of questions. Yet, this is precisely what African Americans and Native Americans are demanding in the name of epistemic and democratic freedom and equality. It is the way of decolonization. For example, in the 1990s Robert Williams and I offered red and white dialogical ways of seeing and decolonizing the structural injustice underlying the Canadian and American constitutions.[116] Instead, as we have seen, neocolonialism offers the extension of "truncated" liberal norms of freedom and equality to all, and the right to inhabit them in a reasonable pluralism of ways.

Consequently, through the lens of neocolonial liberalism, the social system of de facto segregation appears as a case of individual inequality of opportunity requiring affirmative action. Fred Harris explains that this "color-blind" misrecognition generates a perverse "tug of war" that fails to address the underlying injustice.[117] On the one hand, affirmative action consists in helping disadvantaged blacks to enter into the mainstream competitive systems and adopt their forms of subjectivity: politics, economics, education, military, sports, and so on. Many take this path and are successful in it. They give expression to their multicultural differences in their professions and often enact decolonial praxis within them. Moreover, many try to help their sisters and brothers in the communities they left. On the other hand, black communities lose members who would have worked in black communities and been roles models for children. The collective strength of black communities suffers and the grip increases of the oppressive system of segregation, poverty, poor education, unhealthy food, pollution, racial profiling and militarized policing, and incarceration.

Consequently, misrecognizing and responding to the effects of the racist system as if it were a liberal color-blind problem of inequality of opportunity makes the racist system worse. If liberals would move around and see the underlying racist system from the perspectives of those subject to it, as Michelle Alexander and Ruth Wilson Gilmore have done, they would be able to see the systemic injustice their parochial mode of representation misrecognizes and the damage its policies cause.[118] Moreover, they would learn about the responses community members are enacting on the basis of their vernacular traditions. Yet, neocolonial liberalism forecloses this kind of deparochializing and enlightening dialogue of reciprocal elucidation.

Colonizing Civil Disobedience

When African Americans try to bring these injustices to the attention of their liberal fellow citizens by means of nonviolent deeds as well as words, liberal theorists redescribe their activities in the liberal language of civil disobedience. Civil disobedience is justifiable insofar as it is oriented to the achievement of liberal civil rights of freedom and equality. This form of nonviolent action is important and it has brought about many gains. Notwithstanding, this liberal redescription colonizes, mischaracterizes, and severely limits the much broader and richer African American tradition of nonviolence as an integrated way of life oriented to decolonization.[119] It recasts black struggles for emancipation into the means of making them subjects of liberal norms.[120]

Conclusion

The double tragedy of neocolonial liberalism is that, from the perspective of its language and institutions, it appears that liberal norms of freedom and equality are being extended to African Americans through inclusion, subalternization, and guidance up the deliberative steps to becoming free and equal liberal citizens by means of their own participatory powers. We have seen this in each aspect of liberalism discussed above. Moreover, blacks and other colored citizens are free to bring their traditions and give expression to them in the ways they participate in liberal modernity. This structure of argument is the continuation of the imperial, racist civilizing, and modernizing mission, with the addition of the inclusive and participatory features I have surveyed here, and more generally in "Dialogue and Decolonization."[121] It enables some people of color to cross the formal color line. This theory is a prototype of countless programs of liberal modernization of people of color around the world in education, democratization, building civil society, business, social work, conflict resolution, constrained self-determination, and constitutional assistance programs since formal decolonization. In practice it is often called "transitional justice": that is, transition to liberal justice.[122]

This form of liberalism includes AMPT and provides a place for it in universities. It does not foreclose and exclude at the outset. However, as Mills notes, AMPT is rarely taken up in philosophy departments by white liberal philosophers. When it is taken up, it tends to be interpreted as not that different from liberalism, since they share the language of freedom and equality. If it is seen as different in kind, then there is no compelling reason within neocolonial liberalism to enter into deparochializing dialogues to see their shared polity from other perspectives. The hegemonic status accorded to the liberal framework forecloses the self-critical need to do so, not only for reasons of epistemic and democratic justice but also for their own reciprocal enlightenment. It thus prevents liberals from seeing and understanding the way liberalism colonizes AMPT, de facto segregation, the three underlying injustices, the tug of war, and nonviolence *from* the critical perspectives of those subject to them, as well as their proposed solutions to them. Since such dialogues among all affected are the democratic way of decolonizing the unjust systems and co-creating a just America together, transformative justice is ruled out, and transitional justice remains firmly in place.

All these neocolonial obstacles to dialogue and transformative justice can be seen as examples of looking yet not seeing and listening yet not hearing by liberals in false dialogues with colored subalterns. They finesse the ethical steps of genuine deparochializing dialogue and the underlying racist framework remains in place. The exposure of this foreclosure or evasion by scholars across the humanities and social sciences today is not new. By 1963, perceptive blacks and whites realized that liberal support for black demands had this neocolonial character. Howard Thurman, King, James Baldwin, and Thomas Merton wrote devastating critiques. In "Letters to a White Liberal" Merton presented a careful analysis of both the overt southern racist and the liberal racist:[123]

> Most of us are congenitally unable to think black, and yet that is precisely what we must do before we can even hope to understand the crisis in which we find ourselves, and our best considered and most sympathetic consideration of the Negro's plight is one calculated to antagonize him because it reflects such pitiful inability to *see* him, right before our nose, as a real human being and not a higher type of domestic animal. Furthermore, we do not bother really to listen to what

he says, because we assume that when the dialogue really begins, he will already be thinking just like ourselves.

The actions and attitudes of white Christians all, without exception, contain a basic and axiomatic assumption of white superiority, even when the pleas of the Negro for equal rights are hailed with the greatest good will. It is simply taken for granted that, since the white man is superior, the Negro wants to become a white man.

What he [the black] expects of us is some indication that we are capable of seeing a little of the vision he has seen, and of sharing his risks and his courage ... He asks us to listen to him, and to pay some attention to what *he* has to say. He seriously demands that we learn something from him, because he is convinced that we need this, and need it badly.

Merton argued that America needs "a complete reform of the social system which permits and breeds such injustices," and, second, this work "must be carried out under the inspiration of the Negro whose providential time has now arrived ... to free the white man in freeing himself from the white man."[124] In April 2020, Jamelle Bouie wrote a short genealogy of the patterns of systemic racism and inequality from slavery to the high rates of infection and death among blacks during the coronavirus pandemic. He concluded that "as long as those patterns remain, there is no path to a better society. We have to break them, before they break us."[125] The crisis continues.

The hegemony of neocolonial liberalism in practice is closely associated with neoliberal capitalism and its massive economic inequality. The result has been the backlash and resurgence of overt racism among whites excluded from neocolonial liberalism and done down by neoliberal economic inequality.[126] The political success of racist, authoritarian neoliberal capitalism in the United States is replicated in many other states. The contest for hegemony between liberal and authoritarian neoliberalism makes it appear that they are the only alternatives, but this is not the case.[127]

As we have seen, local and global decolonial dialogues and practices of freedom and "black radicalness" in education, politics, and communities of practice are continuing to grow.[128] Mills is showing how liberalism can be decolonized from within and opened to dialogue with Du Bois and other members of AMPT. Anthony Laden is quietly removing the foreclosing scaffolding of neocolonial liberalism from the inside and showing how an open, dialogical, and pragmatic liberalism can be created on the basis of its underlying commitment to democratic freedom and equality.[129] Comparative political thought among black, red, brown, Latinx, Asian, and white political traditions is also alive and well. In the spirit of these intellectual movements, I will now attempt to begin a dialogue with one black political tradition, the beloved community tradition, and suggest what can be learned by means of comparisons and contrasts.

The Beloved Community Tradition

Introduction

The concept of "beloved community" was introduced by the late nineteenth-century pragmatist philosopher Josiah Royce.[130] He used it to describe communities based on the solidarity of cooperation, compassion, mutual aid, and inclusiveness (the solidarity of solidarity). Royce was a cofounder of the black and white Fellowship of Reconciliation (FOR). Du Bois, Gregg, and King became its members.[131] It stands for anti-imperialism, anti-militarism, and the reconciliation and integration of all races. Howard Thurman and King adapted the concept of a beloved community from Royce and used it creatively to redescribe and reanimate the black church, cooperative, and political tradition to which they both belonged.[132]

Like most pragmatist traditions, it begins with the here and now: the unfree and unequal *interdependent* hegemon-subaltern social relationships of power-over/under in which we are all differently situated. "It really boils down to this: that all life is interrelated. We are all caught in an inescapable network of mutuality, tied into a single garment of destiny. Whatever affects one directly, affects all indirectly."[133] From this perspective, the liberal starting point of free and equal independent individuals is exposed as the mythological self-understanding of the masters who present themselves as independent and autonomous agents to hide their dependency on slaves, servants, and wage slaves.[134] Despite the foreground dominance of these unjust social systems, life-sustaining webs of interdependent, cooperative spiritual, social, and natural relationships of love exist in the background. Participation in the hegemon-subaltern relationships alienates or "dis-inherits" humans from them. The role of critique and emancipatory practice is to free ourselves, as much as possible, from these oppressive relationships that induce despair and engage in the ethical and social practices of reconnecting with and building inclusive, interdependent relationships and communities of cooperation and love (*agape*).[135]

These counter-modernity beloved communities exist in the long history of black churches, cooperatives, unions, local community-based associations, organizations such as FOR and Black Lives Matter, and the many movements for the nonviolent contestation, negotiation, and transformation of hegemon-subaltern relationships into inclusive, free, and equal relationships.[136] The long-term goal is to spread, by nonviolent transformative means, beloved communities around the world—our "world house."[137]

For Thurman and King, the black church tradition is the primary exemplar of beloved communities. Thurman argued that the tradition goes back to Jesus and his disciplines in their nonviolent struggle against the Roman Empire. They taught how to overcome the despair of systemic, intergenerational oppression, root out fear, deception, anger, and hatred, and cultivate love and inclusiveness. For both, the songs, gospels, and prophetic sermons of the black church provided the language of description of beloved communities. The churches are inclusive communities of Christian love and infused grace that enable the cooperative, personal self-realization of their members.[138]

In his PhD dissertation, King found philosophical expression of somewhat similar views in the social philosophy of Henry Wieman and Paul Tillich.[139] He then went through the western tradition dialectically, putting various philosophies in dialogue, selecting the best and rejecting the worst from each, and creating new syntheses that exhibit beloved community features.[140] Many of his multiracial partners and allies from other traditions held similar views: Glenn Smiley, Richard Gregg, A.J. Muste, Dorothy Day, Daniel Berrigan, Thomas Merton, Thích Nhất Hạnh, and Barbara Deming. King spoke out against the genocide of Native Americans and supported their struggle for decolonization and self-determination. He connected with John Echohawk, a member of the Pawnee Tribe and executive director of the Native American Rights Fund.[141] He reached out to the engaged Buddhist tradition by nominating Thích Nhất Hạnh for the Nobel Peace Prize. He spoke out against the US war in Vietnam and war in general. He also supported the War Resisters' League and the anti-war and peace movements of the 1960s.[142]

One of the best examples of beloved communities is the long history of black cooperatives—the black economic alternative to the capitalist corporation. Despite their differences, Du Bois, A Philip Randolph, Bayard Rustin, King, and Malcolm X agreed on their importance in building economic self-reliance. They are analogous to constructive programs in the Gandhian tradition and they continue today.[143] However, in remembrance of Richard Iton (1961–2013), I will try to describe some of the main features of beloved communities through another famous exemplar: the black jazz ensemble.[144]

The members of a jazz ensemble play their diverse instruments with each other without a conductor/conducted relationship. It is a community of participatory democracy. The players exercise and coordinate the intersubjective co-conductive power of music *with* each other through their distributed intelligence. They bring into being a distinctive kind of intersubjective freedom, equality, and power *with* each other, in contrast to the individual and collective independent conceptions of freedom, equality, and power of liberalism. These conceptions of freedom-with, equality-with, and power-with are at the heart of the beloved community tradition in all its manifestations.[145] Based on the intersubjective animacy this cooperative activity generates, each player contributes by improvising freely in his or her own distinctively creative and self-realizing way. This personal freedom of expression within and based on beloved communities is black, Christian, and philosophical personalism, in contrast to liberal individualism. It displays the legendary creative and transformative power of love (agape).[146] The others listen and then reciprocate by integrating the gift of this personal performance into the way they play together. The ensemble is racially inclusive. The pianist in the classic *Kind of Blue* (1959) is white (Bill Evans). Moreover, the audience participates in its own ways.

Thus, although the beloved community and liberal traditions share the language of freedom, equality, and power, they use the concepts in very different ways. Moreover, the basic concept of power-with rules out power-over, and thus hegemon-subaltern relationships. King argues dialectically that it combines the best features of love, power, and participation.[147] It is difficult for modern political theorists to enter into a comparative dialogue that provincializes their conceptions of power as power-over, freedom as individual and collective freedom from and to, equality as equality of opportunity in competitive economic and social systems, and self-determination. And, it is equally difficult to then attempt to understand these interdependent "being with" or "interbeing" conceptions of freedom, equality, and co-determination through participatory democracy (social integration). Nevertheless, it is a duty of epistemic and democratic justice that brings with it a new kind of diversity-aware Enlightenment: the realization that other worlds are not only possible but actual. From this perspective, it is possible to see clearly the destructiveness of the history and present of the racist system. At the same time, the beloved community tradition presents a just alternative that is not some imaginary thought experiment but a way of being in the world *with* others that exists and has survived centuries of oppression.

It is important to realize that this is not some minor change within the modern, western political traditions that, as we have seen, foreclose self-transformation. The impetus for change has to come from outside these traditions, and, I agree with Merton, from traditions that have been oppressed by it. Such a transformative change is exemplary of Foucault's general insight in his dialogue with a Buddhist monk[148]:

> It is true, European philosophy finds itself at a turning point. This turning point, on a historical scale, is nothing other than the end of imperialism. The crisis of Western thought is identical to the end of imperialism. For it is the end of the era of Western philosophy. Thus, if the future exists, it must be born outside of Europe, or equally born in consequence of meetings and impacts between Europe and non-Europe.

The Beloved Community and Gandhian Traditions: Integral Nonviolence

Beginning in the 1920s, members of the beloved community tradition entered into a dialogue of comparative political thought with the Gandhian decolonization movement in India.[149] Three members visited Gandhi and described their movement in the United States as a partner in the global decolonization struggles: Thurman, Benjamin Mays, and Stuart Nelsen. Du Bois corresponded with Gregg in 1926 and sent him a copy of *Darkwater*.[150] Gregg replied and sent a copy of his *Gandhiji's Satyagraha* in 1929. Du Bois invited Gandhi to the United States. Gandhi replied that he supported the African American decolonization struggle.[151] King learned of Gandhi and attended a lecture on him by A.J. Muste as a graduate student. However, he realized the importance of the Gandhian tradition for the beloved community tradition in the context of the Montgomery bus boycott:[152]

> As the days unfolded, I came to see the power of nonviolence more and more. Living through the actual experience of the protest, nonviolence became more than a method to which I gave intellectual assent: it became a commitment to a way of life. Many of the things I had not cleared up intellectually concerning nonviolence were now solved in the sphere of practical action.

On February 26, 1956, Bayard Rustin and Glenn Smiley arrived in Montgomery to help King and teach him the basics of nonviolent transformation of unjust hegemon-subaltern relations. They brought copies of Gregg's *The Power of Nonviolence* with them as the philosophy of, and user's guide to, nonviolence as both a technique for effective social change and an integrated way of life grounded in constructive programs.[153]

Rustin and Smiley knew about *The Power of Nonviolence* because it was widely studied and used in earlier freedom struggles since its first publication in 1934. King distributed the text to black churches and committees organizing nonviolent campaigns. It became the training manual for nonviolent campaigns throughout the following phase of freedom struggles (1956–1968), referred to as a "civil rights" movement by liberals. On May 1, 1956, King wrote to Gregg to thank him for his book and to express the fundamental importance of it in understanding the way of social change. "I don't know when I have read anything that has given the idea of non-violence a more realistic and depthful interpretation. I assure you that it will be a lasting influence in my life."[154] Gregg and King corresponded, met, and lectured together in 1958–9. King wrote the Preface to the 1959 edition of *The Power of Nonviolence*, which contained a new chapter on Montgomery. King wrote, "I hope it gets a wide readership, particularly among those, in this country, and throughout the world, who are seeking ways of achieving full social, personal, and political freedom in a manner consistent with human dignity."[155]

The importance of the dialogue between these two traditions is twofold. First, it provided a comparative example of active, nonviolent resistance and transformative change as an effective alternative to either ineffective passive resistance (acquiescence) or violent resistance, which is immoral and impractical because it generates counter-violence due to the autotelic character of means and ends. Thus, King argues, the "third way open to oppressed people in their quest for freedom is the way of nonviolent resistance":[156]

> The principle of nonviolent resistance seeks to reconcile the truths of two opposites—acquiescence and violence—while avoiding the extremes and immoralities of both. The nonviolent resister agrees with the person who acquiesces that one should not be physically aggressive towards his opponent, but he balances the equation by agreeing with the person of violence that evil must be resisted. He avoids the nonresistance of the former and the violent resistance of the latter. With nonviolent resistance, no individual or group need submit to any wrong, nor need anyone resort to violence in order to right a wrong.

A Phillip Randolph, James Farmer, Bayard Rustin, Du Bois, King, the Harlem Ashram, and white allies, such as Smiley, Harris Wofford, Muste, and Dorothy Day, could compare and contrast their history of passive, violent, and nonviolent resistance with the Indian examples. As a result, an ongoing, pragmatic dialogue about the strengths and weaknesses of passive resistance, violence, and nonviolence became a central feature of this tradition.

Second, the comparative dialogue enabled members of the beloved community to appreciate what Gandhi and Gregg came to see as the most original feature of their model of nonviolent change. In addition to the detailed features of the dynamics of effective nonviolent interaction with violent opponents, *The Power of Nonviolence* presents the equally detailed arguments that, to be effective and transformative, nonviolent agonistics (*satyagraha*) have to be grounded in a nonviolent way of life: that is, in constructive programs of *swadeshi* and *swaraj*. Episodic campaigns are ineffective without this sturdy counter-modernity as training for disciplined nonviolent contestation, a safe home to return to and recover after the suffering of the campaign and jail time, and as a dramatic presentation of the actual existing counter-modernity for which *satyagrahis* are willing to fight and suffer. It provides a crucial living alternative to the injustices of modern capitalism, militarism, poverty, inequality, and racism that the defenders and bystanders of the status quo can see and compare. Gandhi and Gregg discussed this internal relationship in their correspondence on Indian campaigns, especially in 1938–1940. Gregg wrote a short book on the connection in 1940 and Gandhi wrote the Preface.[157] He then incorporated and expanded his analysis in the revised 1944 edition of *The Power of Nonviolence*. This may be the edition Smiley and Rustin brought to Montgomery for King to study and use.[158]

The importance of this practice-tested connection of *satyagraha*, *swaraj*, and *swadeshi* for members of the beloved community tradition is obvious. Comparatively, it highlights and substantiates the internal relationship between their nonviolent campaigns and the cooperative beloved communities that provide the empowering basis of them. This relationship preexists the comparative dialogue with the Gandhian tradition, as Du Bois shows in exposing the falsehoods of white historians about black cooperatives and businesses during Reconstruction. King praises Du Bois for this.[159] The comparison with the Indian case reinforces the point and gives them reasons to deepen the relationship.

This is thus the fourth model of social change. It is not passive resistance, violence, or episodic nonviolence resistance. It is active, militant, mass nonviolent resistance grounded in beloved communities of practice in everyday life.[160] I call this integral nonviolence. The members are being the change that they are fighting for in their nonviolent campaigns. It provides the daily basis for non-cooperation campaigns. It also enables others to see the alternative and compare it with the unjust status quo. In defending this comprehensive view of nonviolence as an integrated way of life, King also explained he was not opposed to organized, episodic nonviolent protests. Participation in them often provides the first step toward a more comprehensive view of nonviolence.[161]

The organization of the Montgomery bus boycott provides an influential example of integrated nonviolent contestation and beloved communities of practice. King's nonviolent research, training, speeches, campaigns, negotiations, jail time, and reviews were organized around him as the charismatic leader, preacher, activist, and prophet. Black feminists' grass roots and participatory democratic communities of practice provided the less visible yet essential basis for the nonviolent campaigns. Here, leadership is by example and consciousness-raising dialogue. Rosa Parks, Jo Ann Gibson Robinson, and Ella Baker preceded King and were already experts in this kind of organization and action when King came along and coordinated with them.[162]

In the heat of the nonviolent campaigns of 1957 Stuart Nelsen published an article entitled "Satyagraha: Gandhian Principles of Non-Violent Non-Cooperation."[163] By succinctly summarizing Gandhi's philosophy and practice, he reminded his readers that *satyagraha* is an integrated nonviolent way of life—a counter-modernity. The coordination of these two types of beloved communities and nonviolent campaigns is now a common feature of decolonization struggles throughout the world.

On Dialogue and Social Integration

Dialogue is central to this pragmatic tradition. Once interdependency and the perspectival character of knowledge are accepted, dialogues of reciprocal elucidation are necessary to understand each other and change the unjust relationships we inhabit. Dialogues of love and inclusiveness are the only way that respects the dignity of all members. They are used for action coordination and dispute resolution among members, as well as for interaction with other traditions.

The philosophical defense of the centrality of dialogue comes from Henry Wieman, *The Source of Human Good*, 1949.[164] Wieman taught Thurman and King wrote his PhD dissertation on Wieman and Paul Tillich. Wieman argues that the social systems humans are socialized into, and thus take to be good as a matter of course, are limited "created goods." To free themselves from socialization, they need to enter freely into radical dialogues that reciprocally call their created goods into question (deparochialize them). These dialogues have the revolutionary capacity to create new "created goods" that both partners can affirm. These created goods are new social systems that combine the best features of competing ones in a new synthesis. He calls this form of dialogue "creative integration." Thus, this radical form of dialogue is the only "creative" good. It is humanity's "ultimate commitment."[165]

Thurman developed his own account of creative dialogue and placed it at the center of his philosophy of personal and social growth and transformation.[166]

He called the outcome of creative dialogue "dynamic integration" and associated it with the beloved community.[167] As Kipton E. Jensen explains, dynamic integration and wholeness can only emerge out of a "natural communal association" sustained by meaningful experiences of togetherness that are "multiplied over an extended time." Thurman contrasted this dynamic integration with the kind of integration brought about by legal desegregation alone.[168]

Like Thurman, King argues that there are two distinct types of "integration" in his philosophy of integration. The first is legal, de jure desegregation.[169] This is the liberal concept of integration. It removes the laws of segregation, but it leaves intact the racist social system of de facto segregation and its processes of socialization into superior/inferior self-understandings. A patina of legal desegregation and formal equality hides systemic social racism. Racist subject formation in the relationships of de facto segregation then corrupts the operation of the de jure desegregation of the justice system. When nonviolent protests irrupt over systemic legal and social racism, the normal response is to reform only the legal system.

The second type of integration is "social integration." The law cannot achieve social integration. It is merely a first step. Social integration involves the social processes of moving from I-It relationships of legal integration and de facto segregation to dialogical I-thou relationships, as described by Martin Buber. It involves treating each other as "persons," as ends rather than means.[170] This requires mutual respect for the development of personal freedom, which can be fully realized only in a socially "*integrated* society." Thus, social integration also includes the recognition of the "unity of humanity" in communities of mutual cooperation. "The self cannot be self without other selves" and "we cannot truly be persons without other persons." Social integration cannot be enforced because it entails always treating each other as persons. Thus, it is brought about by ethical activity, not politics or law. It begins "only as men are possessed by the invisible law which etches on their hearts ... that love is mankind's most potent weapon for personal and social transformation. True integration will be achieved by true neighbors who are willingly obedient to unenforceable obligations." Nonviolence plays a crucial, "double-barrelled" ethical role in the transformation. In using it, the "segregated" gain a sense of "somebodyness" in "destroying the system that has shackled" them, while also respecting "the personhood of their opponent."[171] In bell hooks' moving tribute to King, she describes this nonviolent ethics or ethos as "love as the practice of freedom."[172]

Nonviolent Contestation and Decolonizing Dialogue

King's insight is that nonviolent contestation grounded in the power of beloved communities has the capacity to prod socialized adversaries and bystanders into potentially deparochializing dialogues of reciprocal elucidation, negotiations of the unjust relationships they bear, and coauthoring free and equal relationships of reconciliation and "social integration." Nonviolent campaigns are not coercive. Rather, they extend the persuasive arts and relationships of creative dialogue from the world of words to the world of words and deeds. "We adopt the means of nonviolence because our end is a community at peace with itself. We will try to persuade with our words, but if our words fail, we will try to persuade with our acts."[173] By means of their persuasive words and deeds, nonviolent actors invite and encourage adversaries and bystanders into dialogues among free and equal participants over the unjust relationship in question. These assertive, disruptive, non-cooperative, and truth-speaking acts, along with their open-handed and trust-engendering offers of listening to all sides, move them to see the advantages of becoming partners in dialogues of reciprocal elucidation.[174] This moral jiu-jitsu dynamic has the power to lead to negotiations and social integration. Thus, the "with" relationships of freedom, equality, and love in beloved communities, Wieman's creative dialogues, nonviolent contestation, and social integration are all members of the same family of cooperative human relationships.

In *Pilgrimage to Nonviolence* King argues that this kind of dialogical transformation occurred during the Montgomery bus boycott. The power of nonviolent dialogues of words and deeds moved many whites, despite their socialization, to see the justice of the demands, support the campaigns, and join hands with the campaigners. He explains this transformative experience in the following way:[175]

> It did not spring into being full grown as Athena sprang from the head of Zeus; it was the culmination of a slowly developing process. Mrs. Parks' arrest was the 'precipitating factor' rather than the cause of the protest. The cause lay deep in the record of similar injustices .... But there comes a time when people get tired of being trampled by oppression. There comes a time when people get tired of being plunged into the abyss of exploitation and nagging injustice. The story of Montgomery is the story of 50,000 Negros who were willing to substitute tired feet for tired souls, and walk the streets of Montgomery until the walls of segregation were finally battered by the forces of justice.

He goes on to say that this is not the whole explanation. Other black communities suffer similar or worse injustices, so the abuses cannot be the whole explanation. It cannot be explained by a preexisting unity because the community "was marked by divided leadership, indifference, and complacency." Nor can it be explained by the appearance of "new leadership" (i.e., by his leadership). "The Montgomery story would have taken place if the leaders of the protest were never born."

Thus, "every rational explanation breaks down at some point. There is something about the process that is suprarational; it cannot be explained without a divine dimension." He then describes this coming together in nonviolent response to injustice in the terms of the philosophers he studied in his PhD dissertation: Whitehead's "process of concretion" (which Whitehead used to describe Gandhi's Salt March and Roundtable negotiations), Wieman's dialogical "process of integration," Tillich's "being-itself," and the "personal god" of the personalism tradition (King's own spiritual view). He accepts these convergent descriptions of the same phenomenon from different philosophical traditions, but he goes on to put it in his own words:

> Whatever the name, some extra-human force labors to create a harmony out of the discords of the universe. There is a creative power that works to pull down mountains of evil and level hilltops of injustice. God still works through history His wonders to perform.

That is, the culminating factor is that the participants connected with, exercised, and were moved by the intersubjective, personal, social, and spiritual relationships of creative love and inclusiveness that animate and sustain the harmony of life on earth: the beloved community.

How did white participants describe the experience? Harris Wofford was a liberal democratic lawyer from a southern family who lived in the north and attended Howard University before transferring to Yale University. He participated in the boycotts and arrests with King. In 1957 he gave a speech entitled "Law and Non-violence." Nelsen published it in his journal, right after his article on *satyagraha*. Wofford explains the experience as "[u]nder the inspired leadership of Martin Luther King and his brother ministers the Gandhian alchemy, as in India and South Africa, made heroes out of common clay."[176] Moreover, drawing on Socrates, Thoreau, and Gandhi, Wofford redescribes the experience theoretically as the equiprimordial coordination of the rule of law (liberalism) and dialogical democratic participation (participatory democracy):[177]

> The principle of ... democracy ... is learning. The law will play its full role as a teacher only when we look upon it as a question. The law is not some final arbiter. It is the voice of our body politic with which we must remain in dialogue.

For the proposition to which we are dedicated is self-government. We must respond to the law, resist it, change it, and fulfill it, even as it challenges, changes, and educates us.

Barbara Deming was a white, lesbian feminist activist who participated in many nonviolent campaigns and arrests in the 1960s. In her famous 1968 article, "Revolution and Equilibrium," she describes nonviolent contestation as the revolutionary equilibrium of masculine assertion of truth to power with one hand, and feminine reassuring offer of nonviolent dialogue to negotiate a just reconciliation with the other. In another article, she describes this reconciliation of the male and female characteristics that exist in all human beings as the "androgynous" reconciliation of humanity with itself.[178]

Turning to Du Bois, he wrote two articles on King and the Montgomery bus boycotts in 1957. In the first, "Will the Great Gandhi Live Again?," he was skeptical.[179] "Gandhi's nonviolence gained freedom for India, only to be followed by violence in all the world." The same dialectic is happening in Montgomery. Nonviolent campaigns, "led by a man who had read Hegel, knew of Karl Marx, and followed Mohandas Karamchand Gandhi," did not bring peace and reconciliation. It triggered the unrelenting violence of "white police and city administration," "egged on" by white supremacists. "Most white people of the city say nothing and do nothing." The result is "race war, jails full of the innocent, and ten times more money spent for mass murder than for education of children."

Du Bois concludes that there can be "no possible synthesis" until there is first "education for all children and education all together, so as to let them grow up knowing each other as human." Until this happens, their socialization into a racist system of superiority-inferiority relationships and ignorance of the Negro will cause them to respond to nonviolence with violence. "It will spread war and murder." Therefore, if we can "solve our antithesis [of nonviolence leading to overwhelming counter-violence], great Gandhi lives again. If we cannot civilize the South, or will not even try, we continue in contradiction and riddle."[180]

King agrees with Du Bois regarding the need for coeducation to decolonize the ignorance and lies of segregated education. He praises Du Bois for his work on exposing the falsehoods that whites learn in their schools concerning blacks during Reconstruction, and for his teaching career in the South.[181] King also agrees that two responses to nonviolence are white supremacist backlash out of ignorance and white liberals doing little or nothing. However, as we have seen, King's view is that nonviolent prodding of whites is itself an immensely powerful form of practical coeducation of both whites and blacks that has the capacity to move them to desegregate schools and institute social integration co-education.

In July 1957, Du Bois wrote a second article, "Gandhi and the American Negroes."[182] He begins with a brief account of his lifelong engagement with Gandhi and quotes Gandhi's letter to African Americans in 1929. He says that he was initially puzzled by the turn to Gandhian nonviolence in Montgomery, because he saw the contradiction that Gandhi's success in India was followed by war and violence throughout the world. However, now, with the current situation of the Soviet Union blocking neocolonial imperialism, "[p]erhaps in this extraordinary impasse, the teachings of Mahatma Gandhi may have a chance to prevail in the world." He then turns to Montgomery and gives a remarkably positive endorsement of the possibility of nonviolent emancipation.

He explains the power of the boycott with many of the same factors as King mentions above. Rather than being defeated by white backlash, "[b]lack workers led by young, educated ministers began a strike which stopped the discrimination, aroused the state and the nation and presented an unbending front of non-violence to the murderous mob which hitherto has ruled the South. The occurrence was extraordinary." Du Bois writes that leaders "like Martin Luther King" and educated businessmen knew of Gandhi and nonresistance. Yet, this is not the explanation of the transformative power of the movement:

> [T]he rise and spread of this movement was due to the truth of its underlying principles and not to direct teaching or propaganda. In this aspect, it is a most interesting proof of the truth of the Gandhian philosophy.

This remarkable description of the "extraordinary" power of the nonviolent movement is completely complementary to King's description in *Stride toward Freedom*. Du Bois concludes that the "American Negro is not yet free. The recent court decisions in his favor are excellent but are as yet only partial." However, "it may well be that the enforcement of these laws and real human equality and brotherhood in the United States will come only under the leadership of another Gandhi." It is difficult to imagine a stronger endorsement of King's philosophy and practice, and the beloved community tradition.

In conclusion, this philosophy and practice of nonviolence seems to be the answer of the beloved community tradition to Mills' question of how to initiate a decolonizing dialogue with members of a tradition that are foreclosed to deparochializing. As King summarizes, "[w]e will try to persuade with our words, but if our words fail, we will try to persuade with our acts."[183] Nonviolent contestation moves recalcitrant opponents into dialogues of reciprocal elucidation, which lead to negotiations of equals over the decolonization of the unjust relationships they bear, and on to democratic social integration "in a manner consistent with human dignity."[184]

Conclusion: Contextualizing Our Dialogue

The theory and practice of the beloved community counter-modernity tradition animated many of the black and white organizations and movements for racial justice in the 1950s and 1960s. In dialogue with other traditions, it also contributed to the democratic movements against racism, war, militarism, imperialism, inequality, and patriarchy of the 1960s and 1970s. These radical democratic, nonviolent movements often joined hands with students, professors, and activists exercising practices of freedom within mainstream traditions and institutions. As we have seen, these coalitions formed dialogues and networks of comparative political thought with similar decolonizing, multicolored movements around the world.

The turn to violence and the assassination of John F. Kennedy, Malcolm X, King, and Robert Kennedy appeared to marginalize the nonviolent traditions. The "chaos" that King predicted followed and continues today.[185] Neocolonial liberal political philosophy came to prominence in elite universities as the mainstream alternative to the radical democratic traditions domestically, as well as internationally with neoliberal theories of global justice.[186] It tends to foreclose dialogue with some of these traditions and subalternize others. It also misrepresents and so tends to perpetuate the underlying injustices that subalterns are trying to bring to public awareness and address. Yet, as we have seen, the dogmatic attachment to the "created good" of contemporary liberalism as the meta-language of public reasoning makes it appear as if the subaltern is being recognized and treated as free and equal. It thereby forecloses the "creative good" of a deparochializing genuine dialogue of equals that would bring the liberal language into the space of public reasoning as one tradition among others. This is a sophisticated mode of linguistic or "secondary explanation" *inclusionary* foreclosure to add to Mills' deeper analysis of other modes of foreclosure.

Decolonial practitioners show that this inclusion and subalternizing way of dealing with difference is typical of neocolonial modernization in general. They have learned how it works and how to contest and transform it, from within liberalism, as with Mills and Laden, or without, as with the world of counter-modernity traditions. As we have seen, these traditions of political thought and action appear marginal from the perspective of modern political traditions. Yet, from their perspectives, the modernist traditions appear parochial, alienated, and self-destructive. In their different languages and ways, they disclose a world in which we are all interdependent members and citizens of larger, older, and more powerful social, ecological, and spiritual communities, animated by "some extra-human force that labors to create a harmony out of the discords of the universe."[187] As Howard Thurman argued, this hypothesis of the ground of our being in relationships of dialogical cooperation—described in different ways in different traditions—can overcome despair and empower decolonizing struggles. The present-day decolonizing practices of freedom and the differences they make constitute pragmatic evidence for the hypothesis. They are "experiments" that test this "truth," as Gandhi would put it. For example, one meaning of the Black Lives Matter's nonviolent protest slogan "defund the police" is to fund and support black democratic governance of black communities. This is the beloved community under another description.[188]

Our dialogue of comparative political thought can be seen as a small contribution to this renaissance. I am most grateful to my four multiracial and multi-traditional interlocutors for bringing this dialogue into being. I am sure that my responses from my limited white, male perspective from the northwest coast of North America-Turtle Island contain mistakes, misinterpretations, and aspect-blindness. In the spirit of pragmatic dialogue traditions, I present them with the hope that they will be corrected and creatively integrated by the four outstanding interlocutors and readers of this collection in further dialogues.[189]

Notes

1 Mills, "Decolonizing Western Political Philosophy," 23.
2 For more detail on this step and its importance, see Tully, *Democracy and Civic Freedom*, 13–70, and Kuusela, *Struggle against Dogmatism*. For this philosophical tradition, see below "Response to Sudipta Kaviraj," 119.
3 Mishra, *Age of Anger*.
4 King, *Stride toward Freedom*, 90–5.
5 Gregg, *Power of Nonviolence*, 49–72, 148–65.
6 Wieman, *Source of Human Good*.
7 Williams, *Deparochializing Political Theory*.
8 Said, *Orientalism*.
9 Said, *Culture and Imperialism*.
10 For a dialogue on various practices of freedom, see Tully, *On Global Citizenship*, and Nichols and Singh, *Freedom and Democracy*.

11 Said, *Culture and Imperialism*, 18, 66–7, 194, 259. See, further, Tully, *Imperialism and Civic Freedom*, 243–310.
12 de Sousa Santos, *Epistemologies of the Global South*.
13 See Tully, *Democracy and Civic Freedom*, 13–38.
14 For an introduction to changes in meanings of "colonial" and "decolonial" and their cognates, see Young, *Postcolonialism: An Historical Introduction* and Young, *Postcolonialism: A Very Short Introduction*.
15 Tully, "Lineages of Contemporary Imperialism," 3–30.
16 Getachew, *Worldmaking after Empire*.
17 Young, *Postcolonialism: An Historical Introduction*.
18 Tully, *Imperialism and Civic Freedom*, 195–222, See responses to Kaviraj and Mills for examples.
19 Nkrumah, *Neo-Colonialism*, xi.
20 Immerwahr, *How to Hide an Empire*.
21 Pitts, "The Society of Nations, Imperialism, and the Color Line" and *Boundaries of the International*, Bell, *Empire, Race and Global Justice*; Morefield, *Empires without Imperialism*.
22 King, *Stride toward Freedom*, xxvi–vii.
23 Manuel and Posluns, *The Fourth World*.
24 Coates, *A Global History of Indigenous Peoples*.
25 Ryser, "'The 'Blue Water' Rule and Self-Determination of Nations."
26 Starblanket and Stark, "Towards a Relational Paradigm," 175–208.
27 Tully, "Rediscovering the World of Franz Boas," 111–46. For Boas, see below, "Response to Mills."
28 Tully, "Rethinking Human Rights and Enlightenment," 3–34.
29 See Sripati, *Constitution-Making under UN Auspices*.
30 Ivison, *Postcolonial Liberalism*.
31 See below "Response to Sudipta Kaviraj."
32 Laden and Owen, *Multiculturalism and Political Theory*; Payrow Shabani, *Multiculturalism and Law*; Brown, *The Rise of Antidemocratic Politics in the West*.
33 For example, Santos, *Epistemologies of the South*; Sripati, *Constitution-Making under UN Auspices*.
34 Scott, *Conscripts of Modernity*.
35 Mills, *Black Rights/White Wrongs*.
36 For example, Wilson, *Social Conquest of Earth*.
37 Crenshaw, Harris and Lipsitz, *The Race Track*.
38 Truesdell, "Black Decolonial Praxis"; Dhamoon, *Identity/Difference Politics*.
39 See Howard, *Gandhi's Ascetic Activism*; Easwaran, *Gandhi the Man*.
40 See my "Response to Mills."

41 Foucault, *Courage of Truth*; Hadot, *Philosophy as a Way of Life*.
42 Parallex Press, *Essential Writings on Engaged Buddhism*.
43 Palmer, *The Practice of Freedom*.
44 Camus, *Rebel*.
45 See Ober, "Original Meaning of Democracy," 3–9; Tully, "On the Power of Integral Nonviolence."
46 See Tully, "Editor's Introduction: Integral Nonviolence," xxi–lxii.
47 Gregg, *Power of Nonviolence*, 49–72.
48 King, *Stride toward Freedom*, 221.
49 See, Bromell, *Political Companion to W.E.B. Du Bois*; Shelby and Terry, *To Shape a New World*; Joseph, *Sword and the Shield*; Valdez, *Transnational Cosmopolitanism*.
50 Slate, *Colored Cosmopolitanism*; Chakrabarty, *Confluence of Thought*; Kapur, *Raising Up a Prophet*; Getachew, *Worldmaking*.
51 Benton, *Law and Colonial Cultures*.
52 The inspiration for this paragraph comes from Thurman, *Luminous Darkness* and Deming, *Revolution and Equilibrium*. They were written in the 1960s as black and white activists became aware of the limits whites placed on desegregation. For the ways nonviolence moves violent actors, see Gregg, *Power of Nonviolence*, 49–72. For this context, see "Response to Mills" below.
53 Nietzsche, *Gay Science*, Section 337, 190–1. Richard Gregg refers to this passage to describe the transformative nonviolent power of Gandhi's Satyagraha. It "outshines" the violent opponents. See, Gregg, *Gandhiji's Satyagraha*, 318, 433–7. He compares it to the gift-reciprocity relation at 341–2. Nietzsche calls for unilateral disarmament in "The Means to Real Peace," 380–1.
54 King, "Where Do We Go from Here," 161–80, 171–2. He criticizes Nietzsche for separating power and love, so he had not read passage 337 of *Gay Science*.
55 See, for example, the chapters in Williams, *Deparochializing Political Theory*.
56 A good example of this kind of colonization is the history of the dialogue on human rights at the United Nations by Normand and Zaidi, *Human Rights at the UN*. Kaviraj calls this "false dialogue" (Kaviraj 72). Compare Tully, "Rethinking Human Rights."
57 Tully, *Imperialism and Civic Freedom*, 243–310.
58 See, for example, Marx, "British Rule in India."
59 Bowden, *Empire of Civilization and Civilization and War*.
60 Santos, *Epistemologies of the South*.
61 Kant, "Idea for a Universal History with a Cosmopolitan Purpose," 46.
62 Mantena, *Alibis of Empire*.
63 See Mills, *Black Rights/White Wrongs*.
64 For this interpretation of Socratic dialogue and its relation to Wittgenstein (below), see Rowe, "Wittgenstein, Plato, and the Historical Socrates," Kuusela, "Wittgenstein's Reception of Socrates," Moore, *Brill's Companion to the Reception*

of Socrates. These articles modified my interpretation of Socratic dialogue from "Deparochializing." I over-emphasized the search for universal definitions.
65 Kaviraj mentions that Hobbes claimed his theoretical science of politics was new. Relative to the Aristotelian and humanist traditions with their acceptance of *paradiastole*, Hobbes' insistence on the univocal definition of terms by himself and the sovereign, it was new. Along with Descartes, it initiated the quest for certainty contra skepticism in modern philosophy. See Skinner, *Reason and Rhetoric* and Havercroft, *Captives of Sovereignty*.
66 King, *Stride toward Freedom*, 81–3.
67 Aeschylus suggests that this tradition is the basis of Athenian democracy: "Deparochializing," note 100.
68 Stern, "How Many Wittgensteins?"; Pichler and Saatela, *Wittgenstein*, 205–29.
69 Tully, "Situated Creatively," *Democracy and Civic Freedom*, 39–70.
70 For an introduction, see West, *American Evasion of Philosophy* and Chin, *Practice of Political*. For the concept of pragmatic judgment (*phronesis*), see Zerilli, *Democratic Theory of Judgment*.
71 Jensen, *Howard Thurman*.
72 Hildebrand, "Neopragmatist Turn." The quotation at the end is from Dewey, *Middle Works*, 12, 256. Hildebrand claims that Rorty collapses experience into linguistically expressed experience. I disagree. On my interpretation, and like Kaviraj and Hildebrand, Rorty distinguishes between experience and the languages in which it is articulated. In the beginning is the deed. The difficulty in making the distinction is that language use is both expressive and representative.
73 See Sripati, *Constitution-Making under UN Auspices*.
74 Scott, "Traditions of Historical Others," 1–8.
75 Gilligan, *In a Different Voice*; Gilligan and Richards, *Darkness Now Visible*.
76 See the section on "Dialogue and Decolonization" above.
77 I adopt the term "vernacular" from Goldsmith, *The Way*; Santos, *Epistemologies of the South*, 16.
78 Gandhi, *Hind Swaraj and Other Writings*. Gandhi referred to Socrates in the *Apology* as a "story of the soldier of truth" and a "pilgrimage of truth." He translated parts of the *Apology* and commented on it extensively: Gandhi, *Collected Works*: 8: 196–241, 21: 457, 33: 245–47.
79 Gandhi, *Hind Swaraj*, 27.
80 Compare Kochi, "The End of Global Constitutionalism."
81 For the use of "countermodernity" to describe the tradition of Gandhi and Gregg, see Kosek, *Acts of Conscience*, and Kosek, "Richard Gregg, Mohandas Gandhi, and the Strategy of Nonviolence."
82 For Gandhi's integration of *satyagraha* and *swaraj* into a nonviolent way of life, see Dalton, Mahatma Gandhi, and Tully, "Editor's Introduction: Integral Nonviolence."

83 Agarwal, *Gandhian Constitution for a Free India*, 11–12.
84 Gregg, *Which Way Lies Hope?*
85 Gregg, *Power of Nonviolence*.
86 Gandhi, *Non-Violent Resistance (Satyagraha)*, v.
87 Hardiman, *Gandhi in His Time and Ours*.
88 Freire, *Pedagogy of the Oppressed*.
89 Sharma, *Alternative Economics*.
90 Caradonna, *Sustainability*.
91 See Harding, *Animate Earth*.
92 See, for example, Tully, "Life Sustains Life 1," and "Life Sustains Life 2," 163–204; Caradonna, *Sustainability*.
93 Suzuki and McConnell, *Sacred Balance*; Turner, *Earth's Blanket*; Shiva, *Earth Democracy*; Capra and Luisi, *Systems View of Life*.
94 Taylor, *Secular Age*.
95 Hawken, *Blessed Unrest*; Tully, *On Global Citizenship*.
96 Tully, "Editor's Introduction: Integral Nonviolence," lix–lxx.
97 Shiva, *Earth Democracy*, 14–15, 52.
98 Suzuki, *Sacred Balance*.
99 It is somewhat similar to what Mills calls the "foreclosure" of liberalism to black political traditions.
100 This "erasure" of non-modern and non-western traditions by their classification as premodern in the modern political theory worldview is what Santos calls "abyssal thinking" in *Epistemologies of the South*, 118–36.
101 Wittgenstein, *Philosophical Investigations*, remarks 104 and 115 at 50 and 115.
102 For the dialogue, see Fell McDermott, Gordon, Embree, Pritchett, and Dalton, *Sources of Indian Traditions*, 388–95.
103 Ostergaard and Currell, *The Gentle Anarchists*.
104 Goldsmith, *The Way*, 256–66, 331–74, Compare Suzuki, *Sacred Balance*.
105 Tendulkar, *Mahatma*, Vol. 3, 167; Guha, *Gandhi*, 422–3. I am indebted to Dennis Dalton for drawing my attention to this dialogue and for many immensely helpful comments on this chapter.
106 I refer to race at DPTB, 12. I refer to an important article by David Scott on racism and modern political theory at note 38, where he argues that the stadial view of progress disguises racism. We then engaged in a dialogue on reparations in Nichols and Singh, 101–21, 249–50. See also the dialogue with Sahle and Norval in the same volume. The work I have done on racism has been primarily with respect to Indigenous peoples.
107 Lebron, *The Making of Black Lives Matter*.
108 See also Mills, *Black Rights/White Wrongs*.
109 Wilner, "Introduction," ix–xxii.
110 Appiah, "The Defender of Differences."

111 See, for example, the recent works cited in *supra* note 50.
112 The major texts of procedural liberalism are Rawls, *Political Liberalism* and "The Idea of Public Reason Revisited," 765–807, and Habermas, *Between Facts and Norms*. In this section I summarize and discuss the general, neocolonial features of procedural liberalism in these texts. For detailed analysis, see Tully, *Democracy and Civic Freedom*, 39–70, 291–316, *Imperialism and Civic Freedom*, 91–124, 127–65, "On the Global Multiplicity of Public Spheres," 169–204, and *On Global Citizenship*.
113 Primitive accumulation refers to the historical processes that divide the population into a minority class who control access to the means of reproducing life and differentiated majority classes who have to work for them. See Tully, *Imperialism and Civic Freedom*, 243–310. For the conjunction of race and class, see Mills, *From Class to Race*. For dispossession and primitive accumulation, see Nichols, *Theft Is Property*.
114 See Rogers, "Being a Slave of the Community."
115 This foreclosure of enquiry into the foundations of a modern liberal state goes back to Kant's notorious theory of founding. For him, it is a crime even to enquire into the foundations of any state, no matter how unjust its foundation (Kant, *Metaphysics of Morals*, 49 and "General Remark," 129–131 [318–20]).
116 Williams, *Linking Arms Together*; Tully, *Strange Multiplicity*.
117 Harris and Lieberman, *Beyond Discrimination*.
118 Alexander, *New Jim Crow*; Wilson Gilmore, *Golden Gulag*. For the militarization of policing, see Shrader, *Badges without Borders*.
119 See "Beloved Community Tradition" below.
120 Livingston, "Power for the Powerless" and "Tough Love."
121 See also Allen, *End of Progress* for a similar analysis of the contemporary Critical Theory tradition.
122 See Tully, "Middle East Legal and Governmental Pluralism."
123 Merton, "Letters to a White Liberal," 511, 510, 513. For a comparison of Merton and Thurman, see Apel, "Mystic as Prophet," 172–87. Compare King's comments on white liberals and white churches in 1963 "Letter from a Birmingham Jail," 127–45, 135–45.
124 Merton, "Letters to a White Liberal," 514.
125 Bouie, "Why Coronavirus Is Killing African-Americans More Than Others."
126 Di Angelo, *White Fragility*.
127 Kochi, "The End of Global Constitutionalism."
128 Burden-Stelly, "Martin Luther King Jr. and the Tradition of Black Radicalness."
129 Mills, *Black Rights/White Wrongs*; Laden, *Reasoning*.
130 Jensen, "Growing Edges of Beloved Community."
131 For the many roles of FOR in this period, see Kosek, *Acts of Conscience*.
132 For an excellent introduction to the vast literature on the beloved community, see Jensen, *Howard Thurman*; Fluker, "They Looked for a City."

133 King, "Christmas Sermon on Peace," 254.
134 Patterson, *Freedom in the Making of Western Culture*.
135 Thurman, *Jesus and the Disinherited*; King, *Stride toward Freedom*, 77–96, 103–6, 206–21.
136 For a genealogy of Black Lives Matter in this tradition, see Lebron, *Making of Black Lives Matter*.
137 King, *Where Do We Go from Here*, 177–202.
138 Cone, "Martin Luther King, Jr., Black Theology—Black Church."
139 See King, "Chapter IV [of dissertation]."
140 King, "Pilgrimage to Nonviolence," *Stride toward Freedom*, 77–95.
141 Bender, "Dr. King Spoke Out against the Genocide of Native Americans"; Cook, "I have a Dream for All God's Children."
142 King, "Beyond Vietnam."
143 Gordon Nembhard, *Collective Courage*; King refers to them as "constructive programs" in *Stride toward Freedom*, 218–20, and discusses them in detail in *Where Do We Go from Here*, 130–75.
144 Iton, *Solidarity Blues* and *In Search of the Black Fantastic*.
145 For the power of participatory democracy and how it co-generates somebodyness, see King, *Where Do We Go from Here*, 55f, and Moses, *Revolution of Conscience*.
146 King, "The Power of Nonviolence" and "An Experiment in Love."
147 King, *Where Do We Go from Here*, 171–2.
148 Foucault, *Religion and Culture*, 113–14.
149 See references at *supra* note 51.
150 For correspondence, see Du Bois papers: http://credo.library.umass.edu/view/full/mums312-b033-i394, and https://credo.library.umass.edu/search?q=Richard+Gregg&fq=FacetSeriesID%3A%22mums312-s01%22&search=.
151 See Kosek, *Acts of Conscience*.
152 King, *Stride toward Freedom*, 89.
153 Kosek, "Richard Gregg, Mohandas Gandhi, and the Strategy of Nonviolence."
154 King to Gregg, May 1, 1956, https://kinginstitute.stanford.edu/king-papers/documents/richard-bartlett-gregg-0.
155 King, "Foreword to the 1959 Edition of *Power of Nonviolence*," 13–14.
156 King, *Stride toward Freedom*, 207–9.
157 Gregg, *Discipline for Nonviolence*.
158 See, Tully, "Editor's Introduction: Integral Nonviolence."
159 King, "Honoring Dr. DuBois."
160 King, *Stride toward Freedom*, 206–21.
161 King, "Outline" and "Address at the Thirty-sixth Annual Dinner of the War Resister's League."
162 The daily coordination of these two male and female ways of organization was itself an exercise in nonviolent conflict resolution. See Gibson Robinson, "The

Montgomery Bus Boycott and the Women Who Started It: The Memoir of Jo Ann Gibson Robinson"; Ransby, *Ella Baker and the Black Freedom Movement*; Gibson Robinson; Taylor, Ula, "It's about Harnessing the Leader Within," Taylor, Ula, "The Montgomery Bus Boycott and the Women Who Made It Possible."

163 Nelsen, "Satyagraha," 15–24.
164 Wieman, *Source of Human Good*, 6.
165 Wieman, *Man's Ultimate Commitment*.
166 Thurman, *Mysticism and the Experience of Love*, "Mysticism and Social Action."
167 Thurman, "Desegregation, Integration, and the Beloved Community."
168 Jensen, *Howard Thurman*, 134–6.
169 King "The Ethical Demands for Integration."
170 Ibid., 118. He also refers to Martin Buber and I-thou dialogue in "Letter from a Birmingham Jail," 133.
171 Ibid., 118–25.
172 bell hooks, *Outlaw Culture*.
173 King, *Stride toward Freedom*, 211–12.
174 King puts the assertive hand of nonviolence more strongly in 1963. See "Letter from a Birmingham Jail," 130: "Nonviolent direct action seeks to create such a crisis and foster such a tension that a community which has constantly refused to negotiate is forced to confront the issue." He draws a comparison with Socrates creating tension in the minds of Athenians. Like Gregg in *Power of Non-Violence*, he describes it as dramatizing the issue.
175 King, *Stride toward Freedom*, 54–5.
176 Wofford, "Non-Violence and the Law," 29.
177 Ibid., 31. It is difficult to think of a more elegant formulation of the equality of law and democracy. Mills' former colleague, Anthony Laden, another radical liberal democrat, shows how this can be done from within a radically democratized liberalism: Laden, "The Authority of Civic Citizens."
178 Deming, "On Revolution and Equilibrium" and "Two Perspectives on Women's Struggles."
179 Du Bois, "Will the Great Gandhi Live Again?"
180 Du Bois' dialectic here is violence (thesis), nonviolence (antithesis), and synthesis (justice through social integration). Nonviolence fails and produces counterviolence. King's dialectic is different: passive resistance based on love (thesis), active violent resistance (antithesis), synthesis (active mass nonviolent resistance based on love), and King, *Stride toward Freedom*, 207–9.
181 King, "Honoring Dr. DuBois."
182 Du Bois, "Gandhi and the American Negroes."
183 King, *Stride toward Freedom*, 211–12.
184 King, "Foreword to the 1959 Edition," Gregg, *Power of Nonviolence*, 13–14. King's account of nonviolence as the way to decolonizing dialogues and transformative

negotiations is similar to Gandhi and Gregg (Tully, "Editor's Introduction," *Power of Nonviolence,* xxvii–xxviii). For the realism of their shared form of nonviolence, see Mantena, "Another Realism," and "Showdown for Nonviolence."
185 King, *Where Do We Go from Here: Chaos or Community?*
186 See Forrester, *In the Shadow of Justice.*
187 King, *Stride toward Freedom,* 55, see above.
188 Compare Lebron, *The Making of Black Lives Matter.*
189 I am most grateful to Jennifer Pitts, Jeanne Morefield, Anthony Laden, and Dennis Dalton for their important comments on the draft, and to Melvin Rogers for an immensely helpful lecture and conversation on African American political thought. My greatest debt is to Monika Kirloskar-Steinbach for her insightful discussions of successive drafts.

References

Agarwal, Shriman Narayan. *Gandhian Constitution for a Free India.* Foreword by Mohandas Karamchand Gandhi. Daryaganj, New Delhi: Manohar Book Service, 1945.

Alexander, Michelle. *The New Jim Crow: Mass Incarceration in the Age of Color Blindness.* New York: New Press, 2010.

Allen, Amy. *The End of Progress: Decolonizing the Normative Foundations of Critical Theory.* New York: Columbia University Press, 2015.

Apel, William. "Mystic as Prophet: The Deep Freedom of Thomas Merton and Howard Thurman." *Thomas Merton Annual,* 16 (2003): 172–87.

Appiah, Kwame Anthony. "The Defender of Differences." *New York Review of Books,* 67, no. 9, May 28, 2020.

Bell, Duncan, ed. *Empire, Race and Global Justice.* Cambridge: Cambridge University Press, 2019.

Bender, Albert. "Dr. King Spoke Out against the Genocide of Native Americans." *People's World,* February 13, 2014, https://www.peoplesworld.org/article/dr-king-spoke-out-against-the-genocide-of-native-americans/.

Benton, Lauren. *Law and Colonial Cultures: Legal Regimes in World History.* New York: Cambridge University Press, 2002.

Bouie, Jamelle. "Why Coronavirus Is Killing African-Americans More Than Others." *New York Times,* April 18, 2020, https://www.nytimes.com/2020/04/14/opinion/sunday/coronavirus-racism-african-americans.html.

Bromell, Nick., ed. *A Political Companion to W.E.B. Du Bois.* Lexington: University Press of Kentucky, 2018.

Brown, Wendy. *The Rise of Antidemocratic Politics in the West.* New York: Columbia University Press, 2019.

Bowden, Brett. *Empire of Civilization: The Evolution of an Imperial Idea*. Chicago: University of Chicago Press, 2009.

Bowden, Brett. *Civilization and War*. London: Edward Elgar, 2013.

Burden-Stelly, Charisse. "Martin Luther King Jr. and the Tradition of Black Radicalness." *Black Perspectives*, January 23, 2018, https://www.aaihs.org/martin-luther-king-jr-and-the-tradition-of-radical-blackness/.

Camus, Albert. *The Rebel: An Essay on Man in Revolt*. New York: Vintage Books, 1991.

Capra, Fritjof and Pier Luigi Luisi. *The Systems View of Life*. Cambridge: Cambridge University Press, 2015.

Caradonna, Jeremy L. *Sustainability: A History*. New York: Oxford University Press, 2014.

Chakrabarty, Bidyut. *Confluence of Thought: Mahatma Gandhi and Martin Luther King, Jr.* Oxford: Oxford University Press, 2013.

Chin, Clayton. *The Practice of Political Theory: Rorty and Continental Thought*. New York: Columbia University Press, 2018.

Coates, Ken. *A Global History of Indigenous Peoples: Struggle and Survival*. London: Palgrave Macmillan, 2004.

Cone, James H. "Martin Luther King, Jr., Black Theology—Black Church." *Theology Today*, 40, no. 4 (1984): 409–20.

Cook, Roy., ed. "I Have a Dream for All God's Children." http://americanindiansource.com/mlkechohawk.html.

Crenshaw, Kimberly, Luke Charles Harris, and George Lipsitz. *The Race Track: Understanding and Challenging Structural Racism*. New York: New Press, 2018.

Dalton, Dennis. *Mahatma Gandhi: Nonviolent Power in Action*. New York: Columbia University Press, 2012.

de Sousa Santos, Boaventura. *Epistemologies of the South: Justice against Epistemicide*. London: Taylor and Francis, 2015.

Deming, Barbara. *Revolution and Equilibrium*. New York: Grossman Publishers, 1971.

Deming, Barbara. "Two Perspectives on Women's Struggles." In *We Are All Part of One Another: A Barbara Deming Reader*. Edited by Jane Meyerding. 220–31. Philadelphia: New Society, 1984.

Dewey, John. *The Middle Works*, 14 volumes. Carbondale: Southern Illinois U. Press, 1976–88.

Dhamoon, Rita. *Identity/Difference Politics: How Difference Is Produced, and Why It Matters*. Vancouver: University of British Columbia Press, 2007.

Di Angelo, Robin J. *White Fragility: Why It Is so Hard for White People to Talk about Racism*. Boston: Beacon Press, 2018.

Du Bois, W. E. B. *Darkwater: Voices from within the Veil*. New York: Harcourt, Brace, and Company, 1921.

Du Bois, W. E. B. "Will the Great Gandhi Live Again?" *National Guardian*, February 11, 1957, 6–8, https://credo.library.umass.edu/view/full/mums292-b001-i104.

Du Bois, W. E. B. "Gandhi and the American Negroes." *Gandhi Marg*, July 1957, https://www.mkgandhi.org/articles/civil%202.htm.

Easwaran, Ekanth. *Gandhi the Man: How One Man Changed Himself to Change the World*. Tomales, CA: Nilgri Press, 2011 [1972].

Fell McDermott, Rachel, Leonard A. Gordon, Ainslie T. Embree, Frances W. Pritchett, and Dennis Dalton. *Sources of Indian Traditions: Third Edition, Volume Two*. New York: Columbia University Press, 2014.

Fluker, Walter Earl. "They Looked for a City: A Comparison of the Idea of Community in Howard Thurman and Martin Luther King, Jr." *Journal of Religious Ethics*, 8, no. 2 (Spring 1990): 33–55.

Forrester, Katrina. *In the Shadow of Justice: Postwar Liberalism and the Remaking of Political Philosophy*. Princeton: Princeton University Press, 2019.

Freire, Paulo. *Pedagogy of the Oppressed*. New York: Continuum, 1982 [1968].

Foucault, Michel. *Religion and Culture*. Edited by Jeremy R. Carette. New York: Routledge, 1999.

Foucault, Michel. *The Courage of Truth: Lectures at the College De France 1983–1984*. Edited by Frederic Gros, translated by Graham Burchell. London: Picador, 2012.

Gandhi, Mohandas Karamchand [Mahatma]. *Collected Works of Mahatma Gandhi*. Delhi: Ministry of Information and Broadcasting, 2000.

Gandhi, Mohandas Karamchand [Mahatma]. *Non-Violent Resistance (Satyagraha)*. New York: Dover Books, 2001 [Schocken Books, 1961].

Gandhi, Mohandas Karamchand [Mahatma]. *Hind Swaraj and Other Writings*. Edited by Anthony Parel. Cambridge: Cambridge University Press, 2009.

Getachew, Adom. *Worldmaking after Empire: The Rise and Fall of Self-Determination*. Princeton: Princeton University Press, 2019.

Gibson Robinson, Jo Ann. "The Montgomery Bus Boycott and the Women Who Started It: The Memoir of Jo Ann Gibson Robinson." http://nationalhumanitiescenter.org/pds/maai3/protest/text5/robinsonbusboycott.pdf.

Gilligan, Carol. *In a Different Voice: Psychological Theory and Women's Development*. Cambridge, MA: Harvard University Press, 1982.

Gilligan, Carol and David A.J. Richards. *Darkness Now Visible: Patriarchy's Resurgence and Feminist Resistance*. New York: Cambridge University Press, 2018.

Goldsmith, Edward. *The Way: An Ecological World-View*. Athens: The University of Georgia Press, 1998.

Gordon Nembhard, Jessica. *Collective Courage: A History of African American Cooperative Economic Thought and Practice*. University Park: The Pennsylvania State University Press, 2016.

Gregg, Richard Bartlett. *A Discipline for Nonviolence*. With an Introduction by Mohandas Gandhi. Ahmedabad: Navajivan Press, 1941.

Gregg, Richard Bartlett. *Which Way Lies Hope? An Examination of Capitalism, Communism, Socialism and Gandhiji's Programme*. Ahmedabad: Navajivan Publishing, 1952.

Gregg, Richard Bartlett. *Gandhiji's Satyagraha*. Delhi: Facsimile Publisher, 2016 [1930].

Gregg, Richard Bartlett. *The Power of Nonviolence*. Edited and Introduced by James Tully. Cambridge: Cambridge University Press, 2018.

Guha, Ramachandra. *Gandhi: The Years That Changed the World: 1914–1948*. New York: Alfred A. Knopf, 2018.

Habermas, Jürgen. *Between Facts and Norms: Contributions to a Discourse Theory of Law and Democracy*. Cambridge MA: MIT Press, 1994.

Hadot, Pierre. *Philosophy as a Way of Life: Spiritual Exercises from Socrates to Foucault*. Edited by Arnold Davidson. Oxford: Blackwell, 1995.

Hardiman, David. *Gandhi in His Time and Ours: The Global Legacy of His Ideas*. New York: Columbia University Press, 2003.

Harding, Stephen. *Animate Earth: Science, Intuition and Gaia*. Second Edition. Cambridge: Green Books, 2013.

Harris, Frederick C. and Robert C. Lieberman, eds. *Beyond Discrimination: Racial Inequality in a Post-Racist Era*. New York: Russell Sage, 2013.

Havercroft, Jonathan. *Captives of Sovereignty*. Cambridge: Cambridge University Press, 2010.

Hawken, Paul. *Blessed Unrest: How the Largest Movement in the World Came into Being, and Why No One Saw It Coming*. New York: Viking, 2007.

Hildebrand, David L. "The Neopragmatist Turn." *Southwest Philosophy Review*, 19, no. 1 (2003): 79–88.

hooks, bell. *Outlaw Culture: Resisting Representations*. New York: Routledge, 2006, chapter 20, https://collectiveliberation.org/wp-content/uploads/2013/01/hooks_Love_As_The_Practice_Of_Freedom.pdf.

Howard, Veena R. *Gandhi's Ascetic Activism: Renunciation and Social Action*. Albany: State University of New York, 2013.

Immerwahr, Daniel. *How to Hide an Empire: A Short History of the Greater United States*. London: Bodley Head, 2019.

Iton, Richard. *Solidarity Blues: Race, Culture and the American Left*. Chapel Hill: University of North Carolina Press, 2000.

Iton, Richard. *In Search of the Black Fantastic: Politics and Popular Culture in the Post-Civil Rights Era*. Oxford: Oxford University Press, 2008.

Ivison, Duncan. *Postcolonial Liberalism*. Cambridge: Cambridge University Press, 2002.

Jensen, Kipton E. "The Growing Edges of Beloved Community: From Royce to Thurman and King." *Transactions of the Charles S. Peirce Society*, 52, no. 2 (Spring 2016): 239–58.

Jensen, Kipton E. *Howard Thurman: Philosophy, Civil Rights, and the Search for Common Ground*. Columbia: University of North Carolina Press, 2019.

Joseph, Peniel E. *The Sword and the Shield: The Revolutionary Lives of Martin Luther King Junior and Malcolm X*. New York: Basic Books, 2020.

Kapur, Sudarshan. *Raising Up a Prophet: The African-American Encounter with Gandhi*. Boston: Beacon Press, 1992.

Kant, Immanuel. *The Metaphysics of Morals*. Translated by Mary Gregor. Cambridge: Cambridge University Press, 1993.

Kant, Immanuel. "Idea for a Universal History with a Cosmopolitan Purpose." In *Kant: Political Writings*. Edited by H.S. Reiss. 41–53. Cambridge: Cambridge University Press, 2009.

King, Jr., Martin Luther. "Chapter IV [of dissertation 1956], 'A Comparison of the Concepts of God in the Thinking of Paul Tillich and Henry Nelson Wieman.'" https://kinginstitute.stanford.edu/king-papers/documents/chapter-iv-comparison-conceptions-god-thinking-paul-tillich-and-henry-nelson.

King, Jr., Martin Luther. "To Richard Bartlett Gregg." May 1, 1956, https://kinginstitute.stanford.edu/king-papers/documents/richard-bartlett-gregg-0.

King, Jr., Martin Luther. *Stride Toward Freedom: The Montgomery Story*. Boston: Beacon Press, 2010 [1958].

King, Jr., Martin Luther. "Address at the Thirty-sixth Annual Dinner of the War Resister's League," February 2, 1959, https://kinginstitute.stanford.edu/king-papers/documents/address-thirty-sixth-annual-dinner-war-resisters-league.

King, Jr., Martin Luther. "Outline: The Philosophy of Nonviolence." Student Nonviolent Coordinating Committee, Atlanta, Georgia, October 14, 1960, https://kinginstitute.stanford.edu/king-papers/documents/outline-philosophy-nonviolence.

King, Jr., Martin Luther. *Where Do We Go from Here: Chaos or Community?* Boston: Beacon Press, 2010 [1967].

King, Jr., Martin Luther. "A Christmas Sermon on Peace." In *A Testament of Hope: The Essential Writings and Speeches of Martin Luther King, Jr*. Edited by James W. Washington. 253–8. New York: HarperCollins Publishers, 1986.

King, Jr., Martin Luther. "An Experiment in Love." In *A Testament of Hope: The Essential Writings and Speeches of Martin Luther King, Jr*. Edited by James W. Washington. 16–20. New York: HarperCollins Publishers, 1986.

King, Jr., Martin Luther. "The Power of Nonviolence." In *A Testament of Hope: The Essential Writings and Speeches of Martin Luther King, Jr*. Edited by James W. Washington. 12–15. New York: HarperCollins Publishers, 1986.

King, Jr., Martin Luther. "The Ethical Demands for Integration." In *A Testament of Hope: The Essential Writings and Speeches of Martin Luther King, Jr*. Edited by James W. Washington. 117–25. New York: HarperCollins Publishers, 1991.

King, Jr., Martin Luther. "Beyond Vietnam: A Time to Break Silence." (April 4, 1967). In *The Radical King*. Edited by Cornel West. 210–17. Boston: Beacon Press, 2015.

King, Jr., Martin Luther. "Letter from a Birmingham Jail." In *The Radical King*. Edited by Cornel West. 127–45. Boston: Beacon Press, 2015.

King, Jr., Martin Luther. "Where Do We Go from Here." August 16, 1967. In *The Radical King*. Edited by Cornel West. 161–80. Boston: Beacon Press, 2015.

King, Jr., Martin Luther. "Foreword to the 1959 Edition." In *Richard Bartlett Gregg. The Power of Nonviolence*. Edited and Introduced by James Tully. 13–14. Cambridge: Cambridge University Press, 2018.

Kochi, Tariq. "The End of Global Constitutionalism and the Rise of Antidemocratic Politics." *Global Society*, 2020, https://doi.org/10.1080/13600826.2020.1749037.

Kosek, Joseph Kip. "Richard Gregg, Mohandas Gandhi, and the Strategy of Nonviolence." *Journal of American History*, 91, no. 4 (2005): 1318–48.

Kosek, Joseph Kip. *Acts of Conscience: Christian Nonviolence and Modern American Democracy*. New York: Columbia University Press, 2011.

Kuusela, Oskari. *The Struggle against Dogmatism: Wittgenstein and the Concept of Philosophy*. Cambridge MA: Harvard University Press, 2008.

Kuusela, Oskari. "Wittgenstein's Reception of Socrates." In *Brill's Companion to the Reception of Socrates*. Edited by Christopher Moore. Leiden: Brill, 2019, https://www.academia.edu/32449517/Wittgensteins_Reception_of_Socrates.

Laden, Anthony Simon and David Owen, eds. *Multiculturalism and Political Theory*. Cambridge: Cambridge University Press, 2007.

Laden, Anthony Simon and David Owen. *Reasoning: A Social Picture*. Oxford: Oxford University Press, 2012.

Lebron, Christopher J. *The Making of Black Lives Matter: A Brief History of an Idea*. New York: Oxford University Press, 2017.

Livingston, Alexander. "Power for the Powerless: Martin Luther King Jr.'s Late Theory of Civil Disobedience." *Journal of Politics*, 82, no. 2 (2020): 700–13.

Livingston, Alexander. "Tough Love: The Political Theology of Civil Disobedience." *Perspectives on Politics* (forthcoming 2020).

Mantena, Karuna. *Alibis of Empire: Henry Maine and the Ends of Liberal Imperialism*. Princeton: Princeton University Press, 2010.

Mantena, Karuna. "Another Realism: The Politics of Gandhian Nonviolence." *American Political Science Review* 106, no. 2 (2012): 455–70.

Mantena, Karuna. "Showdown for Nonviolence: The Theory and Practice of Nonviolent Politics." In *To Shape a New World: Essays on the Philosophy of Martin Luther King, Jr*. Edited by Tommie Shelby and Brandon M Terry. 78–101. Cambridge, MA: Harvard University Press, 2018.

Manuel, George and Michael Posluns. *The Fourth World: An Indian Reality*. Introduction by Glen Sean Coulthard. Minneapolis: University of Minnesota Press, 2018 [1974].

Marx, Karl. "British Rule in India." *New York Daily Tribune*, June 25, 1853, https://www.marxists.org/archive/marx/works/1853/06/25.htm.

Merton, Thomas. "Letters to a White Liberal." *Blackfriars*, 44. 522 (December 1963): 503–16.

Mills, Charles W. *From Class to Race: Essays in White Marxism and Black Radicalism*. New York: Rowman and Littlefield, 2003.

Mills, Charles W. "Decolonizing Western Political Philosophy." *New Political Science* 37, no. 1 (2015): 1–24.

Mills, Charles W. *Black Rights/White Wrongs: The Critique of Racial Liberalism*. New York: Oxford University Press, 2017.

Mishra, Pankaj. *Age of Anger: A History of the Present*. New York: Picador, 2017.

Morefield, Jeanne. *Empires without Imperialism: Anglo-American Decline and the Politics of Deflection*. Oxford: Oxford University Press, 2014.

Moses, Greg. *Revolution of Conscience: Martin Luther King, Jr., and the Philosophy of Nonviolence.* New York: Guilford Press, 1997.
Nelsen, William Stuart. "Satyagraha: Gandhian Principles of Non-Violent Non-Cooperation." *Journal of Religious Thought* (1957–8): 15–24.
Nichols, Robert. *Theft Is Property! Dispossession and Critical Theory.* Durham and London: Duke University Press, 2020.
Nichols, Robert and Jakeet Singh, eds. *Freedom and Democracy in an Imperial Context: Dialogues with James Tully.* New York: Routledge, 2014.
Nietzsche, Friedrich. "The Means to Real Peace." In *Human, All Too Human: A Book for Free Spirits.* Introduction by erich haller. 380–1. Cambridge: Cambridge University Press, 1986.
Nietzsche, Friedrich. *The Gay Science.* Edited by Bernard Williams. Cambridge: Cambridge University Press, 2001.
Nkrumah, Kwame. *Neo-Colonialism: The Last Stage of Capitalism.* London: Nelsen, 1965.
Normand, Roger and Sarah Zaidi. *Human Rights at the UN: The Political History of Universal Justice.* Bloomington and Indianapolis: Indiana University Press, 2010.
Ober, Josiah. "The Original Meaning of Democracy." *Constellations*, 15 (2008): 3–9.
Ostergaard, Geoffrey and Melville Currell. *The Gentle Anarchists: A Study of the Leaders of the Sarvodaya Movement for Non-Violent Revolution in India.* Oxford: Clarendon Press, 1971.
Palmer, Wendy. *The Practice of Freedom: Akido Principles as a Spiritual Guide.* Berkeley, CA: Rodmell Press, 2002.
Parallex Press, ed. *Essential Writings on Engaged Buddhism: True Peace Work.* Berkeley: CA: Parallex Press, 2019.
Patterson, Orlando. *Freedom in the Making of Western Culture.* New York: Basic Books, 1991.
Payrow Shabani, Omid A., ed. *Multiculturalism and Law: A Critical Debate.* Cardiff: University of Wales Press, 2007.
Pitts, Jennifer. *Boundaries of the International: Law and Empire.* Cambridge MA: Harvard University Press, 2018.
Pitts, Jennifer. "The Society of Nations, Imperialism, and The Color Line: Three Conceptions of the International." In *The 2019 Annual Lecture of the Center for the Study of Law and Society in a Global Context.* Queen Mary, University of London, January 15, 2018.
Ransby, Barbara. *Ella Baker and the Black Freedom Movement.* Chaple Hill NC: University of North Carolina Press, 2003.
Rawls, John. *Political Liberalism.* New York: Columbia University Press, 1993.
Rawls, John. "The Idea of Public Reason Revisited." *University of Chicago Law Review*, 64, no. 3 (1997): 765–807.
Rogers, Melvin. "Being a Slave of the Community: Race, Domination, and Republicanism." Victoria Colloquium, University of Victoria, March 8, 2019, https://www.uvic.ca/victoria-colloquium/events/index.php.

Rowe, M. W. "Wittgenstein, Plato, and the Historical Socrates." *Philosophy*, 82 (2007): 45–85.
Ryser, Rudolph C. "'The 'Blue Water' Rule and Self-Determination of Nations." *My Word*. September 21, 2017, https://intercontinentalcry.org/blue-water-rule-self-determination-nations/.
Said, Edward W. *Orientalism*. New York: Vintage Books, 1978.
Said, Edward W. *Culture and Imperialism*. New York: Knopf, 1994.
Schell, Jonathan. *The Unconquerable World: The Power of Nonviolence and the Will of the People*. New York: Henry Holt & Company, 2003.
Schell, Jonathan and Taylor Branch. "The Power of Nonviolence." *The Nation*, January 14, 2009, https://www.thenation.com/article/archive/power-nonviolence/.
Scott, David. *Conscripts of Modernity: The Tragedy of Colonial Enlightenment*. Durham NC: Duke University Press, 2004.
Scott, David. "Traditions of Historical Others." *Symposia on Gender, Race, and Philosophy*, 8, no. 1 (Winter 2012): 1–8.
Sharma, Jai Narain. *Alternative Economics: Economics of Mahatma Gandhi and Globalization*. New Delhi: Deep & Deep Publications, 2004.
Shelby, Tommie and Brandom M. Terry, eds. *To Shape a New World: Essays on the Political Philosophy of Martin Luther King Jr*. Cambridge MA: Harvard University Press, 2018.
Skinner, Quentin. *Reason and Rhetoric in the Philosophy of Hobbes*. Cambridge: Cambridge University Press, 2000.
Shiva, Vandana. *Earth Democracy: Justice, Sustainability, and Peace*. Cambridge, MA: South End Press, 2005.
Shrader, Stuart. *Badges without Borders: How Global Counterinsurgency Transformed American Policing*. Berkeley: University of California Press, 2019.
Slate, Nico. *Colored Cosmopolitanism: The Shared Struggle for Freedom in the United States and India*. Cambridge MA: Harvard University Press, 2012.
Sripati, Vijayashri. *Constitution-Making under UN Auspices: Fostering Dependency in Sovereign Lands*. Oxford: Oxford University Press, 2019.
Starblanket, Gina and Heidi Stark, "Towards a Relational Paradigm—Four Points for Consideration: Knowledge, Gender, Land, and Modernity." In *Resurgence and Reconciliation: Indigenous-Settler Relations and Earth Teachings*. Edited by Michael Asch, John Borrows and James Tully. 175–208. Toronto: University of Toronto Press, 2018.
Stern, David G. "How Many Wittgensteins?" In *Wittgenstein: The Philosopher and His Works*. Edited by Alois Pichler and Simo Saatela. 205–29. Frankfurt: Ontos Verlag, 2006.
Suzuki, David and Amanda McConnell. *Sacred Balance: Rediscovering Our Place in Nature*. Vancouver: Greystone, 1997.
Taylor, Charles. *A Secular Age*. Cambridge MA: Harvard University Press, 2007.
Taylor, Ula Y. "It's about Harnessing the Leader Within," 2020, https://news.berkeley.edu/2018/02/28/podcast-black-history-month-interview-ula-taylor/.

Taylor, Ula Y. "The Montgomery Bus Boycott and the Women Who Made It Possible," 2020, https://news.berkeley.edu/2020/02/11/podcast-montgomery-bus-boycott-womens-political-council/.
Tendulkar, D. G. *Mahatma: The Life and Death of MKG*. Vol. 3. Delhi: Navjivan Press, 1961.
Thurman, Howard. *Jesus and the Disinherited*. Boston: Beacon, 1996 [1949].
Thurman, Howard. *Mysticism and the Experience of Love*. 115. Wallingford PA: Pendle Hill Publication, 1961.
Thurman, Howard. *Luminous Darkness: A Personal Interpretation of the Anatomy of Segregation and the Ground of Hope*. New York: Harper and Row, 1965.
Thurman, Howard. "Desegregation, Integration, and the Beloved Community." In *Benjamin E. Mays: His Life, Contributions, and Legacy*. Edited by Samuel D. Cook. Franklin, Tennessee: Providence House, 2009 [1966].
Thurman, Howard. "Mysticism and Social Action," October 1978. Edited by Richard Boeke and Patrick Wynne-Jones. United States: International Association for Religious Freedom, 2015.
Truesdell, Nicole. "Black Decolonial Praxis: A Liberation Story." *The Lansdowne Lecture*, Department of Anthropology, University of Victoria, September 24, 2019.
Tully, James. *Strange Multiplicity: Constitutionalism in an Age of Diversity*. Cambridge: Cambridge University Press, 1995.
Tully, James. *Democracy and Civic Freedom, Public Philosophy in a New Key*, Volume I and *Imperialism and Civic Freedom, Public Philosophy in a New Key*, Volume II, Cambridge: Cambridge University Press, 2008.
Tully, James. "Lineages of Contemporary Imperialism." In *Lineages of Empire: The Historical Roots of British Imperial Thought*. Edited by Duncan Kelly. 3–30. Oxford: Oxford University Press, 2009.
Tully, James. "Middle East Legal and Governmental Pluralism: A View of the Field from the Demos." *Middle East Law and Governance*, 4, nos. 2–3 (2012): 225–63.
Tully, James. "Rethinking Human Rights and Enlightenment: A View from the Twenty-First Century." In *Self-Evident Truths? Human Rights and the Enlightenment: The Oxford Amnesty Lectures*. Edited by Kate E. Tunstall. 3–34. London: Bloomsbury, 2012.
Tully, James. "On the Global Multiplicity of Public Spheres: The Democratic Transformation of the Public Sphere?" In *Beyond Habermas: Democracy, Knowledge, and the Public Sphere*. Edited by Christian Emden and David Midgley. 169–204. New York: Berghahn, 2013.
Tully, James. *On Global Citizenship: James Tully in Dialogue*. London: Bloomsbury, 2014.
Tully, James. "Editor's Introduction: Integral Nonviolence." In Richard Bartlett Gregg. *The Power of Nonviolence*. Edited and Introduced by James Tully. xxi–lxx. Cambridge: Cambridge University Press, 2018.
Tully, James. "Rediscovering the World of Franz Boas: Anthropology, Equality/Diversity, and World Peace." In *Indigenous Visions: Rediscovering the World of Franz*

Boas. Edited by Ned Blackhawk and Isaiah Lorado Wilner. 111–46. New Haven: Yale University Press, 2018.

Tully, James. "Life Sustains Life 1" and "Life Sustains Life 2." In *Nature and Value*. Edited by Akeel Bilgrami. 163–204. New York: Columbia University Press, 2019.

Tully, James. "On the Power of Integral Nonviolence: The Significance of Gandhi Today." *Politika*, 2019, https://www.politika.io/en/notice/the-power-of-integral-nonviolence-on-the-significance-of-gandhi-today.

Turner, Nancy. *Earth's Blanket: Traditional Teachings for Sustainable Living*. Vancouver: Douglas & McIntyre 2007.

Valdez, Ines. *Transnational Cosmopolitanism: Kant, Du Bois, and Justice as a Political Craft*. Cambridge: Cambridge University Press, 2019.

Williams, Melissa S., ed. *Deparochializing Political Theory*. Cambridge: Cambridge University Press, 2020.

Wilson, Edward O. *The Social Conquest of Earth*. London: W.W. Norton, 2012.

West, Cornel. *The American Evasion of Philosophy: A Genealogy of Pragmatism*. Madison: University of Wisconsin Press, 1989.

Wieman, Henry N. *Man's Ultimate Commitment*. Carbondale: Southern Illinois University Press, 1958. See http://www.creativeinterchange.org/.

Wieman, Henry N. *The Source of Human Good*. Atlanta, Georgia: Scholars Press, 1995 [1946].

Williams, Robert A. *Linking Arms Together: American Indian Treaty Visions of Law and Peace 1600–1800*. New York: Oxford University Press, 1997.

Wilner, Isaiah. "Introduction." In *Indigenous Visions: Rediscovering the World of Franz Boas*. Edited by Ned Blackhawk and Isaiah Lorado Wilner. ix–xxii. New Haven: Yale University Press, 2018.

Wilson Gilmore, Ruth. *Golden Gulag: Prisons, Surplus, Crisis, and Opposition in Globalizing California*. Berkeley: University of California Press, 2007.

Wittgenstein, Ludwig. *Philosophical Investigations*. Revised fourth edition. Edited by P.M.S. Hacker and Joachim Schulte. Oxford: Blackwell Publishing, 2009.

Wofford, Jr., Harris. "Non-Violence and the Law; The Law Needs Help." *Journal of Religious Thought*, 2 (1957–8): 25–36.

Young, Robert J. C. *Postcolonialism: An Historical Introduction*. Oxford: Blackwell Publishing, 2001.

Young, Robert J. C. *Postcolonialism: A Very Short Introduction*. Oxford: Oxford University Press, 2003.

Zerilli, Linda. *A Democratic Theory of Judgment*. Chicago: University of Chicago Press, 2016.

Afterword: Concluding Reflections

Monika Kirloskar-Steinbach

How should one engage with world philosophies, that is to say, the attempts people have made in different cultural contexts to make sense of their experiences, within the academy in general and within the discipline of philosophy in particular? This is one of the many aspects that the exchange collected in this volume has brought to the fore. Within the scope of this concluding chapter, my main focus will be on this very aspect. My contention is that the conceptual vocabulary that one currently uses in academic discourses around issues pertaining to world-philosophical traditions will have to be reconstituted. Currently, salient philosophical concepts like rationality, freedom, self-consciousness, progress, and modernity tend to be spelt out solely through the lens of the European, and building up on it, the Euro-American tradition. They, as well as the conceptual frameworks they operate in, are based on methodological whiteness. Although presented as being universal due to their supposed neutrality and objectivity, these concepts reflect, in general, the experiences of a specific social group of Europeans in one particular segment of human history. The contention I make in these pages is well known. One detailed account of the Eurocentric bias of academic discourses is to be found in the proliferous writings of W. E. B Du Bois (1868–1963). Du Bois has in my view provided a powerful account of the faultlines of the knowing self that is posited as a given in academic inquiry about human beings. In addition, he has also indicated reasons for implementing a thorough ideational and symbolic reorientation.

Section 1 will revisit the connection Du Bois makes between sociopolitical capital and participation in academic debates. It will also put into the spotlight his proposal that those who are placed at the margins of concept-making should seek to generate concepts that are better aligned with their own experiences such that a fit between their own experiences and the concepts they use to make sense of their lives is obtained. To put it differently, they should free themselves from the mastery that concepts generated by a small group of powerful European and Euro-American individuals have on their lives.

Du Bois' diagnosis of academic bias, as well as his recommendation to resist it, would be shared by the authors of this volume in my reading, as also by those who endorse changes in the manner in which world-philosophical traditions are currently studied. Section 2 will work out their shared ground by focusing on what I term methodological whiteness. Section 3 will briefly illustrate current approaches that seek to upend this shortcoming. Section 4 will elaborate how James Tully's genuine dialogues offer a means for members of historically hegemonic groups to decenter their selves. Inasmuch as these dialogues shift the focus from parochial takes on the world to the interconnectedness of all life, they have the potential to offer these members one way of engaging with world philosophies.

The Biased Academic World: A Du Boisean Analysis

Du Bois observes that the conceptual vocabulary used in academe reflects the experiences of powerful and resourceful European and Euro-American elites in the early decades of the twentieth century. He highlights the link between trade and European conceptual dominance to make this point. Europe's unfazed geopolitical power in global trade that was established through imperial and colonial projects allowed its academics to attribute positive concepts solely to members of their own groups. "Everything 'great,' 'good,' 'efficient,' 'fair' and 'honorable'" became "white," he noted in his essay collection *Darkwater* that was published in 1920 after the First World War.[1] These groups projected a monolithic whiteness on members of their own groups. In contrast, the rest of the world population was first divided up into supposed distinct racial groups and then attributed specific negative concepts depending on their alleged ranking in these groups. A biased pattern of conceptual attribution arose. Through it, the so-called white world veiled itself off from the rest of the world. Du Bois observes how this pattern of conceptual segregation enabled Euro-descended peoples in his contemporary formally segregated United States to police the boundaries of whiteness and restrict concepts like self-consciousness and agency solely to their own members. Negative appraisive concepts were then systematically deployed on African Americans to establish social dominance. During the Reconstruction Era in the United States, for example, African Americans perceived how "the concepts of crime and slavery were inseparably linked as equivalent forms of oppression by whites," he wrote in his journal article for the *Archiv für Sozialwissenschaft und Sozialpolitik* in 1906.[2] Importantly, he saw no plausible reason to accept and follow the ascription pattern of concepts that reflected white sociopolitical capital, both in the national and/or international context.

In thinking through a path that could lead African Americans and/or other structural minorities out of a disfavorable pattern of concept attribution, Du Bois brings into play a process between "double-consciousness," "second sight," and "true self-consciousness." His "double-consciousness" gestures toward the mismatch between concepts from the white world and one's experiences as a member of a (racialized) structural minority. When applied without further reflection, a hermeneutical gap arises when these concepts do not fit the experiences one has when being in the world. This gap is sensed by some, whose bodies are not covered by the social imaginary of whiteness. They feel "a peculiar sensation, [...] this sense of always looking at one's self through the eyes of others, of measuring one's soul by the tape of a world that looks on in amused contempt and pity."[3] They become conscious of the lack-of-fit between the general universal concept that is supposed to be deployed and their own experience. However, merely sensing double-consciousness will not suffice to change the dehumanizing effects the white (conceptual) world has on oneself. A "second sight" will be needed.

Paget Henry teases out its specific Du Boisean understanding by highlighting that it is a "potentiated second sight."[4] It can help to resist the negative reactions which ensue from the inner experience of double-consciousness. One would be better positioned to develop a critical and empowering sense of "I" such that the "twoness" of one's identity is not perceived as a weakness but as an advantage. A "true self-consciousness"[5] could grow. The formation of a critical "I" would abet racialized structural minorities to distance themselves from the caricature of themselves created by the aforementioned universal measuring tape.[6] This second sight can, in other words, abet understanding that the racialized image projected on one's group by the white world can be resisted.

Du Bois urges African Americans in his *Souls of Black Folk* to appropriate select concepts like self-consciousness—a concept which the white world traditionally attributed only to its own members. Were this concept appropriated by African Americans, they would not need to accept the image of themselves portrayed through "the revelation of the other world."[7] Subsequently, they might then not be predisposed to resignedly accept their fate. They would develop a better understanding of their own distinct selves. Through the latter, they would be able to conceptually make sense of the disconnect between this so-called revelation of the other world and their own selves. Once laid bare in self-reflection, this disconnect would very likely enable them not to identify with the caricature of their selves projected on them by the white world. This, in turn, would enable them to resist the ascription of negative concepts to them. They could begin to initiate changes in their hitherto way of being in the world and take up responsibility for such changes. Through time, this act of resistance would enable African Americans to "attain [their] place in the world."[8] Going forward, it would serve them as a springboard to coalesce with other racialized members even across national boundaries. Let it be added in parenthesis here that group-building was, in the Du Boisean view, imperative to systematically reconstitute the conceptual vocabulary that one used ideationally and symbolically. Lone individuals would not be able to move the "thick sheet of invisible but horribly tangible plate glass"[9] that they experience between themselves and the world. The chances of that plate being shifted could be increased through a cooperation with similarly placed others.

Notably, Du Bois underscored a heightened awareness in implementing appropriated appraisive concepts from the veiled white world. Concepts, Du Bois urged, are not neutral carriers of word-meaning. Being integrated into the social structures of such dominant groups, appraisive concepts reflect the manner in which these groups would like to perceive themselves. If a concept were to be appropriated mindlessly, certain aspects of its meaning would remain intact after appropriation. The new context in which it would be used would continue to be informed by the self-perception of the dominant group. If African Americans were to appropriate the concept of self-consciousness mindlessly, they would very likely entomb their souls. As a result, they would be unable to make sense of their experience in the worlds they did not share with the privileged. In fact, the very inability to do so would escape them. Furthermore, Du Bois encourages members of (racialized) structural minorities to become aware of at least two relatively stable factors: actual concept-use in the white world and the role of higher educational institutions in the propagation of whiteness.

In distinguishing their own racial group from other groups, sociopolitical white elites attribute positive concepts to all members of their own racial group, Du Bois observed. However, not all those to whom these concepts are attributed, exhibit behavioral patterns that indicate that they make deliberate use of the positive concepts attributed to them. Some are not sufficiently informed about the intricacies of concept-use, while others deploy concepts pre-reflexively or habitually. This is to say, the homogeneity of the white world is a construct made by its own elites to distinguish their whole group from other societal groups that it divides up using the category of "race." The homogeneity of the constructed world cannot be substantiated empirically though. Accordingly, Du Bois argued in his *Dusk of Dawn* that African Americans should their use their "intelligent reason" to work against, and resist, ideas arising from the white world, ideas that rested "on blind unreason and often irresistible urges of sensitive matter."[10]

In addition, Du Bois directed the attention of structural minorities toward educational institutions, especially universities. Through educational training, these institutions, he claimed, systematically propound and sustain the dominant status of those they deem white. Underscoring the global dimension of such an education, Du Bois claimed that educational institutions around the world systematically centered on concepts predetermined by the privileged white world. Professionals in these institutions deliberated about the meaning of concepts and determined, in their view, legitimate criteria for concept-use. Knowledge was imparted through an education which was "so arranged that the young learnt not necessarily the truth, but that aspect and interpretation of the truth which the rulers of the world wished them to know and follow."[11] Du Bois' observation that white educational institutions foster an educated ignorance about their own group and others racial groups is especially shared by those academics today who endorse conceptual decolonization, that is to say freeing oneself from conceptual frameworks that are based on the experiences of a nonrepresentative subsection of the European population in the eighteenth and nineteenth centuries.

Methodological Whiteness: Scope and Extent

Proponents of conceptual decolonization argue that the distribution of ideational goods continues to be skewed in favor of the white privileged world. Substantial changes have yet to unfold for "concepts, assumptions, norms, values, and framing perspectives that reflect the experiences and group interests of [this] privileged group"[12] continue to be the norm since European imperialism and colonialism. Theory continues to be made for the world from a position of what Charles W. Mills terms *"conceptual or theoretical* whiteness."[13] It arose in modern history by abstracting from the "white supremacy that was originally planetary [and] a racial political structure that was transnational."[14] Specific individuals who, one could say, shared specific European spatiotemporal coordinates built theories using these concepts; conceptual whiteness led up to theoretical whiteness. As these concepts populated frameworks and were implemented, theoretical whiteness developed into a methodological whiteness. Disciplines like philosophy distilled an understanding of philosophical method using concepts and theories that, despite being drawn from experiences of specific individuals, were perceived to be—and touted as being—universal. Doing proper philosophy entailed using this method as the default philosophical position. The claim being that universal concepts could be generated only through this method. These concepts, in turn, could be fed into theories of universal scope. But this is not all.

Using the space afforded to them by the firmly entrenched "universal-instructor-of-the-world"[15] mode, academics have more recently begun initiating a global dialogue that is said to instantiate their commitment to critical thinking. Typically, theory is produced in this space without "bringing aspects of one's background horizon of disclosure" into the foreground (Tully 4). It continues to have a European (and derivatively: Euro-American) bias. Powerful partners in this global dialogue listen to the less powerful and then "translate what they hear into presumptively universal or higher languages of their hegemonic discourses" (Tully 22). A "hegemonic ventriloquism" ensues (Tully 22). Furthermore, this supposed global dialogue is self-serving. It affords, as Garrick Cooper highlights, a means to garner "performance awards," awards that reward conformity to disciplinary and intellectual boundaries.[16]

Authors of this volume would agree with Sudipta Kaviraj that methodological whiteness is disseminated by intellectuals in the wider society who "disseminate forms of thinking incubated in [the academy's] esoteric institutions across various expanses of a society's intellectual culture" (Kaviraj 55). Many of these intellectuals continue to spin the story about "the Europeans' discovery of the world, in which the world and its inhabitants had nothing to do except to exist passively as objects of the western cognitive initiative."[17] Other experiences which would possibly contest this narrative tend to be simply "whited out."[18] A societal narrative is continued that since the heydays of imperialism and colonialism posits all "newly un-civilized non-Euro-American cultures ... along the steep slopes running down from the pinnacles in London and Paris" (Kaviraj 63).

Within the discipline of philosophy, methodological whiteness determines the manner in which world-philosophical traditions are studied, if they are studied at all. It allows those who adopt its perspective to claim epistemic authority when they pit positions from different world-philosophical traditions against what David H. Kim calls the "monotradition core"[19] of the discipline. In such work, pointers are drawn out from this core that in different ways mark out the unique rational enterprise adopted by "western" philosophy. Some of these pointers indicate the presence of supposed intellectual precursors to one's own rational tradition, while others are said to mark out geographical regions that apparently failed to develop thought that can even be set in comparison to the core. In both cases, only Europe remains the sole repository of academic philosophy.

Notably, while methodological whiteness is sustained by powerful European and Euro-American academics, it reigns globally. As Sor-Hoon Tan notes in her intervention in this volume, students in Asia—a region in which many of the so-called eastern spiritual traditions are said to be located—"feel little sense of ownership for Asian traditions, if they think about it at all, but they also assume that these are obsolete pre-modern ways of thought and living that their parents have already rejected, and that they are better off without" (Tan 47).

Indeed, the current status of local world-philosophical traditions outside Europe and Euro-America reflects recent historical developments, as least in some cases. Jonardon Ganeri points out that the binary between the so-called spiritual Indian tradition and the rational "western" tradition has a colonial history.[20] It tells the tale of individuals on the subcontinent, who sought to hammer out an indigenous self-identity under conditions of coloniality. Notably, though, the culturally essentialist position that served some of them as a foil to counter, and even assuage, the colonial impact has outlived political colonialization. Appeals to the authentic nature of this supposed spiritual bent of the "Indian mind" continue, apparently with the expectation that tradition can serve as a bulwark against conceptual colonization. It remains unclear though whether such appeals to a supposed pristine authentic traditional culture can counter or shift methodological whiteness.[21] Conceptual, theoretical and methodological whiteness is being reproduced today also by non-white bodies.

Upending Methodological Whiteness

Imagine that a tailor-made approach to upend methodological whiteness is developed in academic philosophy from one such location from which it once emanated: Germany. Imagine that philosophers initiate this approach and work out several implementation steps. For example: They first study how individual concepts do the work in imagining a German collective through the use of shared conceptual and material interpretative registers. They then work out a cluster of concepts that continue to posit Germany as the center of the world in myriad ways and concomitantly characterize other regions as being principally inferior. In a further step, they analyze whether concepts from this cluster have been, or are being, questioned and recalibrated over a specific time frame. Finally, they deliberately introduce content from world-philosophical positions into the practice of academic philosophy in order to facilitate the interrogation of problematic concepts.

However, at the time of writing, this approach seems to be largely absent. The status of the German intellectual tradition in general and the philosophical tradition in particular reign uncontested in most philosophy departments. Arguably, centering this local tradition is itself an outcome of history, as Peter P. Park illustrates.[22] It reflects the development of scientization within this philosophical tradition. Established as the default position in philosophy since the nineteenth century, this scientization allows its practitioners to hold that their discipline operates with the notion of a generic, centered, seamless, universal self. This notion enabled (and enables) those who adopt its perspective to claim that they are able to generate universal concepts that remain unchanged across space and time. These concepts are, in turn, deployed to generate methodologies to deal with problems that the discipline sets for itself. In short: philosophy becomes in this understanding a self-sustaining academic practice that establishes ideals and procedures modeled on idealized agents. A hermetic self-perception of one's own discipline arises.

Against the backdrop of scientization, a concept is typically considered as being, to borrow from Reinhart Koselleck, a single word which adequately captures the "plentitude of a politico-social context of meaning and experience."[23] Concepts track larger politico-social contexts accurately in this understanding. Unlike words, they can be applied "in a generalized manner"; one can "construct ... types or disclos[e] comparative insights" with concepts.[24] When used across time, they track and capture the rich meaning and experience of a politico-social context adequately when the experience of people in the past is set in relation to that of the researcher using the concept. Concepts, thus, do not "merely serve to define given states of affairs, [but] reach into the future."[25] They can hold the past and future together in a "permanent present in which the past and the future are contained."[26] Arguably, when concepts are understood thus, independently of the positionality of the knower, those who use them tend to presume that the "we" and the "them" are part of the same group that extends across time. The "we" in the present will subscribe to the "them" in the past. They will thread a continuity between both these groups separated across time.

However, authors (including those collected in this volume) who perceive continuities between current practices of knowledge production and past practices that since imperialism and colonialism spawn a theorizing that does not stray away from the center, do not subscribe to this "we." Instead, they endeavor to *discontinue* such a practice of an almost reflexive subscription. They highlight how a discipline that perceives itself as being removed from time and space, curiously engages in practices associated with territorial defense. Situating their discipline in space and time, these philosophers seek to substitute current academic practices of boundary marking and defense, with the "philosophical practice of interrogation," as Mickaella Perina puts it.[27]

One trenchant critique of this one-size-fits-all standard universal self as it pertains to the study of world philosophies is found in the writings of Henry Rosemont, Jr. In a thought-provoking text with the title "On Relativism" (1988), Rosemont seeks to decenter the standard philosophical position. He illustrates how a whole barrage of cultural assumptions like beliefs, attitudes, intentions, and so on influence the translation and interpretation of sources from world philosophies. To deal with the source material judiciously, Rosemont proposes that one work out these assumptions in the form of a "concept-cluster." The idea being that this step would enable one to become more aware about how a whole cluster of concepts works in the background during translation and interpretation. Once one becomes aware of the variegated conceptual background informing translation, one might hesitate to make, and subsequently be satisfied with the results of unidimensional one-to-one translations into one's own language.

Rosemont substantiates the need for work with concept-clusters using the example of classical Chinese used by Confucian-Ruist authors. This language did not have a lexical item for "moral." It also lacked corresponding terms for "freedom," "autonomy," "liberty," "rationality," etc., and also a term for "ought."[28] For Rosemont, there is no plausible reason to infer from this observation that the Chinese tradition lacked a sense of morality. Rather, he appeals to scholars working on world philosophies to work on themselves to develop a methodological sensitivity that would enable them to avoid such facile claims. To this end, they should refrain from one-to-one equivalences between terms in the source language and discourses in academic philosophy. They should widen their focus when terms from the source language are translated. Equally, he proposes that they become more aware of the role of "cultural determinants" in the understanding process.[29] Rather than implementing perspectives from the European and Euro-American philosophy tradition as hooks into texts from other traditions, he submits that one ask: "to what extent do these texts suggest that we should be asking very different philosophical questions?"[30]

Rosemont's concept-cluster approach that seeks to avoid facile comparisons between concepts in the source and translated languages could be strategically deployed by Indigenous philosophers when they decide to leave philosophical terms in Indigenous languages untranslated, especially when their communities "perceive translations as a perversion, corruption, or unfair appropriation of indigenous epistemologies"[31] in the light of the assimilative power of the academy's Eurocentric knowledge making.[32] The work on concept-clusters might also draw the attention of researchers to the material source in which some of these assumptions are to be found, namely print culture and the accompanying claim that only it can serve as the sole repository of academic knowledge. As is well known, this assumption has led many a researcher to (inadvertently) exclude material that either does not adhere to one's understanding of a standard text (commentaries for example) or material that was handed down through another medium (orally for instance).

Similar choices are being made by scholars to resist the "deep structural biasing"[33] of European and Euro-American academic philosophy and the effects of its "white miscognition"[34] on the study of world philosophies. They aim to illustrate that philosophy is permeated through and through with the way we human beings make meanings of our own selves and our places in the world through exchanges with our communities.[35] "[T]hrough conceptual labor and in the company of others,"[36] these scholars coalesce to create spaces through which the hitherto hegemonic "language of description of the global order"[37] can be gradually critiqued, overturned, and rewritten. Forms of epistemic liberation are explored that can free one's gaze from the "hegemonic and parochial universalism" of academic philosophy such that a shift toward a philosophizing which delves into "the boundless universality of our creative potential as human beings" can be made.[38] Pedagogic practices are developed "for the sake of intellectual hygiene" that will enable one "not to speak about the facts of one history always through the language of the other."[39] The hope is that they can upend curricula that "continue to operate with implicitly colonial historiographies that organize the canonical periodizations of western philosophy and its geographical borders."[40] Tully's "deep listening" through "genuine dialogues" share this commitment (Tully 1). His understanding of genuine dialogues offers, especially members of historically hegemonic communities, a path to resist methodological whiteness and, as I have argued elsewhere,[41] point out one way through which they can engage with world philosophies.

Tullyean Genuine Dialogues

Tully envisions genuine dialogues as those that lead to a transformation of the self. While they might not be restricted to academic spaces, these dialogues can be conducted in these very spaces too. Genuine dialogues are dialogues of "reciprocal elucidation."[42] They presuppose an *askesis*, a deliberate acting on the self when it engages in routine activity. Their participants bring to the table the willingness to engage in deep listening and the readiness to heed "embodied and place-based dimensions of the dialogue" (Tully 15). These dialogues presuppose that participants are already sufficiently comfortable with practices of moral cultivation, before they come to the discussion table—practices that will enable them to deliberately refrain from using confrontational and combative argumentative strategies during the dialogue. Participants in these dialogues will be ready to understand fellow participants more thoroughly; these practices will enable them to detach themselves from the "background view of [their] world and the assumptions that compose it" (Tully 16). They will be ready to decolonize "the dispositional relationships of self-formation and self-awareness (subject formation) each person bears in such relations" (Tully 113). Through a repeated usage of such practices, the "global network Esperanto [of methodological whiteness] that brings about, at best, a fast-time listening and superficial communication" will slowly be replaced by "learning [our] way around" and "within the lifeworld of living theories, traditions, practices, and places" (Tully 1). In the long run, the spiral of "vicious monological clashes of unequal theories, traditions and civilizations" (Tully 103) will be broken through these practices; they can, for example, make us see the limits of our passion for what others have termed "language-based concepts."[43] Notably, cultivating a detachment from one's own background views will open up our view to other ways of philosophizing. We can in the process look at the world as a whole. However, this opening up will also decenter the place of human beings in the general scheme of things and bring into view our interconnectedness with all forms of life and non-human environments. Consequently, this way of looking at the world can make us more aware of just how "destructive and unsustainable [our hegemonic] social systems" are (Tully 136).

Tully points out that structural minorities have practiced deep listening in an attempt at disrupting the spiral of violence and counter-violence historically. They have challenged the methodological whiteness propagated by academic institutions, without categorically rejecting the ideals and principles found in these institutions. Through their "ethical act of self-oblative freedom and equilibrium," "they have offered the open hand of dialogue and negotiation, rather than a closed fist of counter-violence" (Tully 116). Building up on this practice, Tully endorses that members of historically hegemonic groups learn and implement this practice too, contending that, "critical members of hegemonic traditions" have the "primary ethical responsibility" at taking the first step in cultivating practices of deep listening in the academy (Tully 104).

But what reason would structural minorities have to accept the invitation to engage in a genuine dialogue with members of dominant groups? One could claim that the conventional manner of organizing academic philosophy has, in general, eroded the trust of many, especially those who hold that they have largely served as so-called native informants who can merely lead to the storehouse of commodities instrumental to knowledge-making. In the light of a history of "patriarchies, aristocracies, colonialism and imperialism, and normative gender social roles and labour divisions," the prospect of opening oneself up to "hitherto unexplored possibilities" through a dialogue can be experienced by some of them as being threatening, especially when the new relationship needed to get the dialogue off the ground is "mediated through and by our existing sets of relationships."[44]

In my reading, Tully's answer would point toward the interdependency of our world. The methodological whiteness prevalent in the academy is but a part of a larger process through which a disembedding of "human producing and consuming capabilities and activities from the surrounding social and ecological relationships in which they take place" radiates in our interdependent world from Europe and Euro-America.[45] This disembedding has been followed by a re-embedding in anthropocentric networks centered on what Max Horkheimer and Theodor Adorno famously called "dissolvent rationality,"[46] networks which claim to have mastered the natural environment in extricating commodities from it. Relatedly, knowledge-makers perceive themselves as being part of networks which have accurately mastered non-European and non-Euro-American cognitive systems in order to extricate knowledge from them. In both cases, the socioeconomic and political conditions of (knowledge) production are bracketed out; the world is disclosed as "an external storehouse of proto-commodities."[47] The dominant stratum of today's world makes knowledge for itself, while maintaining its "unsustainable relationship[s]"[48] with non-human environments and other peoples placed on supposedly lower rungs of human development. When initiated by members of historically hegemonic communities, Tully's genuine dialogues, it seems, would offer societal members the opportunity to work together to make a world which is more free, or freed, from oppression irrespective of their social positionality. This world would include both human and non-human beings.

This volume brings together scholars whose work underscores the lack of substantial changes in academic practices since Du Bois began writing about what I have for the purposes of this concluding essay termed methodological whiteness a century ago. The volume as a whole does more though. It references work that much in the spirit of Tullyean-like genuine dialogues seeks to materialize scholarship that deliberately abstains from a monological Eurocentric posturing in our "*post*colonial" and "open, messy, boundary-crossing world."[49] This body of scholarship works toward transforming "mechanisms of production of meaning in academia" such that knowledge can be produced across the world in accordance with the principle of solidarity.[50] In speaking to this point, some authors draw upon what seems to be a constant feature of our human lives: our social roles. In different ways, the typical roles of being a child, a sibling, a partner, a colleague, or a friend reiterate the insight that one's flourishing is interlocked with that of other human beings. And in the performance of one of these roles, I may clear the way for my own path, but I never walk alone. Or to quote Rosemont, "The way is made in the walking of it, but one never walks alone."[51] Indigenous scholars like Cooper, but also Tully, underscore that non-human environments should not be lost from view in generating a scholarship based on solidarity.[52] They draw attention to the dangers of subscribing to the belief that a human being is wholly independent from the "life-sustaining eco-social and ecological webs of life."[53] Instead, in relation with human beings and non-human environments one should seek to be the change[54] such that unsustainable relationships to other human beings and to non-human environments are disrupted and discontinued such that the current "money form of global philosophy,"[55] as Amy Donahue puts it, comes to an end. It remains to be seen whether the current strategies that are being developed to address methodological whiteness are able to change academic practices in the long run.

Notes

1 Du Bois, *Darkwater*, 44.
2 Du Bois, "Die Negerfrage," 257. The *Archiv* was edited by Edgar Jaffé (1866–1921), Max Weber (1864–1920), and Werner Sombart (1863–1941).
3 Du Bois, *Dusk of Dawn*, 9.

4   Henry, "Africana Phenomenology," 8.
5   Du Bois, *Dusk of Dawn*, 9.
6   Henry, "Africana Phenomenology," 9.
7   Du Bois, *Souls of Black Folk*, 9.
8   Ibid., 12.
9   Du Bois, *Dusk*, 66.
10 Ibid., xxxiii.
11 Du Bois quoted in Mills, "W.E.B. Du Bois," 48.
12 Mills, *Black Rights/White Wrongs*, 82.
13 Mills, *Blackness Visible*, 2; emphasis in original.
14 Mills, *Black Rights/White Wrongs*, 33.
15 Kaviraj, "Global Intellectual History," 311.
16 Cooper, "What Is Intellectual Freedom Today?" 94.
17 Kaviraj, "Disenchantment Deferred," 308.
18 Mills, *Black Rights/White Wrongs*, 69.
19 Kim, "Alterity, Analectics," 47.
20 Ganeri, "Indian Logic," 2.
21 A similar claim is made by Tan. See Tan, "Why Study Chinese Classics and How to Go about It," 628.
22 See, Park, *Asia, Africa*, 151.
23 Koselleck, "*Begriffsgeschichte* und Social History," 419.
24 Ibid., 424.
25 Ibid., 413.
26 Koselleck, "Social History and Conceptual History," 317.
27 Perina, "On Doing Philosophy," 151.
28 Rosemont, "On Relativism," 61.
29 Ibid., 66.
30 Ibid., 66.
31 Andreotti, Ahenakew, and Cooper, "Epistemological Pluralism," 44.
32 Also see Mika, "Tokenism."
33 Mills, *Black Rights/White Wrongs*, 103.
34 Ibid., xvii.
35 Cf. Kirloskar-Steinbach and Kalmanson, *The Practical Guide*.
36 Mills, "Ideology," 107.
37 Tully, *Imperialism and Civic Freedom*, 143.
38 Mungwini, "Quest for Epistemic Liberation," 73, 76.
39 Kaviraj, "Disenchantment Deferred," 178.
40 Martín Alcoff, "Philosophy and Philosophical Practice," 403.
41 Kirloskar-Steinbach, "Diversifying Philosophy."
42 Tully, "Deparochializing Political Theory," 60.

43 Cf. Pernau and Rajamani, "Emotional Translations," 48.
44 Cooper, "Responses," 157.
45 Tully, "Reconciliation Here on Earth," 106.
46 Horkheimer and Adorno, "Concept of Enlightenment," 6.
47 Tully, "Reconciliation Here on Earth," 114.
48 Ibid., 85.
49 Kim, "Alterity, Analectics," 44.
50 Andreotti, Ahenakew and Cooper, "Epistemological Pluralism," 44.
51 Rosemont, *Against Individualism*, 96.
52 Also see Mika, Jones, Korab-Karpowicz, Mercier and Verran, "Why Give Up the Unknown"?
53 Tully, "Reconciliation Here on Earth," 111.
54 Ibid., 114.
55 Donahue, "For the Cowherds," 603.

References

Andreotti, Vanessa, Cash Ahenakew, and Garrick Cooper. "Epistemological Pluralism: Ethical and Pedagogical Challenges in Higher Education." *AlterNative: An International Journal of Indigenous Peoples* 7, no. 1 (2011): 40–50.

Du Bois, W. E. B. "Die Negerfrage in den Vereinigten Staaten (The Negro Question in the United States)." Translated by Joseph Fracchia, *CR: The New Centennial Review* 6, no. 3 (2006 [1906]): 241–90.

Du Bois, W. E. B. *Darkwater: Voices from within Veil*. New York: Brace, Harcourt, Brace and Company, 1920.

Du Bois, W. E. B. *The Souls of Black Folk*. A Penn State Electronic Classics Series Publication, 2006.

Du Bois, W. E. B. *Dusk of Dawn: An Essay toward an Autobiography of a Race Concept*. The Oxford W.E.B. Du Bois. Edited by Henry Louis, Gates Jr. Oxford, New York: Oxford University Press, 2007.

Cooper, Garrick. "What Is Intellectual Freedom Today? An Indigenous Reflection." *Continental Thought and Theory: A Journal of Intellectual Freedom*, 1 (2016): 93–5.

Cooper, Garrick, Charles Mills, Sudipta Kaviraj, and Sor-hoon Tan. "Responses to James Tully's 'Deparochializing Political Theory and Beyond.'" *Journal of World Philosophies* 2 (2017): 156–73, https://scholarworks.iu.edu/iupjournals/index.php/jwp/article/view/929.

Donahue, Amy. "For the Cowherds: Coloniality and Conventional Truth in Buddhist Philosophy." *Philosophy East and West* 66, no. 2 (2016): 597–617.

Ganeri, Jonardon. "Indian Logic and the Colonization of Reason." In *Indian Logic: A Reader*. Edited by Jonardon Ganeri. 1–25. London, New York: Routledge, 2001.

Henry, Paget. "Africana Phenomenology: Its Philosophical Implications." *Worlds and Knowledges Otherwise* (2006): 1–22, https://globalstudies.trinity.duke.edu/sites/globalstudies.trinity.duke.edu/files/file-attachments/v1d3_PHenry.pdf.

Horkheimer, Max and Theodor W. Adorno. "The Concept of Enlightenment." In *The Dialectic of Enlightenment: Philosophical Fragments*. Edited by Max Horkheimer and Theodor W. Adorno. 1–34. New York: Herder and Herder, 1972.

Kaviraj, Sudipta. "Global Intellectual History: Meanings and Methods." In *Global Intellectual History*. Edited by Samuel Moyn and Andrew Sartori. 295–319. New York: Columbia University Press, 2013.

Kaviraj, Sudipta. "Disenchantment Deferred." In *Beyond the Secular West: Religion, Culture and Public Life*. Edited by Akeel Bilgrami. 135–87. New York: Columbia University Press, 2016.

Kim, David Haekwon. "Alterity, Analectics, and the Challenges of Epistemic Decolonization." *The Southern Journal of Philosophy, Spindel Supplement* 57 (2019): 37–62.

Kirloskar-Steinbach, Monika. "Diversifying Philosophy: The Art of Non-Domination." *Educational Philosophy and Theory* 51, no. 14 (2019): 1490–503.

Kirloskar-Steinbach, Monika and Leah Kalmanson. *A Practical Guide to World Philosophies: Selves, Worlds and Ways of Knowing*. London etc.: Bloomsbury, 2021.

Koselleck, Reinhart. "*Begriffsgeschichte* and Social History." *Economy and Society* 11, no. 4 (1982): 409–27, DOI: 10.1080/03085148200000015.

Koselleck, Reinhart. "Social History and Conceptual History." *Politics, Culture and Society* 2, no. 3 (1989): 308–25.

Martín Alcoff, Linda. "Philosophy and Philosophical Practice: Eurocentrism as An Epistemology of Ignorance." In *The Routledge Handbook of Epistemic Injustice*. Edited by Ian James Kidd, José Medina, Gaile Pohlhaus. 397–408. London and New York: Routledge, 2017.

Mika, Carl. "Tokenism and te reo Māori: Why Some Things Just Shouldn't Be Translated." *The Conversation*, September 13, 2022, https://theconversation.com/tokenism-and-te-reo-maori-why-some-things-just-shouldnt-be-translated-190140.

Mika, Carl, C. Jones, W. J. Korab-Karpowicz, O. R. Mercier, and H. Verran. "Why Give Up the Unknown? And How"? *Journal of World Philosophies* 7, no. 1 (2022): 101–44, https://scholarworks.iu.edu/iupjournals/index.php/jwp/article/view/5485.

Mills, Charles W. *Blackness Visible: Essays on Philosophy and Race*. Ithaca and London: Cornell University Press, 1998.

Mills, Charles W. *Black Rights/White Wrongs: The Critique of Racial Liberalism*. New York: Oxford University Press, 2017.

Mills, Charles W. "Ideology." In *The Routledge Handbook of Epistemic Injustice*. Edited by Ian James Kidd, José Medina, and Gaile Pohlhaus. 100–11. London, New York: Routledge, 2017.

Mills, Charles W. "W.E.B. Du Bois: Black Radical Liberal." In *The Political Companion to W.E.B. Du Bois*. Edited by Nick Bromell. 19–56. Lexington, Kentucky: University Press of Kentucky, 2018.

Mungwini, Pascah. "The Quest for Epistemic Liberation: What Can Be Done to Be True to Both Philosophy and to Humanity?" In Mungwini, Pascah, Aaron Creller, Michael Monahan, and Esme Murdock, "Why Epistemic Decolonization?" *Journal of World Philosophies* 4 (2019): 70–105, https://scholarworks.iu.edu/iupjournals/index.php/jwp/article/view/3116.

Perina, Mickaella. "On Doing Philosophy: Territory, Discipline and Practices." In *Philosophy by Women: 22 Philosophers Reflect on Philosophy and Its Value*. Edited by Elly Vintiadis. 147–54. New York and London: Routledge, 2020.

Pernau, Margrit and Imke Rajamani. "Emotional Translations: Conceptual History Beyond Language." *History and Theory* 55 (2016): 46–65.

Rosemont, Jr., Henry. "Against Relativism." In *Interpreting across Boundaries: New Essays in Comparative Philosophy*. Edited by Gerald J. Larson and Eliot Deutsch. 36–63. Princeton, New Jersey etc.: Princeton University Press, 1988.

Rosemont, Jr., Henry. "Response to the Contributors." In *Polishing the Chinese Mirror: Essays in Honor of Henry Rosemont, Jr*. Edited by Marthe Chandler and Ronnie Littlejohn. 352–402. New York: Global Scholarly Publications, 2007.

Rosemont, Jr., Henry. *Against Individualism: A Confucian Rethinking of the Foundations of Morality, Politics, Family, and Religion*. Lanham etc.: Lexington Books, 2015.

Tan, Sor-hoon. "Why Study Chinese Classics and How to Go about It: Response to Zongjie Wu's 'Interpretation, Autonomy, and Transformation: Chinese Pedagogic Discourse in Cross-Cultural Perspective.'" *Journal of Curriculum Studies* 43, no. 5 (2011): 623–30, DOI: 10.1080/00220272.2011.577813.

Tully, James. *Imperialism and Civic Freedom*. Cambridge etc.: Cambridge University Press 2008.

Tully, James. "Deparochializing Political Theory and Beyond: A Dialogue Approach to Comparative Political Thought." *Journal of World Philosophies* 1 (2016): 51–74.

Tully, James. "Reconciliation Here on Earth." In *Resurgence and Reconciliation: Indigenous-Settler Relations and Earth Teachings*. Edited by Michael Asch, John Burrows and James Tully. 83–129. Toronto etc.: Toronto University Press, 2018.

Contributors

Garrick Cooper is Senior Lecturer in Aotahi School of Māori and Indigenous Studies at the University of Canterbury, Christchurch, New Zealand. His research is concerned with decoloniality, and the borders between indigenous and non-indigenous knowledge systems, highlighting critical ontological dimensions of indigenous knowledge systems.

Sudipta Kaviraj teaches Indian politics and intellectual history at Columbia University. His research interests are in political theory, historical sociology of the Indian state, and modern Indian literature.

Monika Kirloskar-Steinbach currently holds the chair "Diversifying Philosophy" at Vrije Universiteit Amsterdam. She is the founding coeditor of the *Journal of World Philosophies* and is the journal's current editor-in-chief. Some of her recent publications are: (with Leah Kalmanson) *A Practical Guide to World Philosophies: Selves, Worlds and Ways of Knowing* (2021); "Diversifying Philosophy: The Art of Non-Domination," *Educational Philosophy and Theory* 51, no. 14 (2019): 1490–503; (with Carl Mika) "Refusing the 'Foolish Wisdom of Resignation': kaupapa Māori in Conversation with Adorno," *European Journal of Social Theory* 23, no. 4 (2020): 532–49.

Charles W. Mills was Distinguished Professor of Philosophy at The Graduate Center, CUNY. He worked in the general area of oppositional political theory, with a particular focus on race. He was the author of numerous journal articles and book chapters, and six books: *The Racial Contract* (1997); *Blackness Visible: Essays on Philosophy and Race* (1998); *From Class to Race: Essays in White Marxism and Black Radicalism* (2003); *Contract and Domination* (with Carole Pateman) (2007); *Radical Theory, Caribbean Reality* (2010); and *Black Rights/White Wrongs: The Critique of Racial Liberalism* (2017).

Sor-hoon Tan is Professor of Philosophy at the Singapore Management University. She is the author of *Confucian Democracy: A Deweyan Reconstruction*, and editor of *Bloomsbury Research Handbook of Chinese Philosophy Methodologies*, and *Challenging Citizenship: Group Membership and*

Cultural Identity in a Global Age. She co-edited *The Moral Circle and the Self*; *Filial Piety in Chinese Thought and History*; *Democracy as Culture*; and *Feminist Encounters with Confucius*. Her articles have appeared in publications such as the *Australasian Journal of Philosophy, Journal of Value Inquiry, Political Theory, Philosophy East and West, Journal of Chinese Philosophy, International Philosophical Quarterly, Asian Philosophy*, and various collections on Chinese and Comparative Philosophy.

James Tully, PhD Cambridge, FRSC, is Distinguished Professor Emeritus of Political Science, Law, and Philosophy at the University of Victoria. He has taught at McGill University, University of Toronto, and University of Victoria. His publications include *Strange Multiplicity: Constitutionalism in an Age of Diversity* (1995); *Public Philosophy in a New Key*, 2 volumes (2008); *On Global Citizenship: James Tully in Dialogue* (2014); and Robert Nichols and Jakeet Singh, eds., *Freedom and Democracy in an Imperial Context: Dialogues with James Tully* (2014). He is the co-editor and contributor of *Resurgence and Reconciliation: Indigenous-Settler Relations and Earth Teachings* (2018); and edited of and contributor of Introduction in Richard B. Gregg, *The Power of Nonviolence* (2018), "Life Sustains Life," in Akeel Bilgrami, ed., *Nature and Value* (2020).

Index

Afro-modern political tradition (AMPT) 81–83, 92–96, 112, 139
ahimsa 130, 133

Baker, Ella 113, 158
Baldwin, James 82–83, 91–92, 95, 142–143, 150
bell hooks 113, 125, 159
Bhaṭṭa, Jayanta 73
Bhabha, Homi 107
Biko, Steve 82
Black Lives Matter 152, 165
Boas, Franz 5, 17, 18, 21, 111, 116, 141–142, 166

Césaire, Aimé 82
Chakrabarty, Dipesh 102
Chakravorty Spivak, Gayatri 90, 107 (*see*: Spivak C., Gayatri)
Chatterjee, Partha 65
Chattopadhyay, Kamaladevi 113
Chin, Clayton 125
Crenshaw, Kimberly 113
Confucianism 49–51
Cugoano, Quobna Ottobah ("John Stuart") 81–82

Dalton, Dennis 25, 116, 131
deep listening 14–20, 22, 51, 65, 69, 72–73, 96, 103, 126, 192, 193–194
de facto segregation 92, 141, 143, 144, 147–149, 150, 159
Delany, Martin 81, 82, 92, 94
Deming, Barbara 116, 135, 153, 162
de Sousa Santos, Boaventura 25, 54, 122
dialogues
  as assimilative monologue 2
  cosmopolitan dialogue 2
  false dialogues 3–5, 7, 11, 15, 41, 44, 72, 150, 167
  genuine dialogues 2–7, 9, 10, 12, 13–14, 15, 17–18, 26, 28, 30, 31, 41, 49, 72, 83, 90, 95, 101, 118, 138, 139, 141, 144, 164, 194
  global dialogues 5, 13, 18, 102, 116
Donahue, Amy 195
"double consciousness" 185
Douglass, Frederick 81, 82, 90, 92, 94
W. E. B. Du Bois 82, 84, 88, 92, 94, 108, 109, 111, 116, 125, 151, 152, 153, 155–158, 162, 163, 183, 184, 185, 186, 187

Ellison, Ralph 92
epistemic injustice 47, 90, 93, 95, 106, 197
Equiano, Olaudah ("Gustavus Vassa") 81, 82

Fanon, Frantz 5, 43, 82
Foucault, Michel 1, 36, 42, 53, 54, 107, 113, 125, 141, 155

Gandhi, Mohandas Karamchand 23, 25, 26, 42, 65, 67, 69, 106, 111, 113, 114–115, 118, 128, 129–132, 133, 134–139, 153, 155–158, 161–163, 165 (*see*: beloved community and Gandhian traditions)
Ganeri, Jonardon 189
Garvey, Marcus 82
Getachew, Adom 108, 145
Gibson Robinson, Jo Ann 113, 158
Gilligan, Carol 113
Goldenberg, David 88
Gordon, Lewis R. 42
Gregg, Richard 103, 115, 132–133, 135, 136, 152–153, 155–158
Guha, Ramchandra 139

Harlem Ashram 113, 156
Harris, Cheryl I. 90 (*see*: whiteness as property)

Index

Heng, Geraldine 87
Henry, Paget 185
Heyes, Cressida 113

interdependency 15, 16–20, 51, 113, 135, 158, 194
Isaac, Benjamin 86

James, C. L. R. 82, 108, 110, 150
Jensen, Kipton 125, 145, 159
Joseph, Peniel E. 145

King, Jr., Martin Luther 150, 152–163, 164 (*see*: beloved community tradition)
Kim, David H. 188
Koselleck, Reinhart 190

Lebron, Christopher 142
lifeworld and lifeworlds 7, 13, 18, 19, 25, 51, 64, 82, 92, 96, 119, 193 (*see*: *Mitsein*)

Māori 43–44, 118 (*see*: *tono tūpāpaku*)
Malcolm X 82, 113, 153, 164
Mantena, Karuna 123
Montgomery bus boycott 155–163

Nkrumah, Kwame 82, 108–110

Park, Peter P. 190
Parks, Rosa 158, 160
Perina, Mickaella 191

racism
    anti-black racism 83–86, 88–89, 140, 143, 151 (*see also*: short and long periodizations of race and racism)
    biological racism 84–86, 89, 111 (*see also*: 'scientific' racism)
    colonial white racism 84–85
    and Jews 84–85
Rosemont, Jr., Henry 191–192, 195

Royce, Josiah 152
Rustin, Bayard 109, 153, 155, 156, 157

Said, Edward 21, 82, 101, 105–106, 141
samaja 69, 113, 129, 133, 134, 136, 138
satyagraha 22, 42, 118, 130, 132, 135, 157, 158, 161
Scott, David 112, 127
secondary explanations 5, 6, 12, 14, 83, 91, 141–142, 144, 147
settler colonialism 15, 21, 62, 82, 91, 106, 109, 110, 111, 128, 138 (see: settler colonial dispossession)
Shiva, Vandana 134, 135
swaraj 26, 129, 130, 131, 133, 157
swadeshi 26, 130, 131, 132, 157

Tagore, Rabindranath 67, 69, 138–139
Thích Nhất Hạnh 19, 113, 135, 153
Thurman, Howard 116, 150, 153, 155, 158, 159, 165

universalizing
    and historicizing 123
    mode of 56, 59–61
    and universal 60–61

vernacular and vernaculars 64, 111, 123, 125, 128–129, 130, 131, 133–134, 135, 136–138, 146, 149

Walker, David 81, 82, 92, 94
Wells, Ida B. 82, 92
West, Cornel 125, 145
whiteness
    as property 90
    conceptual and theoretical 184, 187–189
    methodological 183, 184, 185, 186, 187–192, 193, 194, 195
Wilson Gilmore, Ruth 149
Wittgenstein, Ludwig 8, 9, 23, 24, 26, 124, 125, 137, 147

www.ingramcontent.com/pod-product-compliance
Lightning Source LLC
Chambersburg PA
CBHW052116300426
44116CB00010B/1682